21.00
net

D1545298

AESTHETICISM
AND DECADENCE

GARLAND REFERENCE LIBRARY
OF THE HUMANITIES
(VOL. 82)

*Some Persons of "the Nineties" little imagining,
despite their Proper Pride and Ornamental Aspect,
how much they will interest Mr. Holbrook Johnson and Mr. Osbert Burdett*
Max Beerbohm, 1925
Reprinted courtesy of the Ashmolean Museum, Oxford,
and by permission of Mrs. Eva Reichmann

AESTHETICISM AND DECADENCE
A Selective Annotated Bibliography

Linda C. Dowling

GARLAND PUBLISHING, INC. • NEW YORK & LONDON
1977

©1977 by Linda C. Dowling
All rights reserved

Library of Congress Cataloging in Publication Data
Dowling, Linda C   1944-
  Aestheticism and decadence.

  (Garland reference library of the humanities)
  Includes index.
  1. English literature—19th century—History and criticism—
Bibliography. 2. Aestheticism (Literature)—Bibliography.
3. Decadence (Literary movement)—Bibliography. I. Title
Z2013.D68   [PR468.A33]   016.820'7   76-52676
ISBN 0-8240-9891-9

Robert Manning Strozier Library

JUL 14 1978

Tallahassee, Florida

PRINTED IN THE UNITED STATES OF AMERICA

CONTENTS

Frontispiece: Max Beerbohm, *Some Persons of "the Nineties"* . . .

Introduction   vii

List of Abbreviations   xxvii

Bibliography   1

Index   137

INTRODUCTION

> To give an accurate and exhaustive
> account of the period would need a
> far less brilliant pen than mine.
>
> -- Max Beerbohm, "1880"

The myth of the Victorian fin de siècle -- the *l'art pour l'art*
aesthetic eighties, the gay, mauve, yellow, decadent, naughty nineties -- is still green today.   The myth was not merely the focus of
most contemporary discussions of the years 1880-1900, but has powerfully influenced the tenor of modern critical discussion.   After
nearly one hundred years of publicity, denunciation, nostalgia, de-
bunking, rediscovery and correction, the myth still fascinates and
prevails, remains for all its narrowness and lurid exaggeration the
single most important literary fact about the last twenty years of
the Victorian era.   As aestheticism and decadence, the two artistic
ideas with which this bibliography is specially concerned, have rarely been discussed without reference to the myth of the fin de siècle,
we may perhaps consider some of the problems it has raised for literary criticism.
     The myth of the Victorian fin de siècle is, if anything, almost
too well known to both general readers and literary scholars.   Indeed, we may be tempted to paraphrase Ezra Pound and say that the
years 1880 - 1900 did not exist; that, instead, their ambience has
conferred existence upon them. The myth of the fin de siècle, a pervasive sense that the eighteen-eighties and nineties comprise a distinct and significant artistic, psychological and cultural episode,
was originally a creation of the period itself. For as any reader of
fin de siècle memoirists knows, the nineties seemed to the young
writers and artists who crowded London to mark a release from the

mid-Victorian moral dispensation, to offer intoxicating opportunities for experimentation in the two realms that ambitious theory sought to merge -- art and life. The cult of excess ranged from Oscar Wilde's widely reported public performances at the performances of his own plays and his increasingly public, increasingly dangerous flirtations with rented male courtesans to Lionel Johnson's private excess of asceticism and study. Fashionable French theories of cultural decadence only made millenarian expectations of change seem more piquant to the young, more baffling to older outsiders who trusted to *Punch* and the Reverend W.F. Barry to settle the aesthetical hash.

We know, too, that much of the fin de siècle sense of impending doom has been retrospectively projected upon those years by writers like Yeats and Pound who, struggling to understand their own place in literary history, made tragedy out of misfortune. But even more, much of our sense of "the nineties" is, as Ellen Moers has pointed out, the result of the curious and unstable marriage between an aspiring avant-garde and the new media. Wilde's call for the realization of personality, for example, finds its commercial parallel in the aggressive merchandising of literary and artistic talent; Johnson's dandiacal dictum, "One should be quite unnoticeable," must be set beside Richard Le Gallienne's column of whole - souled literary gossip in the *Star*; John Gray's libel suit against the same newspaper for suggesting he was the original of Dorian Gray should be weighed with his letter to Wilde signed "Yours, Dorian." An attentive press, a curious public and complaisant publishers encouraged such persiflage and posturing; but they may also have suggested to avant-garde writers and artists of the early nineties that their art would make a difference in the national life, when in fact Wilde's trial for homosexual practices in 1895 merely ensured that their lives would make a difference in the national arts, propelling them for twenty years along conservative, traditional, patriotic and essentially parochial paths.

Thus, for all its dandiacal disdain and scholarly preoccupations, much of the avant-garde art of the period was deeply and perilously implicated in the machinery of commercial publicity and promotion -- Wilde's disgrace thrust Aubrey Beardsley from the *Yellow Book*, the *Savoy* failed when railway bookstands refused to stock the magazine.   It was all very well to act like superfluous men but, as Beardsley and Symons and Dowson and a number of others discovered, it was quite another thing to eat like one.   One answer was a private income.   Another was Beerbohm's, who cheated fashion by declaring himself to be passé. Still another possibility was, in a sense, to merchandise disaster itself.   When the Wilde trial was succeeded by Beardsley's premature death in 1898 and by Ernest Dowson's death in dire circumstances two years later and by Johnson's death, apparently from the effects of alcoholism, two years after that, the outlines of a compelling myth of heedless talent and headlong disaster had already emerged with some clarity. For survivors like Symons and Le Gallienne and Yeats, the myth of a "tragic generation" made their own experience more comprehensible.   For inheritors like Pound and Eliot, the myth was a benchmark for succeeding explorers to follow or avoid.   For generations of literary scholars and critics, the myth has complicated and obscured an understanding of the literary passage from Victorian to modern, while fitfully illuminating those years with what Johnson once called "the flames of evil ecstasy."

Yet even before this series of personal disasters made the 1890s synonymous with dissipation and self-destruction, an acute Victorian historical self-consciousness combined with a good deal of apocalyptic journalism to engender a sense of chronological difference and discontinuity; some writers sensed an ending, many others a beginning, still others an uncertain sort of interregnum. The question, as readers of the following bibliography will discover, is still at issue in modern scholarship. Thus we hear the fin de siècle described in works written in the last ten years as "fundamentally Victorian" and "Edwardian" and "palaeo-modern" and "[not] the period of our contemporaries, of writers who address themselves, in our kind of language, to the common problems that we recognize."

Like any other literary period surrounded by myth and oversimplification, the years 1880-1900 have attracted literary scholars anxious to replace vulgarization with responsible interpretation. Modern students of the period, especially, have, in their effort to escape the banal and restrictive cliches of the past, stressed the diverse attitudes and energies of the fin de siècle, and have expanded its cast of characters far beyond the stereotypical set of aesthetes,

dandies, decadents and "counter-decadents." But if such careful re-
visionism has made the notion of an aesthetic eighties or naughty
nineties as intellectually untenable as the notion of a medieval Dark
Ages, the myth and its stereotypes nonetheless persist with, it sometimes seems, increasing vigor.

The very persistence of the fin de siècle myth tells us a great
deal both about its indispensability to the modernist imagination and
about certain important affinities between the fin de siècle and late
twentieth-century culture. The fascination with youth and personality, for example, or the belief that a generation identifies itself
through a characteristic style, or the notion that decades will range
themselves cooperatively under alliterative labels, all have a common
source in late nineteenth-century journalistic log-rolling and avant-
gardism. Then too, the myth of the fin de siècle, with its presentation of the self as performance and its conviction of cultural decay,
satisfies certain modern theories of dramatistic behavior and historical decadence. It seems, finally, inevitable that while some writers will deride the myth as a pernicious and ineradicable caricature
of the period, still others will continue to invoke it and its major
emphases, especially as the twentieth - century fin de siècle approaches.

Though it may explain our continuing interest in the years 1880-
1900, we must, of course, recognize that the myth of the fin de
siècle has deeply involved fin de siècle literature in its sensationalism. Modern scholars agree that the corollary myth of the tragic
generation -- so brilliantly expressed by Yeats and Pound -- has for
too long held us in thrall, diverting our attention from far more
complex, if less notorious, aspects of the years 1880-1900. Such indeed is the tremendous prestige of Yeats and Pound that the myth of
the tragic generation has survived exposure of its limitations to
earn a kind of secondary authority as a key to their creative concerns. For Pound, who arrived in London in 1908 affecting a velvet
cloak, a turquoise earring and a set of poetic enthusiasms some ten
or fifteen years out of date, the tragic generation seems to have
been a slightly ludicrous, if monitory, example of utter dedication
to Art; "Though our lips be slain," Pound's poem "The Decadence"
concludes, "We see Art vivant, and exult to die." For Yeats, the

generation of Beardsley, Dowson, Johnson and Wilde symbolized the extortionate price art exacted from life, but Yeats, unlike Pound, never abandoned his belief in the myth nor in the economy of the sacrifice; it was to remain an important and self - renewing imaginative well-spring for him all his life. Three years before he died, Yeats once again summoned the slim, besotted spectres of Dowson and Johnson for a radio audience -- "those elegant, tragic penitents," he called them, "those great men in their triumph."

The partisanship of Yeats and Pound has been on the whole a stroke of extraordinary good fortune for the reputations of the tragic generation poets and, to a lesser extent, for the fin de siècle itself. Yeats's sponsorship, Joyce's fin de siècle affinities, Eliot's indebtedness to and dismissal of the period have earned for the years 1880 - 1900 a scholarly attention that otherwise might not have been won, for the roots of modernism legitimize an interest that the fruits of Pre - Raphaelitism, perhaps, might not. At the same time, the issue of whether or not interest in the fin de siècle is intellectually respectable has been, and to a degree remains, a real problem both for literary criticism and literary history.

During the eighties and nineties the problem of legitimacy was discussed primarily in terms of minor or coterie poetry -- what sort of claim could the work of such poets as Dobson, Symons and Gray have upon the readers of Tennyson, Browning and Tupper? Such groups as the English Parnassians and the Rhymers were, for a number of reasons, quite willing to be known as "minor" poets. The word, like "Decadent," was adopted as an epithet of honor, not least because it expressed the distaste of the aesthetes for the moral ambitiousness and high seriousness of mainstream Victorian poetry even as it modestly aligned their own work with the exquisite achievements of the minor poets among the Elizabethans, Jacobeans and Cavaliers.

And then, of course, the problem of minor poetry and its legitimacy was cruelly complicated for later commentators by the Wilde disaster, which not only plunged Wilde's reputation into an obloquy that lasted for decades, but also cast a deep cloud over the reputations of other artists and writers, only a few of whom were actually Wilde's friends. Wilde's conviction for homosexuality was instantly and universally read as an act of poetic justice almost too richly symbolic to be expected from mere life, whose usual catastrophes, as Wilde himself had once complained, "happen in the wrong way and to the wrong people." In only a few years the trial was seen as marking the end of an era.

The reputation of Wilde both as an artist and as a theoretician of the aesthetic movement is today, after years of serious scholarly endeavor, rated very high, but the period with which his name is identified has fared less well. Though perhaps no scholar writing today consciously equates homosexuality with criminality, a prejudice against homosexuals and homosexual themes in literature, both so conspicuous in the fin de siècle, has long conspired to inhibit serious consideration of the fin de siècle even as it has encouraged an underground and cultish partisanship. The cult of the martyred Wilde, quite as much as the Sunday supplement fatuities purveyed by literary journalists, has placed the fin de siècle in isolation from more respectable fields of literary scholarship.

Yet even if the dubious reputation of the fin de siècle had not alienated scholars, the problem of "minor" literature would remain. Like the critics of the 1890s who denounced the "Decadents," modern critics who have chosen to remain within the tradition of evaluative or "taste" criticism have been reluctant to waste time on works they find meretricious or mediocre. Such writers have, for the most part, chosen to consider the literature of the eighties and nineties as derivative or probationary, to view it either as the exhausted product of a moribund tradition or an unsteady experiment in apprenticeship. The underlying assumption involved here has long since been exposed in modern critical theory; it is, in simple terms, the assumption that such "second-rate" work establishes its claim upon critical attention only as it can illuminate the "superior" literature that preceded or followed it. Even today, when the theoretical argument that evaluation has no place in critical discussion has long been commonplace, to suggest that evaluative critics may mislead us about the fin de siècle as they have in the past misled us about Donne, Pope, Dickens and James, is to risk being chided for the same flash aestheticism to which the fin de siècle was long found lamentably inclined.

If some scholars have dismissed fin de siècle literature on

grounds of its literary "inferiority," their assessment is in part generated by another problem raised for criticism by the myth of the fin de siècle -- the assumption that the artistic achievements of the period are fully represented by a few figures. The tendency of scholars to take the part for the whole -- to find Arthur Symons, for instance, typical of the Rhymers' Club, which is then seen to be typical of fin de siècle poetry, which in turn is found typical of fin de siècle literature in general -- has been encouraged, too, by the very exclusiveness of the tragic generation. By narrowing the focus of critical and scholarly attention to a small circle of flamboyant and apparently fated young men, the myth has long made it appear that there was little of interest beyond. And yet, as recent study and commentary has labored to show, the tragic generation, so far from being representative of the actual literary situation during the years 1880 - 1900, probably ought to be treated as a gorgeous and treacherous fiction.

Although we may find it as difficult to conceive of the fin de siècle without peacock plumes and opium pipes as to imagine George Washington without hatchet and cherry tree, recent scholarship has demonstrated that the effort is well rewarded. If the names and works that some recent scholars ask us to consider seem radically unfamiliar -- Richard Whiteing, Arthur Machen, *Keynotes*, *Silverpoints*-- their aim has been less to urge new elections to the literary pantheon than to assist in the recovery of the authentic literary context of the fin de siècle, a labor that promises to be engrossing, essential and long.

At the same time, new scholarly interest in individual works and writers of the fin de siècle may inhibit, for a time at least, the study of such broader typics as aestheticism and decadence. Such topics have always posed problems for scholars of the period, who have found themselves caught between, on the one hand, the inflated claims made by contemporary publicists and, on the other, the traditional Anglo - Saxon mistrust of -isms and movements in art, particularly French art. The problem has been further complicated both by the notion that neither aestheticism nor decadence is genuinely indigenous to English literature and by the failure of scholars to agree on what constitutes representative examples of either tendency

xiii

in English.

Once they push beyond the richly parodic kingdom of Wilde and his satirists, for example, scholars of aestheticism find themselves in uncertain territory. This is why, undoubtedly, so many scholarly accounts of aestheticism have chosen either to treat the movement historically, emphasizing its sources in Goethe and German idealist philosophy and its refinement in Gautier and Baudelaire, or to consider it as an essentially ahistorical tendency that may be equally located in the art of a John Lyly or of a Wallace Stevens.

For scholars of decadence, the situation has been even more complex. As a literary and cultural phenomenon, decadence was early identified with French artistic ideas that were seen by its foes as destructive and by its friends as liberating. Thus, for instance, the Reverend W.F. Barry's apoplectic attacks on French decadence were met by Grant Allen's demure prose explorations of the "new hedonism." Richard Le Gallienne's stoutly sentimental defense of English poetic innocence and tradition was countered by Arthur Symons' passionate devotion to French experience and innovation. Arthur Waugh's critique of the "new realism," commissioned by the *Yellow Book*, prompted Hubert Crackanthorpe to defend the new frankness in a later number of the same magazine. And Max Nordau's famous diagnosis of cultural hysteria in *Degeneration* inspired G.B. Shaw's witty prognosis for *The Sanity of Art*. In the nineties at least, decadence often seemed less an artistic idea than an occasion for speeches.

The young partisans of the movement, of course, chose "decadence" as the defining term of the new avant-gardism precisely because of its power both to pre - empt and to provoke criticism. Yet the outraged reaction, however much it may have amused them, made it nearly impossible to define the movement in more serious terms -- especially so since the decadents themselves never really made it clear whether the term was meant to refer to the form or the content of their art. In England, where the moral function of literature had been urged at least since Sidney's *Defense of Poetry*, and where critical moralism had attained new heights only a few years before in the works of Matthew Arnold, the problem was particularly acute.

Along with the set of problems engendered by the fin de siècle artists and their adversaries and later by the myth of the fin de siècle, a scholar of the period today confronts a larger problem now much discussed by theorists of literary history -- the problem of period itself. In the case of the fin de siècle, it is a problem considerably complicated by the shifting critical attitudes towards the years 1880 - 1900. Early discussions of period, for example, tended to divide along the lines of the avant-gardist vs. traditionalist controversy of the nineties. Thus younger writers and artists were eager, as we have noted, to declare the advent of a new age, even as they enjoyed a delicious *frisson* at the thought that the accession of the new meant the apocalypse of the old. Older hands like Robert Buchanan and the Reverend Mr. Barry and, to be sure, Max Nordau believed that civilization was seriously threatened by the new art, that the end of culture as they had known it could be at hand. In either case, however, the sense of a breach with the cultural past was sharp.

Yet, as Yeats was regretfully to record several years later, nothing really extraordinary seemed to emerge from the artistic ferment of the fin de siècle; though it trembled very promisingly, the veil of the temple remained unrent. And so, in the absence of any clear artistic issue, early twentieth-century commentators, writing under the influence of the myth of the fin de siècle, turned to biography as a substitute for literary explanation. Literary London of the 1890s, their accounts suggest, had been exclusively populated by Dowson, Johnson, Beardsley and Wilde, with poor Pater hovering fretfully somewhere in a suburb. Similarly, the fin de siècle produced but a single work, variously titled "Cynara" or "Dorian Gray" or the "Conclusion" to *The Renaissance*, and copiously illustrated by the more reprehensible of Beardsley's designs. It clearly served the moral purposes of such critics as Irving Babbitt and P. E. More to portray the fin de siècle this way, as a dead end for fin de siècle art and artist alike. Their opinion had been anticipated by the *Academy* critic who, reviewing the final issue of a "Decadent" magazine, concluded, "the *Yellow Book* literature generally is *cul-de-sac* -- it leads nowhere" and was to be echoed by Pound's "Mr. Nixon," bluffly advising Mauberley, "The 'Nineties' tried your game / And died, there's nothing in it."

Yet curiously enough, this opinion of fin de siècle artists was to be shared by those we now consider their immediate successors, the modernists.   While we are not, perhaps, surprised to hear T.S. Eliot murmuring about "untidy lives," the tone of disdainful superiority and what Le Gallienne called the "feminine ferocity" of the attack on the eighteen-nineties is particularly striking in writers like Pound and Strachey and Woolf whose rejection of the moral and aesthetic assumptions of the Victorians was hardly more vehement than that of the "Decadents" themselves.   What we see here, of course, is what Renato Poggioli has taught us to recognize as the palingenesis of the avant-garde, disavowing its past in order to regenerate itself and gain creative space.   By treating aestheticism and decadence as the last exotic pendants of a hopelessly frumpish Victorianism, modernists made modernism newer, fathering themselves.

Conservative literary critics during the early years of modernism, on the other hand, were quick to point out that new modernism seemed little more than old decadence writ large.. Such was the vigor and brilliance of literary modernism, however, that most discussions ot its sources or models or resemblances to earlier literature rather soon seemed all but irrelevant.   Thus it was that the revolutionary colors of fin de siècle aestheticism and decadence faded to the faint hues of a quaintly outmoded tradition, "late violets," sniffed Edmund Wilson in a review of Ronald Firbank, "of the nineties."   In time, the perception of continuity between fin de siècle and twentieth - century avant-gardism also faded and the earlier movement became, perhaps inevitably, the solace and refuge of literary conservatives.   Again and again in the twenties and thirties readers are urged by conservative critics, exasperated by Mr. Eliot's obscurity or Mr. Joyce's obscenity, to devote their days and nights to Laurence Binyon or Le Gallienne -- to turn, in short, to those poets who carried on the nineties tradition of lyricism and poetic craftsmanship. That theirs was a minority opinion does not lessen its significance.

With the renewal of interest in the Victorian age that began some thirty years ago, scholars once again adjusted their perspective on the fin de siècle and its place in literary history.   The aesthetes and decadents, now perceived as having been "late Victorians," shared in the widened sympathy for the Victorians that was inspired by such influential reassessments as J. H. Buckley's *The*

Victorian Temper (1951) and Walter Houghton's *The Victorian Frame of Mind* (1957). At the same time, however, such works tended to present students of the fin de siècle with a new set of problems. For scholars who had learned to admire Victorian moral and artistic seriousness were, naturally, impatient with works that attacked or parodied such values. Fin de siècle writers, especially those associated with aestheticism and decadence, generally suffered in what was to become an almost obligatory comparison with their Victorian predecessors -- next to Ruskin, Newman and Arnold, for instance, Pater and Wilde were usually made to appear as self - indulgent and essentially frivolous writers whose intellectual flabbiness bred a woeful vulgarization of their predecessors' thought. Thus the long - standing moral bias against aestheticism and decadence submerged itself in other, ostensibly analytical, concerns; but conclusions usually concluded that fin de siècle writers had "failed" in their lives and art, had been too timid, too escapist, too subjective, too temporizing.

It was, instead, the scholars of modernism who most stimulated the current revival of interest in the fin de siècle. Their search for origins led them back to the aesthetes and decadents, whose interest in colloquial speech, in urban themes and, most of all, in "the image," made them seem like genuine, if neglected, antecedents of the very modernists who had once slighted them. This interpretation was strengthened considerably when it was remembered that Yeats, himself considered a modernist, not only had learned his craft during the fin de siècle but had persistently represented the tragic generation as a gallant revolt against Victorian rhetoric and "impurities." The energy, erudition and persuasiveness of this reinterpretation of the fin de siècle is best represented by such works as Frank Kermode's brilliantly suggestive *Romantic Image* (1957), which not only restored Arthur Symons' reputation as a critic at a single stroke but originated a whole line of critical inquiry into the performing arts that even now is not exhausted. Then too, since it appears that the fin de siècle will be a trump card in the hands of modernist scholars hoping to defeat the claims of "post-modernism," it seems likely that the scholarly annexation of the fin de siècle for modernism may indeed become permanent.

As even so brief an account of scholarly responses to the fin de siècle may suggest, it has been the uneasy fate of the fin de siècle to be shuttled back and forth across an imaginary literary historical divide, first as the unruly child of Victorianism, next as the unlikely sire of modernism. Scholars dissatisfied with this situation have recently suggested that the years 1880-1900 might be better understood if they were located firmly within a period of their own, specifically, in the "hidden period," variously set as 1870-1914 or 1880-1920, that many commentators have discerned to lie between the Victorian and modern periods and that some writers have dubbed the "Age of Transition."

At first glance, such a perspective on the fin de siècle seems to offer some obvious advantages. Redrawing the lines of literary history in this way would seem, certainly, to let us view the fin de siècle as both a genuine divergence from Victorian literary culture and as an authentic anticipation of the modernist movement. Then too, the notion of "transition" seems to reflect the wide variety of literary impulses during these years -- aestheticism, Parnassianism, realism, impressionism, decadence, neo-romanticism, symbolism, activism, Edwardianism, neo-classicism, Vorticism, imagism -- without imposing a single reductive scheme upon them all. And, perhaps most important, such a reparcelling of literary territories seems to provide scholars with a useful explanatory paradigm to assist them in the search for unifying themes in works by authors ranging from Abercrombie to Zangwill, a body of literature otherwise distinguished only for its unmanageable heterogeneity.

Unfortunately, whether we are speaking of the Silver Age of Latin classicism, the "pre-romantic" movement in eighteenth-century English literature or, as now, of the Victorian fin de siècle, no genuine theory of literary history allows for the existence of an "age of transition." For the notion of transition is in literary history always implicitly a confession that we are working without a theory, that we remain imprisoned within a borrowed conceptual paradigm. In relation to the fin de siècle, the idea of an "age of transition" means no more than that the attempt of scholars to navigate the waters between the well-mapped territories of Victorianism and modernism remains an uncertain enterprise. Though the notion of transition may well calm the crew, it is of little use in sounding the bottom or charting a course.

In any genuine theory of literary history, that is, the concept of age or period has meaning only as referring to an age or period perceived as having its own coherence and its own center of gravity. This is the context in which scholars of the fin de siècle might do well to recall the long debate over pre - romanticism, a debate that ended only when the very notion of pre-romanticism was exploded in a classic essay by Northrop Frye. Beginning with a description of the later eighteenth century as seen in transitional terms -- "this period has the 'Augustan' age on one side of it and the 'Romantic' movement on the other, and it is usually approached transitionally, as a period of reaction against Pope and anticipation of Wordsworth" -- Frye needed only to expose the consequences of such a view: "as for the term 'pre-romantic,' that, as a term for the age itself, has the peculiar demerit of . . . imposing a false teleology on everything we study. Not only did the 'pre - romantics' not know that the Romantic movement was going to succeed them, but there has probably never been a case on record of a poet's having regarded a later poet's work as the fulfilment of his own."[*]

All we need do is substitute key terms -- "Victorian" for "Augustan," "modernist movement" for "Romantic movement," "age of transition" for "pre-romantic" -- to expose the false teleology now threatening to distort serious study of the fin de siècle. Other areas of contemporary literary study, one suspects, would not have borne the notion of an age of transition for so long -- perhaps because other areas of literary study have not required so much apology and justification from its scholars. Perhaps, too, it is because the notion of transition has borrowed a certain legitimacy from such writers as Yeats -- as when, contemplating the fate of the tragic generation, he wonders, "was it that we lived in what is called 'an age of transition' and so lacked coherence?"

The attempt to view the years 1880 - 1900 as part of an age of transition can, in this sense, be seen as simply one more reaction to the myth of the fin de siècle. Clearly enough, scholars who have accepted the notion have been largely motivated by a praiseworthy

[*]"Towards Defining an Age of Sensibility," *ELH*, 23 (1956), 144.

desire to free fin de siècle works and writers from what one scholar has called the vicious constriction of melodramatic myth and cliche, and so have come to accept a latitude of definition bordering on meaninglessness. Yet it is not this latitude of definition that causes concern: other literary periods have been saddled with effectively meaningless names, and we have long grown accustomed to using such labels as "the Gilded Age" for the sake of their convenience rather than their sense. Nor should we be troubled by Yeats's endorsement of the term; for his notion of the fin de siècle as an age of transition, like his invention of the tragic generation, has meaning not as it guides our inquiries but as it is the object of inquiry. It is itself what we must seek to explain. Instead, the disabling weakness of any approach that views the fin de siècle as part of an age of transition is that it is meaningless in a certain essential way, that in its very nature it denies the possibility of any genuine theory of literary history.

Viewed in another way, however, recent studies undertaken in the name of "transition" do emphasize a larger coherence in modern scholarship of the fin de siècle: for scholars who seek deliverance from the myth of the fin de siècle in the idea of an age of transition are, finally, as dominated by the myth they reject as those scholars who accept and exploit it, who have chosen to treat the myths of the fin de siècle and the tragic generation as necessary fictions, great and unavoidable parables of Romanticism. This last point of view, expressed in the work of such commentators as Harold Bloom, treats the myth with considerably more cleverness than do the literary journalists who work up the "naughty nineties" one more time; for Bloom, for example, the myth is less a description of the erratic careers of Rhymers' Club members than a paradigm of the Romantic imagination as it confronts its Oedipal situation in a failing culture.

Scholars interested in discrediting the myth, on the other hand, who believe it has too long blocked access to the literary truth about the fin de siècle, have for some twenty years looked for encouragement and direction to the journal *English Literature in Transition*. At a time when most treatments of the fin de siècle were ensnared in one way or another by its myth, this journal argued that as long as the vanished context of the fin de siècle was viewed with a jaundiced eye through the lens of the "yellow nineties," the true literary proportions of the period would never be fully known nor would the contemporary sense of the continuity and interconnectedness of fin de siècle literature, of the affinities between George Egerton and George Gissing, Kipling and Symons, Conrad and Gray, Wells and Wilde, ever be recovered. But even more important has been the research into little - known or utterly forgotten writers and works encouraged by *ELT* and its editor, H.E. Gerber; for, as such work as Ian Fletcher's on Herbert Horne or Wendell Harris' on the fin de siècle short story writers indicates, it is this line of inquiry that will contribute significantly to the emerging scholarly reassessment of the fin de siècle.

Although scholars engaged in the reconstruction of the fin de siècle literary context have not by any means reached a final consensus, much of the direction and emphases of their study already seem clear. They will insist, for example, upon the diversity, vitality and experimental richness of fin de siècle literary culture, while the myth of the fin de siècle, no longer utterly rejected or uncritically embraced, will become for them simply a central theme among others. And as they carry their search for other defining concerns and motifs beyond the usual specimen works and writers, scholars, drawing upon previously unconsidered evidence, will endeavor to interpret the fin de siècle in its own terms and attempt to locate the center of gravity in the period as a whole.

A glance at contemporary studies of fin de siècle authors and topics indicates that the redirection of scholarly interest has already begun. Few scholars, it seems, are eager to prolong the reductive domination of the biographical motive in discussions of the period; in recent works, at least, the overemphasis on lives instead of works has continued to be righted. Thus, for example, though presses still pour out biographies of Wilde in the customary profusion, studies like Epifanio San Juan, Jr.'s *The Art of Oscar Wilde* (1967) and Christopher Nassaar's *Into the Demon Universe* (1974) as well as numerous recent essays in scholarly journals increasingly have chosen to concern themselves with the literary dimension of Wilde's career; and the same reorientation of interest is evident in such critical biographies of other period figures as Mark Longaker's

Ernest Dowson (3rd edition 1967) and John M. Munro's *Arthur Symons* (1969).

In the same way, scholars have begun to re-examine our interpretative assumptions about fin de siècle literature. Many literary critics, exasperated by the institutionalization of cliches about the period, are working to return criticism of fin de siècle literature to certain first principles; they point out that although modern critical theory has established analytical reading or explication as the essential first step for any critical interpretation, few fin de siècle works, outside those by Wilde and Yeats and a handful of recitation pieces like "Cynara" and "The Dark Angel," have won this most fundamental critical attention. Close reading of well-known as well as unfamiliar texts, they maintain, must precede any more ambitious plans to distill the literary essence of the period or disestablish journalistic gossip and cliche.

An even plainer sign of enhanced interest in the fin de siècle is the reprinting of many obscure but essential titles. The Beardsley boom of a few years back did much, of course, to resurrect fin de siècle texts; both the *Savoy* and the *Yellow Book*, for instance, have been reprinted, and even Beardsley's own fragmentary *Story of Venus and Tannhäuser* has recently been reissued in an illustrated and unexpurgated form. That scholarly interest persists beyond mere faddish enthusiasm, however, is clear from the continuing efforts to keep important titles in print: *The Eighteen Nineties* (1913), Holbrook Jackson's venerable but sprightly classic, for example, has recently enjoyed yet another reprinting. Perhaps the most ambitious undertaking in this line is the reprint series announced by Garland Publishing; *The Aesthetic Movement and the Arts and Crafts Movement,* edited by Peter Stansky and Rodney Shewan, will make available some forty - eight works connected with the two movements, while *The Decadent Consciousness: A Hidden Archive of Late Victorian Literature,* edited by Ian Fletcher and John Stokes, will reprint forty - one now rare titles.

The emerging scholarly reconstruction of the fin de siècle will depend as well upon the recovery and interpretation of unpublished sources. One such work has already appeared: James G. Nelson's *The Early Nineties* (1971), which in its detailed and deeply informative picture of the literary influence of the Bodley Head, provides a fine model for future contextualist studies, both as it illuminates the fin de siècle literary situation and as it breaks down barren preconceptions about the period based on Symons' poems, Dowson's passion, Johnson's drinking and Yeats's myth. Encouraging, too, has been the recent appearance of such synoptic studies as Barbara Charlesworth's *Dark Passages* (1965), John A. Lester, Jr.'s *Journey Through Despair* (1968) and Tom Gibbons' *Rooms in the Darwin Hotel* (1973), all works that affirm the new seriousness of critical inquiry into the fin de siècle without necessarily managing to surmount the difficulties posed to systematic analysis by a literature as diverse and subtly varying as that written in the fin de siècle.

Yet even if such studies as these should reveal the dangers involved in trying to negotiate a body of literary works so little known and so densely eclectic by the light of a single thesis -- whether that thesis be subjectivism, scientific materialism or evolutionism -- nonetheless they suggest at the same time, in their powers of fresh sympathy, observation and analysis, that scholarship of fin de siècle literature, long wearied by its apparently endless battle with myth and gossip and demoralized by apology and low esteem, is on the threshold of major achievement. Future scholars may well hesitate on the threshold, for the range of tasks before them is wide, but it is hardly likely, having achieved so much, that they will retreat. At the very least they will recognize that fin de siècle literature requires of its scholars some of the qualities most characteristic of itself, qualities of deep and subtle learning, of self-irony, of precision and colloquial ease, of intense curiosity and certainty, tempered, as the scholarly Lionel Johnson himself would have said, by a saving disbelief in certitudes.

If to define is to limit, I should perhaps make clear that this limited bibliography has no covert designs on definition, whether of aestheticism or decadence or fin de siècle. If it should seem to ratify older, more limited notions of "fin de siècle" or "the nineties," it is simply because such treatments predominate historically, while the scholarly and critical work that will extend and deepen our understanding of that period has, for the most part, only begun to be written. What I have endeavored to do is list those studies which, it seems to me, offer the most help in understanding aestheticism, decadence and the fin de siècle. My principles of selection have been roughly these: (1) to include works that deal in a general or specific way with these topics while omitting works that concern themselves exclusively with a single figure or single work without reference to the period as a whole or to the topics of aestheticism and decadence. I have, for example, included relatively few entries from the vast store of Wilde and Yeats studies, so rich in both biographical and textual comment; on the other hand, I have admitted a number of single-author studies if those authors were little known or had received little critical attention. Readers who require more specialized studies of individual figures should consult the standard bibliographies, the Annotated Secondary Bibliography Series of Northern Illinois University Press or the excellent series of primary and secondary bibliographies published in *English Literature in Transition*; many of these are listed in this bibliography.

(2) To favor recent and analytical studies over purely biographical or evaluative accounts. Thus no effort has been made to list all the parodies, reviews or journalistic treatments of aestheticism, decadence and the fin de siècle, for such accounts are legion, predictable and of limited interest to scholars and critics familiar with the period; I have, however, included a few representative samples of such commentary for purposes of historical perspective and general amusement. (3) In the event of any repetition of remarks either through reprinting or revision, to list the most accessible or, in the case of dissertations, the most mature version.

In annotating the entries, I have sought to provide neutral and informative summaries of the authors' chief points or theses. Whenever possible, I have quoted these in the authors' own words, especially if they dealt directly or suggestively with aestheticism, decadence or the fin de siècle. While the focus of this bibliography is British literature 1880 - 1900, I have included a few studies which deal in an illuminating way with Continental, particularly French, ideas of aestheticism and decadence. The bibliography covers books, articles and dissertations written from 1882 to 1975 and includes a number of later studies as well.

Research for this book was largely underwritten by a fellowship from the National Endowment for the Humanities, and was carried out at the Widener, Houghton and Fogg Libraries of Harvard University and at the Zimmerman Library of the University of New Mexico. I should particularly like to thank Ms. Keitha Shoupe, Director of Zimmerman's Inter-Library Loan Department, for her efficiency, ingenuity and wry good humor; she and her staff did their best to make the desert disappear.

ABBREVIATIONS

ABC   American Book Collector

AntigR Antigonish Review

BB   Bulletin of Bibliography

BJA   British Journal of Aesthetics (London)

BNYPL Bulletin of the New York
Public Library

CE   College English

CL   Comparative Literature

CLQ   Colby Library Quarterly

ContempR Contemporary Review

CritQ Critical Quarterly

DA   Dissertation Abstracts

DAI   Dissertation Abstracts International [Supersedes
DA]

E&S   Essays and Studies by Members of the English As-
sociation

EDH   Essays by Divers Hands

EIC   Essays in Criticism (Oxford)

ELH   Journal of English Literary
History

ELN   English Language Notes (U.
of Colo.)

ELT   English Literature in Transition (1880-1920) [Super-
sedes *English Fiction in
Transition*]

EM   English Miscellany

HLB   Harvard Library Bulletin

JAAC   Journal of Aesthetics and
Art Criticism

JRUL   Journal of the Rutgers University Library

KR   Kenyon Review

LitR   Literary Review (Fairleigh
Dickinson U.)

LQHR London Quarterly and Holborn
Review

MLN   Modern Language Notes

MLQ   Modern Language Quarterly

MLS   Modern Language Studies

MP   Modern Philology

N&Q   Notes and Queries

PBSA   Papers of the Bibliographical Society of America

PLC   Princeton University Library
Chronicle

PLL   Papers on Language and Literature

PMLA	Publications of the Modern Language Association	*TSL*	Tennessee Studies in Literature
PR	Partisan Review	*TSLL*	Texas Studies in Literature and Language
QRL	Quarterly Review of Literature		
REL	Review of English Literature	*UR*	University Review
		UTQ	University of Toronto Quarterly
RLV	Revue des Langues Vivantes (Bruxelles)	*UWR*	University of Windsor Review (Windsor, Ontario)
RNL	Review of National Literatures	*VN*	Victorian Newsletter
SAQ	South Atlantic Quarterly	*VP*	Victorian Poetry
SEL	Studies in English Literature, 1500-1900	*VPN*	Victorian Periodicals Newsletter
SoR	Southern Review (Louisiana State U.)	*VS*	Victorian Studies
SP	Studies in Philology	*WTW*	Writers and Their Work Series
SR	Sewanee Review	*YCGL*	Yearbook of Comparative and General Literature
SSF	Studies in Short Fiction (Newberry Coll., S.C.)	*YES*	Yearbook of English Studies
TEAS	Twayne's English Authors Series		

BIBLIOGRAPHY

1. Adams, Elsie B. *Bernard Shaw and the Aesthetes*. Columbus, Ohio: Ohio Univ. Press, 1971.

    Studies GBS's relationship to aestheticism ("Whether one defines aestheticism narrowly as a cult of art or broadly as a concern [overshadowing all others] for creating or comprehending beauty, the aesthetic movement can be seen as encompassing a number of the 'isms' of the late nineteenth century. Aestheticism may be compatible with decadence, with impressionism, or even with naturalism"). Concerned in particular with Shaw's relationship to the "moral aesthetes" (Ruskin, Rossetti, the Pre-Raphaelites, Morris) and the "fin de siècle aesthetes" (Moore, Pater, Swinburne, Whistler, Wilde) who lacked social conscience. Includes chapters on Shaw's view of the artist in his plays and novels and on Shaw as an artist in his own person.

2. Adams, Elsie B. *Israel Zangwill*. NY: Twayne, 1971. [TEAS 121]

    Includes chapters on the fantasies, his criticism and philosophical excursions, on the novels, the short stories and the drama. Concludes with a close examination of *Dreamers of the Ghetto*, stressing Z's characteristic themes: the separation of the generations, the return of the prodigal, his hostility to organized religion, his insistence that art exert a moral force. Finds that Z's humor sets him apart from other writers of the nineties.

3. Adams, Elsie B. "Israel Zangwill: An Annotated Bibliography of Writings About Him," *ELT*, 13 (1970), 209-244.

4. Adlard, John. "Poetry and the Stage-Doors of the 'Nineties," *REL*, 7, iv (1966), 50-60.

    Discusses the survival of the romantic ballet of the 1830s in a decadent form popular in London music-halls where it influenced the poetry of Symons, Wratislaw, Davidson, Kipling and other poets of the nineties. Finds the ballet and especially the figure of the dancer

1

e important inspirations for modernist theories of poetry; believes that if poets like Symons had imitated some of the irony and
gusto of the music-hall *artistes*, they might have been saved from
subsequent banality and absurdity.

5.   Adlard, John. *Yeats, Stenbock and the Nineties*. London:
     Cecil and Amelia Woolf, 1969.

     A biographical account, in the manner of A.J.A. Symons, of the
witty, imaginative, very rich, perverted, generous, short-lived author and eccentric whose opium habit, fantastic Huysmans-esque rooms,
zoöphilia and bizarre obsessions fascinated Yeats and others. Includes an unpublished essay on S. by Symons and a bibliography.

6.   "Aestheticism." *Princeton Encyclopedia of Poetry and Poetics*,
     ed. Alex Preminger. Princeton, N.J.: Princeton Univ. Press,
     1974. Enlarged Edition, pp. 6-8.

     "A term applied to the point of view that art is self-suffi-
cient, need serve no ulterior purpose, and should not be judged by
moral, political, or other nonaesthetic standards." Briefly notes
origins, characteristic expressions and later influences on Anglo-
American modernism. Concludes that the most valid aspect of aestheticism for writers affected by it, "the prime motivating factor in
their lives as artists," was the realization that "the Beautiful has
independent importance and that the poet must be technically scru-
pulous in his work."

7.   Alaya, Flavia. *William Sharp -- "Fiona Macleod" 1855-1905*.
     Cambridge, Mass.: Harvard Univ. Press, 1970.

     Attempts to free WS from the assumptions of biographical cri-
ticism, stressing the variations in his character and interests.
"Fiona Macleod" represents no final resolution; instead, "she was
merely one of a system of pauses and experiments, the whole of which
represented an instinctive anti-nationalism, a convinced cosmopoli-
tanism." Notes the central function in Sharp's work of his search
for place-identity.

8.   Aldington, Richard, ed. *The Religion of Beauty: Selections
     from the Aesthetes*. London: Heinemann, 1950. "Introduction,"
     pp. 1-45.

     Good-humored survey emphasizing personality and anecdote
rather than definition or thorough-going literary history. Believes
aesthetes celebrated an ideal of concrete beauty and saw the function
of art as praise.

2

9.   Alexander, Calvert, S.J. *The Catholic Literary Revival: Three Phases in Its Development from 1845 to the Present*. Milwaukee: Bruce, 1935.

     Believes the Beardsley-Wilde-Dowson phase was "a vital and meaningful drama, arranged and directed by Providence for the salutary benefit of the public."

10. Alford, Norman W. "The Rhymers' Club (Founded 1891): A Study of its Activities and Their Significance," *DA*, 27 (1966), 451A. [Texas]

     Collates the available published materials relating to the RC. Finds term "decadent" only of limited use in describing their work. Group's criticism lacks an "objective, analytical approach," while their poetry is found "remote from the concerns of humanity."

11. Alford, Norman W. *The Rhymers' Club; Poets of the Tragic Generation*. London: Charles Skilton, 1977?

     Not seen.

12. Ali, Raza. "The 'Decadent' View of Life and Dowson's Poetry," *Thoth*, 13, i (1972-73), 19-23.

     Believes the disillusionment characteristic of the decadent poet is an "inevitable consequence" of the aesthetic pursuit of intense sensation. Sees Dowson's idealization of childhood, like the decadent's interest in abnormal sexuality, as a rejection of process. "The irony of the decadent's condition lies in the fact that he has sought to live only in the moment but cannot avoid shadows from the past, nor can he forget the dissolution that lies ahead."

13. Allen, Grant. "The Celt in English Art," *Fortnightly Review*, 49 n.s. (Jan-June 1891), 267-277.

     Sees the aesthetic movement, "which has transformed our houses and profoundly altered our public taste," as a direct result of the Celtic reflux on Teutonic Britain. Finds the Celtic spirit orderly, structural, architectonic: "It delights in Triads, in set forms, in recurrences of measured lines, in arrangements like the Triolet, the Ballade, the Sonnet, the Chant Royal . . . . nothing in it must be bald, dull, flat, amorphous; continuity, regularity, richness with refinement, are its rules of being." Burne-Jones its pre-eminent artistic exemplar.

14. Allen, Grant. "The New Hedonism," *Fortnightly Review*, 55 n.s. (Jan-June 1894), 377-392.

Relying on evolutionistic arguments, declares "everything high and ennobling in our nature springs directly out of the sexual instinct" and "it will be the task ot the new hedonism to restore culture to the place thus usurped by religion."

15.   Altick, Richard D. *Victorian People and Ideas: A Companion for the Modern Reader of Victorian Literature.* NY: Norton, 1973.

Includes consideration of the "artists' reaction against the materialistic tide" and its three successive phases of Pre-Raphaelitism, aestheticism and decadence. Believes "the Aesthetic movement ended the cultural parochialism which had been one of the most deadening aspects of English life under Philistine middle-class rule." Finds that although aestheticism "sometimes is stretched to cover the last phase of the reaction against Victorian orthodoxy in art and morals, the Decadence of the 'Yellow Nineties' is better regarded as a separate, though derivative, phenomenon."

16.   Archer, William. *Poets of the Younger Generation.* London and NY: John Lane, 1902.

"Unscientific appreciations" of poets born after 1850 (thus excluding Henley, Bridges, Dobson) meant to offset the widespread opinion that the age was one of decadence. Attempts to rehabilitate the concept of "minor poet" in discussions of such poets as A.C. Benson, Money-Coutts, Davidson, Hinkson, Hopper, Housman, Kipling, Le Gallienne, Meynell, Nesbit, Newbolt, Phillips, Radford, Santayana, Sigerson, Symons, Thompson, Mrs. Marriot Watson, William Watson and Yeats.

17.   Arvidson, K.O. "Ruskin's Aesthetic: An Approach to the English Elements in the Decadence," *Australasian Universities Language and Literature Association: Proceedings and Papers of the Thirteenth Congress Held At Monash University, 12-18 August, 1970,* ed. J.R. Ellis. Melbourne: AULLA and Monash Univ., 1971.

The abstract of this paper indicates consideration of French and German influences on aestheticism, JR's influence on Pater, on Wilde and the discernibly Ruskinian tendencies among the aesthetes -- their idealism, socialism and religious conversions.

18.   Aslin, Elizabeth. *The Aesthetic Movement: Prelude to Art Nouveau.* NY: Praeger, 1969.

Though primarily devoted to the expression of aestheticist principles in architecture and various crafts, does include chapters on Wilde's role in the movement both in England and America and on the range of satirical comment the movement provoked.

4

19.   Babbitt, Irving. *The New Laocoön: An Essay on the Confusion of the Arts.* Boston and NY: Houghton Mifflin, 1910.

An anti-modernist attack on the mélange of genres, the sensationalism, the "primitivism" of contemporary art forms. "If all the arts are thus restless and impressionistic, the reason is not far to seek; it is because the people who practice these arts and for whom they are practiced are themselves living in an impressionistic flutter. If the arts lack dignity, centrality, repose, it is because the men of the present have no center, no sense of anything fixed or permanent either within or without themselves, that they may oppose to the flux of phenomena and the torrent of impressions. In a word, if confusion has crept into the arts, it is merely a special aspect of a more general malady of that excess of sentimental and scientific naturalism from which, if my diagnosis is correct, the occidental world is now suffering."

20.   Baker, Houston A., Jr. "A Decadent's Nature: The Poetry of Ernest Dowson," *VP*, 6 (1968), 21-28.

"Dowson's use of nature imagery reinforces his dichotomous view of human experience. His major theme is the disparity between the beauty of the ideal moment and the despair of its inevitable loss."

21.   Baker, Houston A., Jr. "The Idea in Aestheticism, 1866-1899," *DA*, 29 (1968), 1862A. [UCLA]

Finds that "a greenery-yallery foreground has greatly obscured the more somber tints in the background" of aestheticist works. Insists that "at the heart of the work of [Swinburne, Rossetti, Pater, Wilde and Dowson] there is always a sound idea -- a meaningful, philosophical conception of the most desirable life -- and the idea is not one that stresses an airy, palace-of-art existence."

22.   Balakian, Anna. *The Symbolist Movement: A Critical Appraisal.* NY: Random House, 1968.

Mainly concerned with French figures and their twentieth-century heirs, but includes consideration of the relationship between decadence and symbolism. Decadence, identified with "the haunting awareness of man's mortality," is used to describe the spirit of the new poetry as distinct from its technique: "What gave symbolism, in its generalized sense, longevity and a power of radiation was that quality called 'decadence,' and the ability to convey via the symbol-image the mood of mysterious, metaphysical restlessness and the lyrical sense of doom." Suggests that without the decadent's anguish, his symbols become monotonous, while without the symbol-image, his view of the world is merely philosophy set to verse.

5

23.   Baldensperger, Ferdinand. "English 'Artistic Prose' and its
      Debt to French Writers," *Modern Language Forum*, 29 (1944),
      139-150.

      Finds that "artistic prose" was little more than "a passing
episode" whose indebtedness to French sources "cannot be over-esti-
mated." Suggests that Wilde's fall was due to the same kind of ex-
cessiveness that marred his prose style. Includes some personal recollections by the author of George Moore.

24.   Balfour, Arthur. *Decadence*. Cambridge: Cambridge Univ. Press,
      1908.

      Decadence as an historical phenomenon. "I do not mean the
sort of decadence often attributed to certain phases of artistic or
literary development, in which an overwrought technique, straining
to express sentiments too subtle or too morbid, is deemed to have
supplanted the direct inspiration of an earlier and simpler age."

25.   Baring, Maurice. *Lost Lectures, or The Fruits of Experience*.
      NY: Knopf, 1932.

      Gives an interesting account of reading tastes among the public
and the highbrows at Cambridge during the early nineties: highbrow
taste favored Verlaine, Ibsen, Meredith, tolerated George Eliot,
Stevenson, Swinburne, and despised the Rhymers' Club poets. "People
spoke then as if the educated world had entered into a new era, and
as if nothing could ever be old-fashioned again."

26.   Barnett, Pat. "Some Aspects of Symbolism in the Work of Aubrey
      Beardsley," *AntigR*, 1 (1970), 33-45.

      A brief treatment of AB's use of candles and candelabra as
stylized signature and symbolic motif. Finds it "a highly appropriate figure to symbolize the warring contrasts and paradoxes" in
AB.

27.   Barry, W.F., Rev. "The French Decadence," *Quarterly Review*,
      174 (Apr 1892), 479-504.

      Finds "the tribe" of Zola, Bourget, Daudet, Maupassant a plague
upon France -- "never was the lightning of indignation, human or
divine, so justly called for . . . to sweep these abominations from
the earth."

28.   Barry, W.F., Rev. "Realism and Decadence in French Fiction,"
      Quarterly Review, 171 (July 1890), 57-90.

      "There is something beyond revolution; and the Renans, Bour-
gets, and Daudets are not slow to pronounce it -- the word 'decadence.'

A putrescent civilisation, a corruption of high and low, a cynical
shamelessness meet us at every turn, from the photographs which in-
sult modesty in the shop windows on the Boulevards, and the porno-
graphic literature on the bookstalls, to the multiplication of di-
vorces and the 'drama of adultery' accepted as a social ordinance."

29.   Bassett, Sharon. "Wordsworth, Pater and the 'Anima Mundi':
       Towards a Critique of Romanticism," *Criticism*, 17 (1975), 262-
       275.

       Studies the "kinship" between the two as expressed in WP's es-
say on Wordsworth in order to question "some conclusions about the
inner tensions that ultimately reduced English romanticism to a program of occult, stylized and private gesture. Remarkably enough it
was not the character flaws of the Aesthetes and Decadents. Instead,
if Pater's assessment is to be credited, the ideology of romanticism
was rooted in an attitude deeply threatened, at least in Wordsworth's
case, by the full range of human creativity."

30.   Baugh, Edward. "Arthur Symons, Poet: A Centenary Tribute,"
       REL, 6, iii (1965), 70-80.

       Seeks to "adjust the balance which has swung too much to the
credit of Symons the critic at the expense of Symons the poet."
Notes the modernist aspects of AS's nineties poetry: urban themes
and sensibility, "simplicity" of language.

31.   Beckson, Karl, ed. *Aesthetes and Decadents of the 1890's: An
       Anthology of British Poetry and Prose*. NY: Vintage, 1966.
       "Introduction," pp. xvii-xl.

       A highly readable account of the major influences, themes and
personalities of the decade. Notes that while the confusion in the
use of the term "decadent" to refer to either an artist's behavior
or to his art persisted through the decade, the decadents who survived the century saw the development of a more mature aestheticism
in Imagism, the work of Eliot and Joyce and the New Criticism. Concludes "English Aesthetes and Decadents command our attention by
their determination to transform their lives into works of art, to
center the meaning of life in private vision in order to resist a
civilization intent on debasing the imagination and thus making man
less human."

32.   Beckson, Karl. "A Mythology of Aestheticism," *ELT*, 17 (1974),
       233-249.

       A systematic examination of the central mythology of the aes-
thetic movement -- the Religion of Art. Briefly discusses the
sources of this particular mythology in Blake, Keats, Ruskin, Poe
and Rossetti, its sacred texts, its idea of art as ritual and its

pervasive image of the artist as priest.

33. Beckson, Karl. "New Dates for the Rhymers' Club," *ELT*, 13
     (1970), 37-38.

     Citing some unpublished sources, suggests 1890-96. See
     and #444 and #521.

34. Beckson, Karl. "The Rhymers' Club," *DA*, 20 (1959), 1021-22.
     [Columbia]

     Believes that though the Rhymers scrupulously avoided the vul-
     garity of manifestoes and doctrines, some shared concerns are evi-
     dent among the members of the group: the importance of craft, small
     forms (though not fixed forms), traditional rhyme schemes and "the
     worn-out diction of much nineteenth-century poetry. Indeed, the tra-
     ditionalism of their poetry is perhaps more striking than their pre-
     sumed *avantgarde* concern with 'purity'."

35. Beckson, Karl and John M. Munro. "Symons, Browning and the
     Development of the Modern Aesthetic," *SEL*, 10 (1970), 687-699.

     Emphasizes the importance of Browning in the development of
     AS's ideas, especially his role in preparing Symons' receptivity to
     the experiments of the French Symbolists. Brownings's isolation of
     dramatic character in a significant moment is seen as crucial for
     AS's own poetic theory. Symons thus linked to such modernist con-
     cepts as Joyce's epiphany, Pound's image and Woolf's moment of being.

36. Beckson, Karl. "Yeats and the Rhymers' Club," *Yeats Studies*,
     1 (1971), 20-41.

     Proposes "an inside view of the Rhymers' Club -- particularly
     Yeats's function as catalyst of various causes -- rather than the
     usual rehearsal of received opinion and error which has marked vir-
     tually all discussion of the group." Refers to a number of unpub-
     lished letters in order to emphasize Yeats's conflicting ambitions
     for the group. Includes some discussion of the first and second
     Rhymers' anthologies and notes that a third was planned.

37. Beebe, Maurice. *Ivory Towers and Sacred Founts: The Artist as
     Hero in Fiction from Goethe to Joyce*. NY: New York Univ. Press,
     1964.

     Traces the development of the artist-novel from the late
     eighteenth century to the early twentieth and considers in detail
     works by Balzac, James, Proust and Joyce. In a chapter on the "ivory
     tower tradition" of art as religion, treats characteristic themes and
     attitudes of Poe, Baudelaire, Mallarmé, Wilde, Rolfe and Conrad.

38. Beer, Thomas. *The Mauve Decade: American Life at the End of Nineteenth Century*. NY: Knopf, 1926.

An anecdotal and highly colored account that includes some mention of American reactions to Wilde and the *Yellow Book* group.

39. Beerbohm, Max. "A Defense of Cosmetics," *Yellow Book*, 1 (Apr 1894), 65-82.

"For behold! The Victorian era comes to its end and the day of sancta simplicitas is quite ended. The old signs are here and the portents to warn the seer of life that we are ripe for a new epoch of artifice." Suggests that the will to cosmetics might "promote that amalgamation of the sexes which is one of the chief planks in the decadent platform."

40. Beerbohm, Max. "1880," *Yellow Book*, 4 (Jan 1895), 275-283.

A parodic attempt to glimpse "through the mists of antiquity" the age of Beauty, Intensity, the Masher and the Lily; "Nincompoopiana the craze was called at first, and later 'Aestheticism'."

41. Beerbohm, Max. "A Letter to the Editor," *Yellow Book*, 2 (July 1894), 281-284.

Deplores the pressmen and their "police-constable mode of criticism" who had attacked his "Defense of Cosmetics" [see 39], an essay intended as a "burlesque upon the 'precious' school of writers."

42. Bellamy, William. *The Novels of Wells, Bennett and Galsworthy: 1890-1910*. NY: Barnes and Noble, 1971.

Sees the Edwardian social novel as "a revolutionary step towards the creation of the acultural 'Brave New World'," as an activist and vitalist response to the "negative apocalyptic myth" and the "convention of sickness" of the fin de siècle: "All the lacks of the 1890's are precisely what Edwardianism remedied: *Angst* was replaced by confidence; the sense of an ending by the sense of a beginning; insecurity by security; invisibility by visual repletion; emptiness by filling."

43. Benamou, Michel, Herbert Howarth, Paul Ilie, Calvin S. Brown and Remy G. Saisselin. "Symposium on Literary Impressionism," *YCGL*, 17 (1968), 40-68.

Among the critical estimates of impressionism offered here are these: "Along with phlegmatic Naturalism, choleric Wagnerism, splenetic Decadentism, Impressionism is one of the four cardinal humors governing *fin de siècle* literature. It is sanguine and thrives on good air, sunshine, and things as they are." And "in British literature the Impressionist effect is best found, not in the borrowings of the colors or the syllables of the cosmos, but in the constant manipulation of rhetoric to capture flow, energy, vibrancy." And "the Impressionist project to fix the fleeting moment can be interpreted on the surface as a love of transience, but its Bergsonian quality is also an attempt to stop time and change it into 'durée' . . . . The euphemization of vital fears by intimations of repose, brightened colors, miniaturized nature, naturalized modernity, illusionistic satisfactions, thematic viscosity and homogenizing luminism, all these converge with hedonistic values and together build the psychological structure of Impressionism."

44.   Benson, E.F. *As We Were: A Victorian Peep Show*. London and
      NY: Longmans Green, 1930.

   Memoirs by the author of *Dodo* which include discussions of the Wilde scandal, Whistler and Swinburne and "the movement of the nineties." Feels that the latter has been overrated; contemporaries did not perceive it as a movement. Poetry of the period most striking for its diversity of aims and techniques.

45.   Bergonzi, Bernard. *The Early H.G. Wells: A Study of the Scien-*
      tific Romances. Manchester: Manchester Univ. Press, 1961.

   Includes discussion of Wells as a fin de siècle writer who shared in the contemporary mood of *fin du globe* -- the sense "that the whole elaborate intellectual and social order of the nineteenth century was trembling on the brink of destruction. *Fin de siècle* was not confined to art or aesthetics; its wider implications affected moral and social and even political attitudes and behavior."

46.   Bergonzi, Bernard. *"Fin de Siècle,"* *The Turn of a Century:*
      Essays on Victorian and Modern English Literature. NY: Barnes
      Noble, 1973, pp. 17-30.

   Prefers *"fin de siècle"* to other terms because it "clearly points to the preoccupations of the last years of the nineteenth century, without being limited to a single decade, and . . . can cover such particular manifestations as 'aestheticism' and 'decadence'." Notes two essential characteristics of this cultural attitude: "the conviction that all established forms of intellectual and moral and social certainty were vanishing, and that the new situation required new attitudes in life and art; and the related belief that art and morality were separate realms, and that the former must be regarded as wholly autonomous." Discusses the central role of Pater and Wilde; surveys the works of the Rhymers' Club poets, Henley, Beerbohm, the short story writers, the *Savoy* and the *Yellow Book*. Stresses the continuity of fin de siècle elements in modernism.

47. Bergonzi, Bernard. "John Gray," *The Turn of a Century: Essays on Victorian and Modern English Literature*. NY: Barnes and Noble, 1973, pp. 114-123.

A biographical and critical discussion that centers in a study of Gray's novel *Park* (1932). Gray seen as primarily a stylist who retained in his later work a number of "ninetyish" traits.

48. Betjeman, John. "Introduction," *The Eighteen-Nineties: A Period Anthology in Prose and Verse*, ed. Martin Secker. London: Richards, 1948, pp. xi-xvi.

Though rebellion was not the predominant note in works of the nineties, it was present and was "largely formulated by the Paterian dictum that Art should not be 'socially conscious', and should have nothing to do with philosophies, morals, ethics, laws of life. It was, as it were, the equivalent in prose and verse, of the abstract painting of more recent years."

49. Biddison, Larry T. "The *Femme Fatale* as Symbol of the Creative Imagination in Late Victorian Fiction," *DA*, 30 (1970), 4976A. [La. St.]

Argues that "the relationship of the *femme fatale* and her victim-lover in certain late Victorian novels is essentially that which exists between art and the artist enamoured of his own aesthetic powers." Discusses *Lesbia Brandon, Dorian Gray, Zuleika Dobson, Under the Hill, Roderick Hudson* and *Victory*.

50. Billhymer, Curtis P. "Some Pagan Writers: A Study in Late Victorian Literary Revolt," *DAI*, 35 (1975), 6703A. [Northwestern]

Chiefly concerned with Pater, Symonds and Carpenter and their "search for more satisfying aesthetic, religious, and social expression of their values in pagan and primitive cultures particularly those of ancient Greece and Rome." Traces common elements and places their thought in the current of advanced intellectual opinion 1870-1900.

51. Bitoun, Armand. "Aubrey Beardsley et l'esthétisme homosexuel," *Les lettres nouvelles* (Mar-June 1967), 119-129.

Argues that the great theme of art and literature in the nineties was hermaphroditism. Believes that the episodes and tone of Beardsley's *Venus and Tannhäuser* indicate his desire to experience a widened range of erotic possibilities. Notes the central place of burlesque in English aesthetic decadence. [In French]

11

52. Block, Edwin F., Jr. "The Transition to Modernism: The Reader's
     Role in Selected Works of Walter Pater, Arthur Symons, W.B.
     Yeats and Hugo von Hofmannsthal," *DAI*, 36 (1975), 300A. [Stan-
     ford]

     Employing the methods of phenomenological textual criticism,
seeks to show the importance of these writers to fin de siècle literature. In particular, "examines visible author or persona and the
conditions for reader response in particular texts."

53. Block, Haskell M. "Some Concepts of the Literary Elite at the
     Turn of the Century," *Mosaic*, 2, ii (Winter 1971-72), 57-64.

     Examines the role of three representative poets -- Mallarmé,
George and Yeats -- in the formation of literary elites, and emphasizes the variations in elitist thought within a common symbolist
tradition. Concludes that fin de siècle poets "were not as isolated
or as alienated as has sometimes been claimed. To at least some
degree, their elitism was the basis for a public role."

54. Bloom, Harold. "The Place of Pater: *Marius, the Epicurean*,"
     Ringers in the Tower: Studies in the Romantic Tradition. Chi-
     cago: Univ. of Chicago Press, 1971, pp. 185-194.

     Emphasizes the modernity of Pater and *Marius*, a work whose bur-
den "is the burden of the modern lyric from Wordsworth to Stevens,
the near solipsism of the isolated sensibility, of the naked aesthetic consciousness deprived of everything save its wavering self and
the flickering of an evanescent beauty in the world of natural objects, which is part of the universe of death." Unlike Wordsworth
or Arnold, Pater welcomed excessive self-consciousness "and by this
welcome inaugurat[ed], for writers and readers in English, the decadent phase of Romanticism, in which, when honest, we still find ourselves."

55. Bloom, Harold. "Walter Pater: The Intoxification of Belated-
     ness," *Yale French Studies*, 50 (1974), 163-189.

     Seeks to "place Pater in his Oedipal context in the cultural
situation of his own time" -- especially his "anxiety-of-influence"
response to Ruskin -- in order to expose his role as "father of Anglo-
American Aestheticism": Pater turned "the Victorian continuation of
High Romanticism into the Late Romanticism or 'Decadence' that prolonged itself as what variously might be called Modernism, Post-Roman-
ticism or, self-deceivingly, anti-Romanticism, the art of Pound's
Vortex." Includes discussion of *The Renaissance, Imaginary Portraits*
and *Appreciations*.

56. Bloom, Harold. *Yeats.* London and NY: Oxford Univ. Press, 1970.

A chapter on the "tragic generation" presents Dowson and John-son as "minor but inevitable poets" and sets them in context of the work of the early WBY. Includes several close analyses of their poems, concluding with a reading of "The Dark Angel," termed the best and most representative poem of the period, "a Romantic poem attacking Romanticism, in prophecy of much Modern poetry." Believes "the poets of the Tragic Generation did not fail for seeking the wrong goal, but because they lacked the human strength to put their faith in art alone, as Pater, Yeats, and Stevens did. The last irony of the Nineties is that its poets, except for Yeats, could not follow their art for art's sake alone."

57. Booth, Robert M. "Aubrey Beardsley and *The Savoy*," *Aylesford Review*, 8 (1966), 71-85.

A short sketch of the magazine's founding, contributors, cri-tical reception and demise, including a volume by volume survey of its contents. Concludes the *Savoy* "easily surpassed *The Yellow Book* as an exponent of fin-de-sièclism. It was indeed the most vital mani-festation of the movement. It stood for the modern note without fear or wavering of purpose; hence it represents the most ambitious and most satisfying achievement of fin de siècle journalism in England."

58. Bowra, C.M. *The Background of Modern Poetry.* Oxford: Oxford Univ. Press, 1947.

Believes that "once poetry has exploited the full resonances of a manner, it seems somehow to lose contact with reality and to be guided by rules which stifle its living breath . . . . the sentimen-tality of the last Victorians [illustrates] this danger and show[s] how even the noblest style dies because in the end it lives for it-self instead of to serve a truly creative outlook." The limits of the Victorians' manner to be seen in the "corrupt following" which adopted their mannerisms without their power or daring. The modern mode which made itself felt ca. 1910 sought realism and contemporane-ity, rejecting the choice archaisms and tone of longing and regret characteristic of the later romantics.

59. Bowra, C.M. *The Heritage of Symbolism.* London and Toronto: Macmillan, 1943. [Rptd. London, 1951]

Notes that "if we compare the poetry written in Europe after 1890 with what preceded it, we must admit that there was a change and that the newer poets had some common qualities which make them look like members of a movement . . . .This movement may be regarded as a later development, a second wave, of those poetical activities which are variously known as Symbolist and Decadent." French Symbol-ism actually " a mystical form of Aestheticism" whose counterpart in

England was the aesthetic movement of Rossetti, Pater and Wilde, though the English group was less transcendentally mystical. Discusses the strengths and defects of the Symbolist heritage with chapters on Valéry, Rilke, George, Blok and Yeats.

60. Boyd, Ernest A. *Ireland's Literary Renaissance*. NY: Knopf, 1922. 2nd Rev. Ed.

Contends that the main purpose of the Irish Literary Renaissance "has not been to contribute to English literature, but to create a national literature for Ireland, in the language which has been imposed on her." Chapters on sources and precursors, on Young Ireland, on Yeats's works, on poetry, drama and narrative prose including remarks on such minor figures as Johnson, Todhunter, Eglinton, Hopper and Tynan.

61. Bradfield, Thomas. "A Dominant Note of Some Recent Fiction," *Westminster Review*, 142 (1894), 537-545.

Concerned over the "unwholesome" preoccupation of the new realism with themes of illicit passion and the moral equality of the sexes in such works as Sarah Grand's *The Heavenly Twins* and George Egerton's *Keynotes*: "Is this tendency in our modern novel to be taken as a sign that English fiction has entered upon a stage of decadence, and that this period of its history is to be similar to that which marked the French novel during the middle of the century, when the 'literature of despair' as it had been termed, was succeeded by a 'literature of decadence'?"

62. Bradley, William A. "What is Decadence?" *Bookman* [NY], 37 (1913), 431-438.

Suggests that the critical attack upon decadence springs from a hatred of experimentalism and genius. "It is the condition of activity which it indicates, and not the immediate result which it may or may not attain, that is the essential thing in artistic experimentation; and it is under such a condition alone that genius, when it arrives, can manifest itself. Genius appears, not when forms are hardened and stiffened to receive it, but when they are still in a more or less indeterminate state of chaos. What, as we have sought to show, is incorrectly called Decadence, is nothing more or less than the attempt to prolong such a state at the very heart of an old and encrusted civilisation."

63. Brennan, Neil. "The Aesthetic Tradition in the English Comic Novel," *DA*, 20 (1959), 1780-81. [Illinois]

Wilde seen as the literary progenitor of the "aesthetic" strain in the English comic novel from Beerbohm, Hichens and Benson through Saki and Firbank to Huxley, Waugh and Powell.

64. Bridgwater, Patrick. *Nietzsche in Anglosaxony: A Study of Nietzsche's Impact on English and American Literature.* n.p.: Leicester Univ. Press, 1972.

Stresses that subjective responses to N. -- often the result of early poor translations -- were in fact creative misconceptions. Chapters on Pater and Symons, on Moore, on Davidson, on Wells and Shaw and on Yeats.

65. Briggs, Asa. "Manners, Morals and Tastes: Changing Values in Art and Society," *The Nineteenth Century*, ed. Asa Briggs. London: Thames and Hudson, 1970, pp. 292-326.

Chiefly concerned with the fate of romanticism in the later part of the nineteenth century: "The *fin de siècle* represents a time when Romantic ideals, still pervasive, were beginning to be devalued, but no corresponding set of ideals had arisen to take their place."

66. Brisau, A. "The *Yellow Book* and its Place in the Eighteen-Nineties," *Studia Germanica Gandensia*, 8 (1966), 135-172.

Finds that the *YB*'s decadent reputation is undeserved; "its table of contents, though, is a perfect mirror of the literary activity of the decade." Short critical accounts of the most characteristic prose and poetry writers appearing in the magazine. Concludes that the *YB* stood for "an organ in which all authors, of whatever school, would be allowed to publish their work."

67. Brooks, Cleanth and William K. Wimsatt, Jr. *Literary Criticism: A Short History.* NY: Random House, 1957.

See #575.

68. Brooks, Michael. "Oscar Wilde, Charles Ricketts and the Art of the Book," *Criticism*, 12 (1970), 301-315.

"The friendship between the two men exemplifies one of the most significant aspects of Wilde's career: the cross-fertilization between his literary work and the pictorial arts."

69. Brown, R.D. "The Bodley Head Press: Some Bibliographical Extrapolations," *PBSA*, 61 (1967), 39-50.

Suggests that questions like "what was the decadence?" must wait upon an answer to the prior question of how the exotic attitudes of the decadence managed to find a public forum. Argues that without John Lane the movement would not have taken the form it did. The Bodley book was less a work of bibliographic art than the product of

shrewd business economies in printing: large type, large leadings
between lines meant cheaper typesetting costs; even though the *Yellow Book* was composed on linotype, Lane contrived to give the impression the magazine was hand composed by using catchwords, a collation-
al guide that had gone out of style a century before.

70.   Bruce, Donald. "Vamp's Progress: A Study in Late Nineteenth-
       Century Affectation," *Cornhill Magazine*, 171 (Autumn 1960),
       353-359.

    Suggests Hawthorne's "Rappacini's Daughter" as a model for the
Pre-Raphaelite vamp; traces the vamp figure from Gautier to Baudelaire to Swinburne to Rossetti to Wilde to Beardsley.

71.   Buchanan, Robert W. "The Modern Young Man as Critic," *Univer-
       sal Review*, 3 (Jan-Apr 1889), 353-375. [Rptd. in *The Coming
       Terror*. NY: Lovell, 1891. 2nd Ed., pp. 143-182]

    Typical product of the Buchanan pen: vitriolic attack on five
types of contemporary criticism which threaten established values --
the Superfine Young Man [James], the Detrimental Young Man [Bourget],
the Olfactory Young Man [Maupassant], the Young Man in a Cheap Literary Suit [Archer] and the Bank Holiday Young Man [Moore].

72.   Buchen, Irving H. "Decadence as Blasphemy," *MLS*, 2, i (1972),
       17-23.

    Sees decadence as the "straddling," the "self-begotten or bas-
tard child" of both classicism and romanticism. Decadence characterized by a "falling away from variety to singularity, from interdepen-
dence to self-sufficiency" and by a "falling away from life to the
art of life." Decadent fear of death translates into a revulsion
from sex which in turn is expressed in satire that is "cosmic," "always concerned with death," a "satire against God."

73.   Buckley, Jerome H. "Pater and the Suppressed Conclusion," *MLN*,
       65 (1950), 249-251.

    Suggests Pater withdrew the "Conclusion" from the second edition
of *The Renaissance* because of the damaging satiric portrait of himself as Mr. Rose in W.H. Mallock's *The New Republic*, first serialized
in the monthly *Belgravia* June through December 1876. [See #455,
#469 and #527]

74.   Buckley, Jerome H. *The Triumph of Time: A Study of the Victor-
       ian Concepts of Time, History, Progress and Decadence.* Cam-
       bridge, Mass.: Harvard Univ. Press, 1966.

    Argues that in discussing decadence "we must distinguish

between a sense of the reality or possibility of cultural decline, which . . . has been common among artists and intellectuals for the past century, and an aesthetic mode or temper most apparent, in England, in some of the fiction, minor poetry, and graphic art of the eighteen nineties." Discusses the sources and expressions of the former from Lord Kelvin to Oswald Spengler. Literary decadence usually characterized by eclecticism and self-expression "even when [the decadent artist] sought to mask the self in exotic disguises." Considers Pater's contributions to the modern temper, the importance of "the moment" to late Victorian artists and the consolations provided them by religion and art.

75. Buckley, Jerome H. *The Victorian Temper: A Study of Literary Culture.* NY: Vintage, 1951.

Includes chapters on the "aesthetic" eighties and the "decadent" nineties. 1880s seen as the decade of the specialist, of a retreat from the High Victorian attempt to integrate mind and soul. Comments upon Gissing, English Parnassianism, aestheticism, Wilde and Whistler. Influence of the aesthetic movement seen to have been short-lived, though it "left its mark on the creativity of later decades," particularly in the "aesthetic" regard for craftsmanship and in the concept of the artist as specialist. Believes that the divorce of art from society encouraged by aestheticism damaged both: "Art suffered the burden of self-consciousness and the blight of exclusive and arbitrary interpretation. And society, intent upon its own specialized pursuits, lost the vision of an integrated pattern, the meaningful experience of a 'transfigured life'." Sees the 1890s as possessed of an apocalyptic vision shared by "decadent" and "counter-decadent" alike. Believes decadent art "demanded no courage of action, no true boldness of execution; it was passive gallantry of style, precious, effeminate, effete." Similarly, the decadent vision of evil was "an artificial growth, the calculated product of a curious sensibility; and as such it reflected not the terrors of the objective world but the spiritual isolation of the artist, striving too deliberately to transcend the moral values of a middle-class convention." Comments upon Wilde, Symons, Beardsley, Crackanthorpe, Johnson, Dowson, Phillips, Davidson, Henley.

76. Buckley, Jerome H. *William Ernest Henley: A Study in the "Counter-Decadence" of the 'Nineties.* Princeton, N.J.: Princeton Univ. Press, 1945.

A general critical treatment of WEH's life and work set against a background of social, intellectual and aesthetic concerns. Includes sections on Victorian activism, Henley's early work, political writings, literary criticism and poetry. "The convenience of such a label [i.e. decadence] has led many a reader virtually to ignore the truly vital writing of the English *fin de siècle*. For if there was in the 'nineties a 'decadent' coterie, there was also a far more vigorous 'counter-decadent' group. If there were Wildean aesthetes, there were also the Young Men of William Ernest Henley. And it was in the theory and practice of the latter that the best in Edwardian letters was to take root."

77.   Bulloch, John M. "Literary Circles of the 'Nineties," *Library Review*, 4 (1933-34), 145-150.

Focusses on the activities of William Robertson Nicoll, founder of *The Bookman*, and Clement K. Shorter, critic, with some discussion of the growth of the literary "business."

78.   Burdett, Osbert. *The Beardsley Period: An Essay in Perspective.* London: John Lane, 1925.

Takes as its premise that "the nineties is not period but a point of view." Thus, "many of those who figure largely in the decade itself, since they did not share this point of view, must be excluded." The true artists of the nineties, then, are Beardsley, Wilde, Symons, Johnson, Dowson, Crackanthorpe, Le Gallienne, Beerbohm, Davidson and the *Yellow Book* writers. The movement is characterized by its French influences, the youth of its members, its reaction against Victorianism. It is at once the last dissipated expression of Romanticism and "an eternal mood of the human mind, a mood only the facetings of which had previously been found, and these in unrelated matters." Believes that the "quality that gives interest to this reaction is that it came from several quarters and occupied several talents, all in some degree related by the sympathies and the common influences that had moulded them. In poetry, in criticism, in the novel, in art, in the drama and the short story, the jaundiced note was heard; and since the protagonists were sympathetic to each other, and in several instances personal friends, we have the always interesting and suggestive fact of a movement to chronicle." Includes chapters on French influences, on Beardsley, on prose writers, on poetry and on the *Yellow Book* and the *Savoy*.

79.   Burne, Glenn S. "Havelock Ellis: An Annotated Selected Bibliography of Primary and Secondary Works," *ELT*, 9 (1966), 55-107.

Includes a brief introduction.

80.   Bush, Douglas. *Mythology and the Romantic Tradition in English Poetry*. Cambridge, Mass.: Harvard Univ. Press, 1937.

Finds the mythological conception of nature dead by the second half of the nineteenth century, while Romantic ideas of the poet, detached from context, are intensified in a positive way by French influences, negatively by hostility to bourgeois standards. Late Victorian minor poets in particular "continued to exploit the old conflicts in much the same way and, in spite of Swinburne and Wilde and all the paganism of the nineties, most writers now as before took the

Christian side . . . . in the tired nineties paganism ran rather to
nostalgia than to full-blooded revival of the antique joys of sense."

81.   Busst, A.J.L.   "The Image of the Androgyne in the Nineteenth
      Century," *Romantic Mythologies*, ed. Ian Fletcher. London:
      Routledge and Kegan Paul, 1967, pp. 1-95.

      In a detailed examination of several representative, primarily
French, images and systems, traces the shift from an optimistic early
nineteenth-century image of the androgyne symbolizing human solidar-
ity and the fundamental goodness of man to a later pessimistic view
of the androgyne as "a symbol of vice, particularly of cerebral lechery, demonality, onanism, homosexuality, sadism and masochism." Believes "disillusionment with the realities of practical life and with
human relationships, foreknowledge of the impossibility of finding
satisfaction in the exterior world, withdrawal into the mind and consequent loneliness and frustration -- all this is expressed by the
tremendous vogue of cerebral lechery which constantly increased after
Mademoiselle de Maupin until the end of the century and which found
its most perfect symbol in the hermaphrodite, which was to dominate
the 1890's."

82.   Campos, Christophe.   *The View of France From Arnold to Blooms-
      bury*. London: Oxford Univ. Press, 1965.

      Attempts to explore real-life apprehensions and prejudices
about the French as they are expressed in literature. Includes chapters on Pater, on James, on George Moore and the nineties. Finds
Moore's works "representative of the large section of unsophisticated
and apparently second-rate literature that can be conveniently
grouped together under the heading of the Nineties. In its view of
France, as in most other things, it is superficial. But this is a
minor shortcoming, for its shallowness is not barren: it is not imi-
tating imperfectly, but creating confusedly . . . . Immorality is
perhaps the main feature of the view of France during this period."

83.   Caron, Evelyne.   "Structures and Organisation de quelques
      thèmes dans les oeuvres d'Arthur Machen," *Littérature*, 8 (1972),
      36-40.

      A brief structuralist treatment of some of AM's stories. [In
French]

84.   Carter, A.E.   *The Idea of Decadence in French Literature 1830-
      1900*. Toronto: Univ. of Toronto Press, 1958.

      A detailed account of the sources, development and principal
themes of French decadence, including extensive description of various representative works. Decadence seen as a protest against nineteenth-century complacency; its chief characteristic -- the cult of

the artificial, paradoxically identified with the modern: "It is
worth noting here that this fusion of the artificial and the modern
which is one of the identifying marks of decadence united two fundamentally opposed ideas: a hatred of modern civilization and a love
of the refinements modern civilization made possible." Chapters on
the decadent myth, on its three phases -- late Romantic, Naturalist
and fin de siècle, and on decadent literary style. Concludes that
though decadence was in some sense a final development of Romanticism,
it was also "in revolt against Romantic theory on two essential
points -- the cult of Nature and the cult of ideal love." Sexual
perversion was typically identified with the anti-natural and the
artificial: "This chase after the abnormal is linked to the main
characteristic of decadent sensibility: its intellectualism, its
will-power." Concludes that in its acceptance of nature as normative
decadence is a perverse form of Romantic primitivism.

85.   Cary, Richard. "Vernon Lee's Vignettes of Literary Acquain-
       tances," *CLQ*, 9, iii (Sept 1970), 179-199.

       Believes that Violet Paget's vitriolic sketches of her literary
contemporaries were composed primarily to impress and divert her difficult mother and her half-brother Eugene Lee-Hamilton, a chronic
psychosomatic invalid. She finds Moore and Sharp underbred; Shaw,
Stevenson and Pater pass muster and Browning and James have her res-
pect.

86.   Casford, E. Leonore. *The Magazines of the 1890's*. Eugene,
       Ore.: Univ. of Oregon Press, 1929.

       An inquiry into the literary quality of the more important
periodicals [*Albemarle, Yellow Book, Savoy*] with briefer treatments
of the *Anti-Philistine, Butterfly, Dome, Hobby Horse, Pageant* and
Quarto. Concludes that the noxious and evil qualities of the nineties are overrated, that writers were serious in their attempt to
express dissatisfaction with existing standards and restraints and
that they deserve commendation for helping to develop a more beautiful and artistic English prose style. Sees the nineties as a period
of transition from conventional morality, respectability and smugness
to the realism and freedom of the French: "This longing after the
fullness of experience was the real heart of the so-called 'decadent
movement' which has been decried in recent years. It was not so much
the whim of a few isolated youths as it was the outgrowth of the doctrine of Rousseau, asserting . . . the rights of personality."

87.   Cassagne, Albert. *La théorie de l'art pour l'art en France
       chez les derniers romantiques et les premiers réalistes*.
       Paris: Lucien Dorbon, 1905.

       Studies French writers influenced in various ways by the theory
during the period 1848-1870; discusses relation of l'art pour l'art
to romanticism, science, pessimism, the plastic arts. [In French]

88. Cazamian, Louis and Emile Legouis. "New Divergences," *A History of English Literature*, trans. H.D. Irvine, W.D. MacInnes and L. Cazamian. NY: Macmillan, 1935, pp. 1218-1365.

A literary historical overview of the period 1875-1914 with critical accounts and bibliographies of period writers. Stresses the extraordinary diversity of the period. Sees decadence as "a confused tentative medley of the tendencies which will renovate the literature of the twentieth century," and as a movement whose only unity is psychological, "the outbreak of instincts which had been repressed by the constraint of the Victorian period."

89. Cazamian, Madeleine L. *Le roman et les idées en Angleterre: l'anti-intellectualisme et l'esthétisme (1880-1900)*. Paris: Publications de la Faculté des Lettres de l'Université de Strasbourg, 1935.

Detailed discussion of the sources and expressions of late Victorian aestheticism with chapters on the evolutionist aestheticism of Vernon Lee and Lafcadio Hearne, the social aestheticism of Morris, the sublimated or diffused aestheticism of Le Gallienne, Beerbohm, Henry Harland and George Egerton, Kenneth Grahame, Maurice Hewlett and J.M. Barrie. Other chapters on Wilde, Pater, Arthur Machen, Celtic Renaissance, aestheticism and decadence. Notes that both aestheticism and decadence seemed to lack positive characteristics; less coherent movements that liberating tendencies in literature, tendencies whose "alchemy" continues to contribute color, nuance and suppleness to contemporary literature. [In French]

90. Cazamian, Madeleine L. *Le roman et les idées en Angleterre: l'influence de la science (1860-1890)*. Paris: Istra, 1923.

Includes chapters on science and intellectualism in the novel, on pessimism in the novel 1875-1900, on Gissing and on Hardy. Distinguishes between the pessimism which touched the rich or cultivated classes -- the fear of degeneration which accompanies a civilization too intense or decadent and a life too artificial and feverish -- from the social pessimism which had its roots in the failure of social philanthropy to ameliorate human misery. [In French]

91. Cevasco, G.A. "John Gray (1866-1934): A Primary Bibliography and an Annotated Bibliography of Writings About Him," *ELT*, 19 (1976), 49-63.

92. Chancellor, E. Beresford. "To the Editor: *The Spirit Lamp*," *London Mercury*, 25 (1932), 387-389.

A brief note on the Oxford undergraduate magazine, later edited by Lord Alfred Douglas, whose contributors included Johnson, Wilde, Symonds, Beerbohm, Pierre Louÿs, Gleeson White. [See #131]

93. Chapple, J.A.V. *Documentary and Imaginative Literature 1880-1920*. NY: Barnes and Noble, 1970.

A thematic study of the views of history and literature during the period, focussing on such topics as the rural crisis, urbanization, imperialism, esoteric beliefs. Includes many brief analyses of representative works. Finds that "in the last decades of the nineteenth century there was a kind of art and literature based upon a rejection of life. Its creators deliberately cut themselves off from major movements of history, and the best that can be said for them is that they provided material of peculiar kind for the imagination of a major poet [i.e. Yeats]."

94. Charlesworth, Barbara. *Dark Passages: The Decadent Consciousness in Victorian Literature*. Madison and Milwaukee: Univ. of Wisconsin Press, 1965.

Believes decadent consciousness characterized by the pursuit of isolation and the cultivation of momentary inward states of ecstasy. Misunderstanding the aesthetics of D.G. Rossetti and Pater, "the Decadents failed in their lives and in their art." Literary and psychological discussions of Rossetti, Swinburne, Pater, Wilde, Johnson and Symons.

95. Chesterton, G.K. *Victorian Age in Literature*. NY: Holt, 1913.

Compares the fin de siècle years that followed the collapse of religious and political idealism to "one long afternoon in a rich house on a rainy day. It was not merely that everyone believed that nothing would happen; it was also that everybody believed that anything happening was even duller than nothing happening." Distinguishes two "positive" movements in the fin de siècle: Shaw and the socialists, and Kipling and the imperialists.

96. Chesterton, G.K. "Writing 'Finis' to Decadence," *Independent*, 89 (1917), 100.

"It was an arithmetical coincidence that the decay of the Victorian comfort and conviction occurred at the end of one hundred arbitrarily selected years."

97. Chew, Samuel C. "Aestheticism and 'Decadence'," *A Literary History of England*, ed. Albert C. Baugh, Tucker Brooke, Samuel C. Chew, Kemp Malone and George Sherburn. NY: Appleton-Century-Crofts, 1948, pp. 1475-84.

A brief account which views the aesthetic movement as an "expression of dissatisfaction with the dominant Utilitarian creed" and concentrates on Pater, Wilde and the writers of the *Yellow Book* and the *Savoy*, among whom Symons is found the most characteristic: "In

his poetry there is a remoteness from contemporary society that expresses the point of view of the entire group of 'Decadents'."

98. Child, Ruth C. *The Aesthetic of Walter Pater*. NY: Macmillan,
    1940.

Examines the prevailing assumptions about art for art's sake,
impressionism and aestheticism that have limited Pater's critical
stature. Emphasizes the progression within Pater's aesthetic theory
from an early stress on art as intensity to the later perception of
art as a soul-enlarging, purifying vision of the ideal. Identifies
the emphases of the aesthetic movement as (1) the demand for freedom
of treatment and subject in art, (2) a social aim to make beauty
available to all, (3) an interest in the sensuous elements of art,
(4) the desire to intermingle or merge the arts, (5) an interest in
exotic themes, (6) the ideal of the perfection of form and (7) the
conception of life as an art.

99. Clarke, Austin. *The Celtic Twilight and the Nineties*. Dublin:
    Dolmen, 1969.

Chapters on the nineties, the Celtic Twilight, Victorian verse
drama and Yeats's plays. Stresses the continuity of Yeats's development, emphasizing the sources and significance of his work of the
Twilight, whose "delicate impressionism, shadowy themes, otherworldly
longings and subtle wavering rhythms" were characteristic of the
poets of the nineties.

100. Coldwell, Joan. "'The Art of Happy Desire': Yeats and the
     Little Magazine," *The World of W.B. Yeats*, ed. Robin Skelton
     and Anne Saddlemyer. Seattle: Univ. of Washington Press, 1965.
     Rev. Ed., pp. 24-37.

Brief description of the character and ambitions of such little
magazines as the *Dome, Yellow Book, Savoy, Dial, Pageant, Beltaine,
Samhein, Arrow* and *Evergreen*; surveys WBY's contributions. Believes
the dual interest in art and literature characteristic of the nineties little magazine "reflects that age's growing sense of the need
for cultural education and also the belief, fostered by continental
theorists, of the inter-relation of all the arts."

101. Colson, Percy. *Close of an Era: 1887-1914*. London: Hutchin-
     son, 1945.

Anecdotal and partisan account that stresses the distinctive
nature of the period, the result of a "new spirit" which was "tired
of the gross Victorian materialism and cult of ugliness; the new
scientific and philosophic ideas were beginning to displace the old
dead conventions, and authority of every kind was being questioned."
Decadence was "just a pose and no one took it seriously, least of all

the artists themselves. For the young and talented the 'nineties were a paradise and most of them knew it." Includes chapters on the nineties, the Wilde affair, contemporary music and entertainment, art and popular books of 1887-1914.

102. Connolly, Cyril. *Enemies of Promise*. Boston: Little, 1939.

Though mostly concerned with modernism, describes the nineties as being governed by "a complicating trend or inflation" as distinguished from the simplifying trend of Georgian poetry and realism. Believes that "one faith unites all the writers [except Shaw and Wells] . . . they believed in the importance of their art, in the sanctity of the artist and in his sense of vocation."

103. Cornell, William Kenneth. *The Symbolist Movement*. New Haven: Yale Univ. Press, 1951.

An interesting chronicle of the symbolist movement in France from 1866 to 1898, concentrating upon the factual data of literary groups, quarrels and publications. Traces the growth of symbolism as a reaction against Parnassianism through "decadence" to the form which stressed the negation of the visible, understanding through intuition, abstention from the rational and the dogmatic, the revelations of silence, and the exploration of fine shadings of sentiment.

104. Court, Franklin E. "Virtue Sought 'As a Hunter His Sustenance': Pater's 'Amoral Aesthetic'," *ELH*, 40 (1973), 549-563.

Pater's concern with the idea of virtue "covers at least the twenty most productive years of his life and serves as a theme unifying his early essays." Finds that the concept "underlies the fundamentally ethical nature of his too frequently minsunderstood aesthetic vision."

105. Cox, J. Randolph. "Ghostly Antiquary: The Stories of Montague Rhodes James," *ELT*, 12 (1969), 197-202.

A brief biographical and critical account of the ghost story writer (1862-1936). Undertakes to examine why James' stories are so effective; "they still compel the reader to sleep with lights on."

106. Crackanthorpe, Hubert. "Reticence in Literature: Some Roundabout Remarks," *Yellow Book*, 2 (July 1894), 259-269.

A response to Waugh [see #547], emphasizing the subjective element in the "new realism": "A work of art can never be more than a corner of Nature, seen through the temperament of a single man." Suggests that the treatment will always be more important than the subject and that "the business of art is not to explain or to describe, but to suggest."

107. Croft-Cooke, Rupert. *Feasting With Panthers: A New Considera-*
     tion of Some Late Victorian Writers. London: W.H. Allen, 1967.

     Stresses the interrelationship of sexual idiosyncrasies and
literary work in an attempt to bring the "so-called Decadent writers"
of the period 1857-1895 down to earth: "they all, it seems to me,
need cutting down to size, need stripping of their false colours,
need to be discussed in earthier terms and with less wonder and pi-
ty." Primarily biographical consideration includes Swinburne, Simeon
Solomon, Symonds, FitzGerald, Whitman, Wilde, Pater, John Gray, Raffalovich, Johnson, Dowson, Stenbock.

108. Crowell, Norton B. *Alfred Austin: Victorian.* Albuquerque:
     Univ. of New Mexico Press, 1953.

     The poet who succeeded Tennyson as Laureate saw as one of his
chief functions the combatting of fin de siècle lassitude. "As much
as Henley or Charles Kingsley, he deplored the enervating, unmanly
spirit; for in it he saw the clammy febrile symptoms of decay."
Believes Austin's later neglect is "the fate of those who lack self-
analysis, judgment and a sense of humor."

109. Cruse, Amy. *After the Victorians.* London: Allen and Unwin,
     1938.

     Chapters on the nineties, French influences, minor poets,
crime fiction, drama, science and romance. For all the pretensions
of decadence, the nineties chiefly useful in breaking up "that underlying uniformity of taste that, towards the end of the Victorian era,
had been tending to solidify."

110. Cruse, Amy. *The Victorians and Their Reading.* Boston: Hough-
     ton Mifflin, n.d.

     Studies patterns and opinions in general reading 1837-1887.
Includes chapters on the New Woman and the aesthetes. Says that its
own extravagance and *Patience* killed aestheticism: "in the late
'eighties it drooped; in the early 'nineties, when newer crazes
arose, it died."

111. Cunningham, A.R. "The 'New Woman Fiction' of the 1890's," *VS*,
     17 (1973), 177-186.

     Discusses the novels of Sarah Grand, George Egerton, Emma Fran-
ces Brooke, "Iota" and Menie Muriel Dowie in which the demand for a
more open approach to female sexuality was linked to the demand for
women's emancipation. Finds these novelists shared no consistent

thesis, but did have certain social ideals in common. Discerns two main types of "new woman" novel: the "purity school" that challenged the cant surrounding Victorian concepts of marriage, and the "bachelor girl" novels that were less committed to monogamous relationships and more interested in psychological problems.

112. Currier, Barbara. "The Gift of Personality: An Appraisal of 'Impressionist Criticism'," *DAI*, 33 (1973), 5673A. [Columbia]

Examines various definitions of impressionism and studies the work of fourteen critics including Pater, Symons and Wilde. Finds their work shares assumptions about the expressive nature of art and criticism; notes the several ways in which impressionist critics practiced self-expression in their criticism.

113. Cushman, Keith. "The Quintessence of Dowsonism: 'The Dying of Francis Donne'," *SSF*, 11 (1974), 45-51.

Finds this story, alone of ED's fiction, a significant achievement and "something of a personal testament." Believes that "the deepest and most profound meaning of the story is that the life of aesthetic detachment is nothing more than a long dying."

114. Daiches, David. "The Earlier Poems: Some Themes and Patterns," *In Excited Reverie: A Centenary Tribute to William Butler Yeats, 1865-1939*, ed. A. Norman Jeffares and K.G.W. Cross. NY: Macmillan, 1965, pp. 48-67.

Examines WBY's "conviction of the essential dichotomy between man and nature" in several early poems, noting that "much of what is often regarded as uniquely belonging to the later Yeats can be found struggling to find expression in the earlier and occasionally succeeding."

115. Daiches, David. *Some Late Victorian Attitudes*. London: Andre Deutsch, 1969.

Studies the late Victorian religious doubt and unbelief, "this mood of what might be called sceptical stoicism combined with sceptical activism." Notes that the passive melancholy of aestheticism and the stoic activism of Kipling and Henley "can be seen as opposite sides of the same medal. It is an over-simplification to say that both represent attempts to compensate for a lost world of absolute value. Yet it is an over-simplification worth asserting, for the germ of truth which it contains is worth further exploration."

116. Dale, Hilda. *La poésie française en Angleterre: 1850-1890. Sa fortune et son influence.* Paris: Didier, 1954.

Not seen.

117. D'Amico, Masolino. "Oscar Wilde Between 'Socialism' and Aestheticism," *EM*, 18 (1967), 111-139.

An analysis of OW as rebel and anarchist. Defines Wilde's peculiar brand of socialism and its influences. Suggests that "anarchism with its assertion of individual independence enables Wilde to
give the aesthete's creed, as it were, a universal scope."

118. d'Arch Smith, Timothy. *Love in Earnest: Some Notes on the
Lives and Writings of English "Uranian" Poets from 1889-1930.*
London: Routledge and Kegan Paul, 1970.

A biographical and critical account of a group of poets whose
pederastic philosophy and poetry was less a movement than "a certain
coherence of purpose, a concentration of precisely similar philosophies at precisely similar times." Includes chapters on Uranian precursors like Symonds and Carpenter, on Uranian poets of the nineties,
on Uranian work 1900-1930, on central Uranian themes and beliefs. Appends a handlist of Uranian verse.

119. Davidson, Donald, ed. *British Poetry of the Eighteen-Nineties.*
NY: Doubleday, Doran, 1937. "Introduction," pp. xix-lii.

Sees the nineties as the "significant and perhaps critical
years in a long process of transition" from Victorianism to modernism.
"Decadence" means that "at the moment when style reached a point of
subtlest refinement, the poet was made aware of the futility of his
own utterance, and had nothing really worth declaring. His highly
developed sense of form had nothing to play upon but his highly
developed sense of frustration and death." Treats "counter-decadents," Celtic Renaissance, Catholic Revival, symbolism.

120. Davis, Edward. *Yeats's Early Contacts with French Poetry.*
Pretoria: Univ. of South Africa, 1961.

Insists that WBY's Irishness contributed little to his technique or artistry compared to the direct and indirect influence of
French sources. Even Symons was "a belated contributor to an affinity which had been growing in Yeats" since his early years.

121. Davis, W. Eugene and Helmut E. Gerber. *Thomas Hardy: An Annotated Bibliography of Writings About Him.* Dekalb, Ill.:
Northern Illinois Univ. Press, 1973.

122. Davis, W. Eugene and Edward S. Lauterbach. *The Transitional
Age: British Literature, 1880-1920.* Troy, NY: Whitston, 1973.

See #302.

123. "Decadence." *Princeton Encyclopedia of Poetry and Poetics*, ed. Alex Preminger. Princeton, N.J.: Princeton Univ. Press, 1974. Enlarged Edition, pp. 185-186.

Lists famous examples of decadence in various nineteenth-century works; cites these characteristics: "search for novelty with attendant artificiality and interest in the unnatural; excessive self-analysis; feverish hedonism, with poetic interest in corruption and morbidity; abulia, neurosis, and exaggerated erotic sensibility; aestheticism, with stress on 'Art for Art's Sake' in the evocation of exquisite sensations and emotions; scorn of contemporary society and *mores*; restless curiosity, perversity, or eccentricity in subject matter; overemphasis on form, with resultant loss of balance between form and content -- or interest in jewel-like ornamentation, resulting at times in disintegration of artistic unity; bookishness; erudite or exotic vocabulary; frequent employment of synaesthesia or *transpositions d'art*; complex and difficult syntax; attempt to make poetry primarily a means of enchantment, with emphasis on its musical and irrational elements; experiments in the use of new rhythms, rich in evocative and sensuous effects, alien to those of tradition and often departing from the mathematical principles of control in established prosody; anti-intellectualism and stress on the subconscious; abandonment of punctuation, and use of typography for visual and psychological effect; substitution of coherence in mood for coherence and synthesis in thought; 'postromantic' irony in the manner of Corbière, Laforgue, and the early Eliot; obscurity, arising from remote, private, or complicated imagery or from a predominantly connotative and evocative use of language, with obvious reluctance to '*name* an object' ('Le suggérer, voilà le rêve.'); an overall aura of something lost -- a nostalgic, semi-mysticism without clear direction or spiritual commitment, but with frequent reference to exotic religions and ritual, or to such mysterious substitutes as Tarot cards, magic, alchemy, Rosicrucianism, Theosophy, the Kabbala, Satanism, and the like."

124. Decker, Clarence R. *Richard Le Gallienne: A Centenary Memoir-Anthology*. NY: Apollo Head, 1966.

A brief biographical account making reference to a number of Le Gallienne's works.

125. Decker, Clarence R. *The Victorian Conscience*. NY: Twayne, 1952.

A study of Victorian literary prejudice centering its discussion in the "movement we call Realism. More than any other of the conflicting currents that swept through this turbulent period, it channeled the main stream of intellectual, moral, and aesthetic controversy." Includes chapters on the "fleshly school" and Baudelaire, on naturalism, on Ibsen and the Russians, and on "the new spirit" of late Victorianism.

126. Deghy, Guy and Keith Waterhouse. *Café Royal: Ninety Years of Bohemia.* London: Hutchinson, 1956.

An anecdotal account of the famous restaurant and gathering place; tells the usual stories about such famous customers as Wilde, Beardsley, Dowson, Smithers, Frank Harris and Beerbohm.

127. de la Mare, Walter, ed. *The Eighteen-Eighties: Essays by Fellows of the Royal Society of Literature.* Cambridge: Cambridge Univ. Press, 1930.

Editor believes the decade "deserves the compliment of being called a *period.* A new life is stirring, these are years of transition, they mark an end and beginning, we become conscious of a lively and refreshing breath of spring in the air." Includes essays by divers hands on the poets of the 1880s, on Owen Meredith, on T.E. Brown, on Newman and Manning, on Pater, on minor fiction, on Gilbert and Sullivan, on Ibsen, on Martin Tupper and on Lewis Carroll. [For T.S. Eliot's revised version of his essay on Pater, see #142]

128. DeLaura, David J. *Hebrew and Hellene in Victorian Literature: Newman, Arnold and Pater.* Austin, Tex.and London: Univ. of Texas Press, 1969.

A brilliantly detailed study of the transmission of ideas, first noted by T.S. Eliot, from Newman through Arnold to Pater "by which the substance of dogmatic Christianity was transformed, within one or two generations, into the fabric of aestheticism." Sections on Arnold and Newman, Arnold and Pater, and Pater, Newman and "the road to the nineties." Special attention paid to the literary echoes of earlier in later writers. "By establishing Arnold's and Pater's extensive indebtedness to Newman and by analyzing the nature of their 'use' of his ideas, it is easier to account for the peculiar and complex role of the traditional religion (especially as mediated through Newman) in their successors, notably Oscar Wilde and Lionel Johnson."

129. Dewsnap, Terence Francis. "T. Sturge Moore's Theory of Poetic Self," *DA*, 21 (1961), 3456-57. [Wisconsin]

Believes that Sturge Moore (1870-1944) "reacted against the eccentric and private intellectual versions of beauty, those sustained by the Blake-Carlyle-Ruskin idealistic tradition and those informing the work of the French Symbolists." Sees in Sturge Moore's preoccupation with craftsmanship "an attempt to evolve from Symbolist techniques a broader, more human significance by a rough blending of ideal and real."

130. D'Hangest, Germain. "La place de Walter Pater dans le mouvement esthétique," *Etudes anglaises*, 27 (1974), 158-171.

Stresses WP's aesthetic conscience and his modernity. Suggests
that when his ideal of conscience became a matter of mere fashion in
the hands of Dowson, Symons and Crackanthorpe, aestheticism lapsed
into decadence, the extremity of the artist's isolation from society.
[In French]

131. Dijkstra, Bram. "The Androgyne in Nineteenth-Century Art and
      Literature," *CL*, 26 (1974), 62-73.

      Seeks to show that the vogue of the androgyne during 1880-1900
"was not simply a futile gesture designed to shock the bourgeoisie,
but was, in fact, the culmination of a slowly developing, ideological-
ly based, counteroffensive among artists against the economic motiva-
tions behind the sexual stereotypes which had become established in
the social environment with the rise of bourgeois industrial society."
Concentrates on eighteenth-century French and English works.

132. Dixon, Charles J., ed. *Fin de Siècle: Poetry of the Late Vic-
      torian Period 1860-1900*. London: Norton Bailey, 1968. "Intro-
      duction," pp. 1-26.

      Believes that ca. 1860 Victorian culture "began to lose its
nerve. It began to show unmistakable signs of decadence." Poets
like Swinburne and the decadents "were the first to reject, and to
suffer from, the civilization whose values, although outwardly
healthy, contained an inner rottenness which eventually displayed itself universally in the First World War. They were the sensitive yet
uncertain antennae of twentieth-century civilization."

133. Douglas, Alfred. "To the Editor: *The Spirit Lamp*," *London
      Mercury*, 25 (1932), 482.

      Corrects Chancellor [see #92], explaining that while a poem
published in the periodical -- Lionel Johnson's "A Friend" -- was
dedicated to Harry Irving ("In those days it was the fashion to dedicate poems in a collection to various friends"), the poem was actually about another friend, Maclise Graham, who had died two years before. Notes that the magazine failed because no one would undertake
its financial responsibility after Douglas went down from Oxford in
1893.

134. Dowling, Linda C. "Pursuing Antithesis: Lionel Johnson on
      Hardy," *ELN*, 12 (1975), 287-292.

      Suggests that in *The Art of Thomas Hardy* Johnson attempts to
deal with his own aesthetic problems by adopting the persona and
values of Samuel Johnson: "In the book's antithesis of [Dr.] Johnson and the Decadents we see the drama of a mind struggling to resolve its own conflict while ostensibly engaged in writing an ordin-
ary critical study."

135. Doyle, A.M. "Aspects of Decadence in the Poetry of Ernest Dowson, Lionel Johnson and Arthur Symons." Unpublished M.A. thesis, Univ. of Liverpool, 1967-68.

Not seen.

136. Duffy, John J. "Ernest Dowson and the Failure of Decadence," *UR*, 34 (1967), 45-49.

Traces the source of ED's "Diary of a Successful Man" to an incident in James' *The American*. "The manner in which he depends on Henry James as his master defines the limits of his own art and, what is more important, contributes to a definition of the limits of one aspect of an esthetic generally associated with . . . the Tragic Generation," namely Wilde's notion that actuality spoils art. ED's story is thrice removed from life, a "source of weakness in this and other prose fiction in the decadent nineties."

137. Duncan, Joseph E. *The Revival of Metaphysical Poetry: The History of a Style, 1800 to the Present.* Minneapolis: Univ. of Minneapolis Press, 1959.

Chapters on the Metaphysical Revival 1872-1912, the Catholic Revival and Yeats and the metaphysicals. Stresses the parallel between symbolists and metaphysicals; discusses influence of Donne on Gosse, Symons.

138. Easton, Malcolm. *Aubrey and the Dying Lady: A Beardsley Riddle.* London: Secker and Warburg, 1972.

Essentially an attempt "to explain the drawings through an account of Aubrey's sexual psychology and his relationship with friends and family," this account of Beardsley's life and work concentrates on such topics as the argument about incest and the trans-vestist and trans-sexual elements in Beardsley's work. Includes a chapter on the homosexual literary *cénacles* in London during the nineties.

139. Eckhoff, Lorentz. *The Aesthetic Movement in English Literature.* Oslo: Oslo Univ. Press, 1959.

A 34-page pamphlet urging a broader application of the term to "the entire movement in English literature which chose to inscribe upon its banner the slogan Art for Art's Sake." Thus would include Keats, Rossetti, Pater, Wilde, Moore, Symons, Yeats and, to a lesser degree, Swinburne and Stevenson. Characteristic feature of the aesthetic movement: the special relationship between artist and audience, "a relationship marked by opposition, reluctance, repugnance, and contempt." Concludes "we should be grateful to the Aesthetic Movement for teaching us one thing, namely that it is dangerous to retire from life."

140. Eddins, Dwight. *Yeats: The Nineteenth Century Matrix*. University, Ala.: Univ. of Alabama Press, 1971.

In a chapter on late Victorian context, discusses WBY's debt to Pre-Raphaelitism and to the Rhymers, whose indecisive personae and lack of form, however, Yeats generally avoided. "If a primary characteristic of literary 'decadence' is the systematic exhaustion of once-vital strains and motifs, then the Neo-Romanticism of the Pre-Raphaelites and the lingering Victorianism of the Rhymers come closer to qualifying for that category than does the early work of Yeats."

141. Egan, Rose Frances. "The Genesis of the Theory of 'Art for Art's Sake' in Germany and England," *Smith College Studies in Modern Languages*, (Part I) 2, iv (July 1921), 5-61; (Part II) 5, iii (Apr 1924), 1-33.

Part I concerns itself with history of the term and seeks to show that "before 1830 there were in Germany and in England already expressed and artistically effective the main elements" of the theory. Offers a working definition of the term as used between 1850 and 1900 characterized by these elements: freedom for the artist, form as distinguishing -- and unique -- quality of art, artistic conscience as the artist's sole guide, art's concern with the expression of an individual vision, the artist's indifference to the effect of his work upon others. Indicates the contributions of Kant, Schiller, Goethe and Schelling to formation of the theory. Part II examines the changing ideas of artist in the theory of art for art's sake as influenced by Kant, Goethe, Schiller, Schelling and Schlegel.

142. Eliot, T.S. "Arnold and Pater," *Selected Essays*. NY: Harcourt Brace, 1950. New Ed., pp. 382-393.

A highly influential estimate which, while it recognizes Pater's role as moralist, portrays him as the representative of the late nineteenth century's dissolution of thought and chimerical attempts at imperfect syntheses: "I do not believe that Pater, in this book [*Marius*], has influenced a single first-rate mind of a later generation. His view of art, as expressed in *The Renaissance* impressed itself upon a number of writers in the 'nineties, and propagated some confusion between life and art which is not wholly irresponsible for some untidy lives. The theory (if it can be called a theory) of 'art for art's sake' is still valid in so far as it can be taken as an exhortation to the artist to stick to his job; it never was and never can be valid for the spectator, reader or auditor."

143. Ellis, Havelock. "The Colour-Sense in Literature," *ContempR*, 69 (May 1896), 714-729.

After studying use of color from Baudelaire to D'Annunzio, concludes "if a love of green, as a writer with some claim to be an authority [Wilde] has somewhat absurdly declared, 'heralds a laxity, if not a decadence in morals,' the end of the last century was certainly such an age, and Wordsworth was its chief prophet." Notes that yellow was a favorite color of classical poets.

144. Ellis, Havelock. "Introduction," *Against the Grain*, by J.K. Huysmans. NY: Dover, 1969, pp. v-xxxii. [Adapted from the essay in the Boni and Liveright edition (NY) of *The New Spirit*]

"Technically, a decadent style is only such in relation to a classic style. It is simply a further development of a classic style, a further specialization, the homogeneous, in Spencerian phraseology, having become heterogeneous. The first is beautiful because the parts are subordinated to the whole; the second is beautiful because the whole is subordinated to the parts." Urges decadence as an aesthetic rather than a moral conception: "We may well reserve our finest admiration for the classic in art, for thereon are included the largest and most imposing works of human skill; but our admiration is of little worth if it is founded on incapacity to appreciate the decadent. Each has its virtues, each is equally right and necessary."

145. Ellis, Havelock. *The New Spirit*. London: George Bell, 1890.

Essays tracing the "evolution of the modern spirit" with chapters on Diderot, Heine, Whitman, Ibsen and Tolstoi. Looks forward optimistically to a new renaissance thanks to the leverage provided by science. "We know that wherever science goes the purifying breath of spring has passed and all things are recreated."

146. Ellis, Havelock. "A Note on Paul Bourget," *Views and Reviews: A Selection of Uncollected Articles, 1884-1932*. London: Harmsworth, 1932, pp. 48-60.

This essay, first published in October 1889, summarizes Bourget's remarks on Baudelaire which include Bourget's notion that decadence occurs in society when "the individual life becomes exaggerated beneath the influence of acquired well-being and heredity." A decadent style is one in which unity gives place to the "independence of the word," an anarchistic style in which everything is sacrificed to the parts.

147. Ellis, Stewart M. *Mainly Victorian*. London: Hutchinson, 1924.

Reprints magazine articles on G.P.R. James, Le Fanu, Dobson, Moore, Machen, Sheilah Kaye-Smith and Theodore Wratislaw. Valuable biographical information on TW, four of whose poems he prints.

148. Ellmann, Richard. "The Critic as Artist as Wilde," *Wilde and the Nineties: An Essay and an Exhibition*, ed. Charles Ryskamp. Princeton, N.J.: Princeton Univ. Press, 1966, pp. 1-21.

An interesting and influential interpretation of Wilde's career, emphasizing his contributions to modern critical theory and his exploration of the artist-criminal connection. "His private equation is that sin is the perception of new and dangerous possibilities in action as self-consciousness is in thought and criticism is in art."

149. Ellmann, Richard. "Introduction," *The Symbolist Movement in Literature*, by Arthur Symons. NY: Dutton, 1958, pp. vii-xvi.

Briefly outlines Yeats's role in influencing Symons' thought. Concludes that "there are moments in literature when the important thing is to suspect, to hint, to leap, and there are moments when the important thing is to conclude, to bring together, to bind. Symons found a moment of the second sort, and, with his marvelous adaptability, took possession of it. The result was to import into modern literature the word 'symbol' much as Wordsworth, a hundred years before, had pressed upon romantic literature the word 'nature'."

150. Ellmann, Richard. "Two Faces of Edward," *Edwardians and Late Victorians*, ed. Richard Ellmann. NY: Columbia Univ. Press, 1960, pp. 188-210. [English Institute Essays, 1959]

Believes "neither age nor self-consciousness determines the private character of a period; if anything does, it is the existence of a community between young and old experimental writers. Such a community existed in the Edwardian period." And further, "if a moment must be found for human character to have changed, I should suggest that 1900 is both more convenient and more accurate."

151. Elwin, Malcolm. *Old Gods Falling*. NY: Macmillan, 1939.

A survey of popular literature 1880-1914 with chapters on Moore, Stevenson, Lang and other critics, H. Rider Haggard, best sellers. Feels the nineties overrated, its fame due to tragic biographies. "The literary history, not only of the nineties, but of the whole era between 1887 and 1914 is the story of art's struggle against Humbug."

152. Engelberg, Edward. "Picture and Gesture in the Yeatsian Aesthetic," *Criticism*, 3 (1961), 101-120.

Yeats's tendency to beautify, together with "the overemphasis on pictorial pattern that Yeats recognized in himself as a residue of the 'nineties, which in turn had taken over the intricacies of Victorian 'design', promised to keep poetry in a kind of lingering trance." In order to combine picture (the "marmorean stillness" of

lyric) with gesture (the "turbulence of life" of drama), Yeats
sought in Maeterlinck, Greek drama, Noh theater, Shakespeare and
other sources the model for a non-mimetic art which would include
"manful energy" as well as "clean outline." "Nourished by his experience with drama, he was . . . able to assume again the role of
lyric poet, convinced that he had learned the secrets of strength,
the recklessness of extravagance, that will keep his art personal but
not egotistical; dramatic but not therefore deprived of all lyricism; symbolic -- still that -- but not vague or abstract."

153. Engelberg, Edward, ed. *The Symbolist Poem: The Development
   of the English Tradition*. NY: Dutton, 1967. "Introduction,"
   pp. 17-46.

   An anthology intended to show "how the English tradition in
poetry from the Romantics onward was predisposed to be 'influenced'
by the French Symbolists." Sections on the development of French
Symbolism and the poetic line of development in England from the
Romantics to the aesthetes and decadents to the post-symbolists.
Notes that English translations of French Symbolist poetry emphasized
the "morbid" or "decadent" elements. "The Aesthetes, the Symbolists,
the Decadents: all were concerned with creating a poetry that would
wed the vagueness of Romanticism with the precision of Realism and
give birth to poems whose success would depend on this tension between the vague precisely expressed (or vice versa)." Concludes that
"if it is true that English poetry produced no great nineteenth-century Symbolist poets, it could at least boast an ambitious, significant (if loosely associated) 'movement' whose collective contribution to the development of modern poetry is increasingly being ac-
knowledged."

154. Esdaile, Arundell J.K. "The New Hellenism," *Fortnightly Review*,
   94 (Oct 1910), 706-722.

   [Review of Ross's edition of Wilde's *Works* and Sherard's biography.] Sees OW as essentially "an evangelist in cap and bells;
underneath the surface of his critical paradoxes lies a real creed,
the hatred of ugliness and the realism which is its face in the
glass." Says that Wilde learned the art of paradox from Pater who
was flippant and paradoxical in company in order to avoid generali-
ties.

155. Evans, B. Ifor. *English Poetry in the Later Nineteenth Century*. NY: Barnes and Noble, 1966. 2nd Rev. Ed. [First pub.
   1933]

   Concerned with poetry written after 1860 excluding the later
work of Tennyson, Browning, Arnold; chapters on Pre-Raphaelites,
Coventry Patmore and Meynell group, light verse, Henley and Stevenson, Davidson, Wilde and the nineties. Sees the Victorian romanticism of the Pre-Raphaelites exhausting itself in the nineties, "one

of the most compact movements of modern times, but poetry had only a
limited share in its significance."

156. Evans, B. Ifor. *Tradition and Romanticism: Studies in English
      Poetry from Chaucer to W.B. Yeats.* London: Methuen, 1940.
      [Rptd Hamden, Conn.: Archon, 1964]

      Stresses the continuity of tradition and the coexistence rather
than conflict between romantic and classic views of poetry; a spirit
of compromise found to moderate the influence of "schools," "movements" or extreme doctrines. "Before the twentieth-century [classi-
cal] reaction set in there developed, with its final expression in
the eighteen-nineties, a last phase of romanticism, more compact
than anything which had preceded it . . . . Even more precisely than
with Swinburne, the indebtedness was to French verse, particularly to
Verlaine, modified by the Latin lyric of Horace and Propertius. Dowson had removed from poetry all its rhetoric; he had equally excluded all the problems which had occupied the endless controversies of
the nineteenth century on religion and science. He had narrowed
poetry to the small circle of his own sensations exquisitely expressed."

157. Fairchild, Hoxie N. *Religious Trends in English Poetry.* Vol.
      V, *Gods of a Changing Poetry, 1880-1920.* NY and London:
      Columbia Univ. Press, 1962.

      "A history of English poetry . . . with unusually heavy empha-
sis on religion as a factor in its development." Includes chapters
on aesthetes and decadents, on aesthetic catholicism and symbolism,
on poetry "chiefly hearty, slightly arty" [e.g. Henley and Kipling]
as well as on traditionalist and "unclassifiable" poets. Sees late
Victorian romanticism dividing between a deep faith in human bound-
lessness and a fascination with "the external shimmer of strangeness
and glamour and witchery," a dichotomy, that is, between romanticism
and romance that grew more marked as the century ended.

158. Fallis, Richard. "Yeats and the Reinterpretation of Victorian
      Poetry," *VP*, 14 (1976), 89-100.

      Examines Yeats's critique of Victorian poets as WBY's exercise
in poetic self-definition. Yeats's discrimination of a radical Romantic tradition, a poetry of vision tracing back to Shelley and Blake,
seen as underlying Yeats's charge that Victorians like Arnold and
Tennyson had pursued a false mode of perception based upon the separation of subject and object. Concludes that "Yeats's evaluations of
Victorianism were part of a fundamentalist revolt, one which sought
to return to the true faith of radical Romanticism by purifying the
perceptions and dialects of the tribe."

159. Farmer, Albert J. *Le mouvement esthétique et "décadent" en Angleterre (1873-1900)*. Paris: Honoré Champion, 1932.

Sees "Decadentism" as an international, essentially psychological, phenomenon, growing out of the pessimistic mood of 1880-1900 and its artistic consequences. Believes that in England there was an identifiable and coherent decadent movement whose leading figure was Wilde and which was characterized by a more reflective, less spontaneous idea of art, by the cult of form and by the evocation of the "moment." Finds decadence marking a decisive moment in English culture in which literature tried to express itself more freely and sincerely. Part I discusses origins, Pater and aestheticism, and Moore and French influences. Part II devoted to Wilde, with chapters on early work, *Dorian Gray*, and later work. Part III includes chapters on the Rhymers' Club, on the *Yellow Book* and some early collections of poetry (Gray's *Silverpoints*, Symons' *Silhouettes*, Wratislaw's *Caprices*), on the *Savoy* and some later representative collections of poetry (Symons'*Amoris Victima*, Wratislaw's *Orchids*, Dowson's *Verses* and *Decorations*, Plarr's *In the Dorian Mood* and Douglas' *Poems*). Concludes "l'apport le plus précieux de la 'décadence' réside peut-être dans la sensibilité plus complexe, plus riche qu'elle a éveillée, et qui s'identifie étroitement avec les préoccupations de l'art moderne." [In French]

160. Fass, Barbara. *La Belle Dame Sans Merci and the Aesthetics of Romanticism*. Detroit: Wayne State Univ. Press, 1974.

A study of the fairy-mistress story whose elements are found to be particularly attractive to romantic artists in search of a personal myth. Chapters on various English, German and French treatments, including Hardy's *The Well-Beloved*, James' *The Last of the Valerii*, Swinburne's *Laus Veneris*, Beardsley's *Story of Venus and Tannhäuser*, Morris' *Hill of Venus*, Davidson's *New Ballad of Tannhäuser* and Yeats' *Wanderings of Oisin*.

161. Felstiner, John. *The Lies of Art: Max Beerbohm's Parody and Caricature*. NY: Knopf, 1972.

Seeks to present an alternative image of Max to the finished dandy, perfect stylist, elfin wit, by examining "the inner frame of his art" and by taking seriously caricature and parody as genres and Max as master of both. Discerns a three-part development in Max's work, proceeding from pure invention or creation to criticism and analysis to parody. Studies this dialectic in Max's 1893-1918 work, with chapters on masks, the 1890s. Concludes that Beerbohm "is still alive in the twentieth century because he wrote himself into a parody of literature that invents and conserves criticisms of itself, asking us not to stop the lies of art but to see through them and with them."

162. Field, Michael. *Works and Days: From the Journal of Michael Field*, ed. T. and D.C. Sturge Moore. London: Murray, 1933.

Incisive, occasionally cutting, descriptions and anecdotes of a number of literary and artistic figures of "little London" in the nineties and after, written by Katherine Bradley and Edith Cooper, the aunt and niece who collaborated as "Michael Field."

163. Findlay, L.M. "The Introduction of the Phrase 'Art for Art's Sake' into English," *N&Q*, 20 n.s. (1973), 246-248.

In an article on Lamartine in the *Westminster Review* (Jan 1839) by Desiré Nisard.

164. Fletcher, Ian. "Amendments and Additions to *The Complete Poems of Lionel Johnson* (1953)," *VN*, No.33 (Spring 1968), 38-43.

Some important modifications of the 1952 "Introduction" to the edition [see #167]: now believes that Johnson's self-transformation into a mystic Irish nationalist began as early as 1891; treats much more cautiously the question of LJ's homosexuality -- evidence for it now found "vestigial."

165. Fletcher, Ian. "Bedford Park: Aesthete's Elysium?" *Romantic Mythologies*, ed. Ian Fletcher. London: Routledge and Kegan Paul, 1967, pp. 169-207.

A detailed account of the origins, first inhabitants and ambitions of Bedford Park, all of which were early linked to the aesthetic movement: "One of the constant elements in Aestheticism was a revulsion from the ugliness and materialism of the contemporary scene and the tendency to look back to 'imaginary' 'spots of time' when the sense of beauty was normative. Historical self-awareness led to a sense of freedom in time: time-travelling might be defined as central to Aestheticism, and this sharply distinguishes it from the cult of the moment, of the 'modern,' which is characteristic of 'Decadence.' The Aesthetes looked back to the eighteenth century, the Jacobean period or the Middle Ages, periods represented in Bedford Park."

166. Fletcher, Ian, ed. *The Collected Poems of Victor Plarr*. London: Eric and Joan Stevens, 1974. "Introduction," pp. xi-xvii.

A brief biographical and critical note on Plarr's life and work. Though a member of the Rhymers' Club, Plarr was "no Bohemian; his French culture was quite distinct from the 'decadent' and *symboliste* affections of Symons and he had sharp reservations about the lost causes that Johnson and Dowson collected and cherished: Latin Catholicism, The White Rose League, Fenian politics." Locates Plarr's work within English Parnassianism: "an impassive verbal surface, a fondness for legend, often exotic legend, the cultivation of detachment, a poetry of ideas rather than images expressed in highly formal stanzas."

167. Fletcher, Ian, ed. *The Complete Poems of Lionel Johnson*.
London: Unicorn, 1953. "Introduction," pp. xi-xliv.

Believes that any just evaluation of LJ's poetry must be preceded "by a sympathetic definition of the age in whose limitations
he unavoidably shared," a period characterized by "hesitancies of
tone and emphasis, the harkings backward and forward and yet [by a]
singularly unified quality [dividing] this time of transience from
the full-blown summer of the Victorian ideal." Brief account of the
sources of and influences upon the artists and writers of the 1890s
whose failures were owing to their lack of critical ability or Arnold's "conscience in intellectual matters." LJ's ideals of Ireland
and the Catholic Church are set in their context as part of a revolt
against the Victorian moral order which took its form as a "retreat
into the interior life." Includes a detailed biographical account
and sections on the influences and characteristics of LJ's English
and Latin poems.

168. Fletcher, Ian. "The 1890's: A Lost Decade," *VS*, 4 (1960-61),
345-354.

Finds both the "yellow nineties" and "tragic generation" interpretations of the fin de siècle "viciously constrictive." Agrees
with Gerber [see #194] that the nineties exist as a process. The
shift of sensibility which began around 1870 and whose effects are
still apparent "exalted and isolated the artist, yet it cannot be
equated with Aestheticism or with that self-conscious notion of literary cycles generally termed 'decadence,' which began in France in
the 1830's with Nisard. Essentially that movement was a guilty ex-
altation of art over nature, equating contemporary writers with
writers of the Alexandrian or Latin Silver Age periods. Its effects
can be traced . . . in perversities of language and attitude, in the
cult of homosexuality, in words used learnedly in their root-sense .
. . spiced with underworld slang, and in the obedience to those
petites églises, whether Theosophical, Rosicrucian, French Gnostic,
or even to the antiquarian and dimly political White Rose League . .
. which are so characteristic of the later nineteenth-century writers
on their Augustinian or Huysmans-like transit to the Latin Church."

169. Fletcher, Ian. "Explorations and Recoveries -- II: Symons,
Yeats and the Demonic Dance," *London Magazine*, 7 (June 1960),
46-60.

Examines the fruitful artistic relationship between the two
poets with specific reference to the effect of AS's Salome image upon
WBY's dancer. Warns against the error of treating Yeats's *Autobiography* both as an "aesthetic modulation of history" and as a historical document. Concludes "the more we examine Symons' work, the more
we realize that the 1890s are not, as they are commonly supposed to
be, a self-enclosed period, but a continuum which must be re-enacted
if we are to 'distance' the 'modern' movement in English poetry."

170. Fletcher, Ian, ed. *Romantic Mythologies*. London: Routledge
      and Kegan Paul, 1967. "Foreword," pp. vii-xiii.

      Notes that the essays included in this volume rightly stress
the interconnections not the coherence of the late Victorian period
which for too long has been subjected to misguided attempts to define
it by a single word: "The imposition of schematic traditions becomes vicious. It can take no account of the variety of potentiali-
ties, of cross-fertilizations; of historical accidents, perhaps,
where one potentiality flares into life at the expense of another . .
. . [S]ense will hardly survive the sensitive pruning-away which will
treat the work of Pater, say, as an aberration of the Arnoldian
stress on Hellenism or confine it in a fish-net stocking of Aestheticism." Essays include A.J.L. Busst,"The Image of the Androgyne in
the Nineteenth Century"; Ian Fletcher, "Bedford Park: Aesthete's
Elysium?"; A.G. Lehmann, "Pierrot and Fin de Siècle"; Michael Hamburger, "Art as Second Nature"; Annette Lavers, "Aubrey Beardsley,
Man of Letters." [See individual authors]

171. Fletcher, Ian. "Herbert Horne: the Earlier Phase," *EM*, 21
      (1970), 117-157.

      An extensively detailed study of the poet cum designer cum
editor cum architect (1864-1916) whose personal influence upon the
Rhymers coterie was significant. HH emerges as a pre-eminently "typical" nineties figure: "Puzzling, unsympathetic, faintly sinister,
contained, are the epithets that seem appropriate to Horne's personality. The final impression is of a man embarrassed by a multipli-
city of competing gifts, who gradually disembarrassed himself of
these by quiet and firm acts of will."

172. Fletcher, Ian. "The Poetry of John Gray," *Two Friends: John
      Gray and André Raffalovich*, ed. Brocard Sewell. Aylesford,
      Eng.: St. Albert's Press, 1963, pp. 50-69.

      Considers JG's various collections of poetry with an informa-
tive discussion of *Silverpoints* (1893), stressing Gray's dandiacal
attitudes in typography, title and poetic technique: "For such a
philosophy the natural is the bad; all that is good is acquired and
artificial. Life and art are one: thus the self becomes an icon,
expressing its self-sufficiency through trenchant silences, muted
gestures, and a tart elegance of clothes. The dandy will have no
disciples: his genius is for obscurity. Woman for him is pure body,
sinuous emblem of the Fall; boredom is his divinity and his mask of
indifference veils an inward despair. Such rejection of nature could
lead to Catholicism." Close analysis of several poems.

173. Fletcher, Ian. "Rhythm and Pattern in 'Autobiographies',"
      An Honoured Guest: New Essays on W.B. Yeats, ed. Denis Donoghue
      and J.R. Mulryne. London: E. Arnold, 1965, pp. 165-189.

Treats the sections *Reveries, The Trembling of the Veil* and *Dramatis Personae* as WBY's essays in "self-transcendence." Particularly helpful in clarifying the extent to which Yeats, through selection and emphasis, created the myth of the "tragic generation" and in suggesting the significance of this invention to Yeats's own creative development.

174. Fletcher, Ian. *Walter Pater*. London: Longmans, Green, 1959. [WTW 114]

Traces the development of WP's ruling ideas with discussions of the major works and special attention to *The Renaissance* and *Marius*, both works which are best understood when set against the background of the dissolution of dogma created by Newman's conversion. The importance to Pater of the ideas of urbanity and temperament helped him '[create] himself for us in his *oeuvre* as a permanently significant symbolical figure: the most complete example, the least trivial, of the aesthetic man."

175. Flower, Desmond, ed. *The Poetical Works of Ernest Dowson*. London: Cassell, 1967. [First pub. 1934] "Introduction," 11-29.

Includes a brief biographical sketch, comments on Dowson biographies and the critical reception of his poetry, and an extended parallel of the 1890s and the Elizabethan age in poetry. "A variety of reasons, of which envy was perhaps not the least, invested the memory of remarkable decade with an undeserved stigma of ineffective wickedness." Predicts a rise in reputation of decade and writers associated with it.

176. "Forum." *ELT*, 6, i (1963), 16-18. James G. Hepburn, "Transition, Decadence and Estheticism: Some Notes" and Russell M. Goldfarb, "Time for Aestheticism."

Hepburn suggests that aestheticism represents one aspect of decadence -- "chiefly a separating of art from morality." "The notions of art for art's sake and realism can be viewed, for example, as final fragmentations of a single earlier view [i.e. the Romantic equation "Beauty is Truth"]"; rejects the assumption that aestheticism is concerned with matters of form while decadence describes content. Goldfarb urges more attention be paid to problem of defining aestheticism.

177. Foster, Milton P. "The Reception of Max Nordau's *Degeneration* in England and America," *DA*, 14 (1954), 1078-79. [Michigan]

Includes chapters on nature of Nordau's attack, the favorable and unfavorable newspaper accounts of it and the arguments of the three books written to refute it: Alfred Egmont Hake's *Regeneration*,

William Hirsch's *Genius and Degeneration* and George Bernard Shaw's *The Sanity of Art*. Believes Nordau's approach foreshadows twentieth-century psychoanalytical criticism. Concludes that by denouncing the chief artistic tendencies of the day, Nordau "stimulated his repliers to defend the new art by explaining its special characteristics and stressing its values."

178.   Fowler, Rowena.   "Ernest Dowson and the Classics," *YES*, 3 (1973), 243-252.

Believes that critics have ignored the influence of Greek and Latin lyric and erotic poetry on fin de siècle verse. Seeks to show that Dowson's use of "classical titles, names, and allusions are not so much pretentious flourishes or period mannerism as an acknowledgement of the fragmentary phrases or ideas which were often his source of inspiration."

179.   Fox, Steven J.   "Art and Personality: Browning, Pater, Wilde and Yeats," *DAI*, 33 (1972), 751A. [Yale]

Argues that the formula of art for art's sake "does not do justice to the seriousness of aesthetic enterprise, which more frequently uses art as a means of integrating the artist's being and as the expression of the achieved personality." Chapters on the Pre-Raphaelite aesthetic, Pater's treatment of the moment and portrait, Wilde's contribution to an art of personality, readings of Yeats's poems.

180.   Fredeman, William.   *Pre-Raphaelitism: A Bibliocritical Study*. Cambridge, Mass.: Harvard Univ. Press, 1965.

An extensive annotated bibliography of studies concerned with virtually every aspect of Pre-Raphaelitism as a literary and artistic movement. Distinguishes between the Pre-Raphaelite Brotherhood, the Pre-Raphaelite Movement and Pre-Raphaelitism, with the latter seen as much more generalized and pervasive, a middle ground between Victorian art morality and fin de siècle aestheticism: "It had its roots in the reaction against the materialism of the Industrial Revolution, and it affirmed and reasserted the values of individuality in an age dominated by materialistic demands for social and artistic conformity. In art and literature, it was a revolt against the rules of the academicians and a reassertion of faith in the truth of the creative expression of the individual artist as opposed to the stereotyped and conventionalized expression of pseudo-'classical' art."

181.   Friedman, Norman.   "From Victorian to Modern: A Sketch for a Critical Reappraisal," *VN*, No.32 (Fall 1967), 20-28.

Predicts "Romanticism" will be found the most significant term for discussion of the last two centuries of literary history. Traces the conflict between aestheticism and Philistinism during the Victorian period. Philistine notions of poetry found ascendant 1840-1860; balance shifts in favor of aestheticism 1869-1900.

182. Frierson, William C. *The English Novel in Transition: 1885-1940*. Norman, Okla.: Univ. of Oklahoma Press, 1942.

Chapters on naturalism, the English "Maupassant School," the reaction against Dickens, fiction of the nineties. Transition begun by French naturalism, completed by Tolstoy and Dostoievsky. Nineties a period of "diverse leanings in literature," thus congenial to the social introspection of naturalism and to innovation in technique. "'Transition' involves, on the one hand, a progress in truth-telling in the light of the broad cosmic view opened by scientific materialism; on the other, a technique, or a variety of techniques, which makes the truth-telling plausible."

183. Frye, Northrop. "Yeats and the Language of Symbolism," *UTQ*, 17 (1947-48), 1-17.

"We shall never fully understand the nineteenth century until we realize how hampered its poets were by the lack of a coherent tradition of criticism which would have organized the language of poetic symbolism for them . . . . When critics forgot how to teach the language of poetic imagery the poets forgot how to use it, the creative counterpart of aesthetic criticism being, of course, aestheticism." Believes Yeats himself fell prey to "the techniques of relentless beautifying" of fin de siècle aestheticism: "Cheshire Cheese poetry, like romantic poetry in general, only more so, depends upon an evocative and intuitive approach to the significance of poetic imagery; hence it depends, not on things, but on qualifications of things, not on a pattern of images, but on a background of attributes. The emphasis in such poetry therefore falls on carefully composed epithets and radioactive adjectives."

184. Fussell, B.H. "The Masks of Oscar Wilde," *SR*, 80 (1972), 124-139.

Interesting treatment of *Salomé* as masque or artificial pastoral and *Earnest* as antimasque; stresses the modernity of OW whose farcical absurdities place him at the head of the line of Beckett, Pinter et al. with special reference to Artaud.

185. Gannon, Patricio, ed. *Poets of the Rhymers' Club*. Buenos Aires: Colombo, 1953. "Preface," pp. 11-21.

A brief survey of the group, retelling most of the usual stories, and stressing their role as "symbolists." Believes "their ultimate aim seems to have been the avoidance of the formless, superfluous performance in verse."

186. Garbáty, Thomas J. "The French Coterie of the *Savoy*, 1896," *PMLA*, 75 (1960), 609-615.

A highly-colored account ("They are all gone now, the *Savoy* people of the Nineties") of the founding, contributors, reception and demise of what is seen to have been an "Anglo-French" periodical.

187. Garbáty, Thomas J. *"The Savoy*, 1896: A Re-Edition of Representative Prose and Verse, with a Critical Introduction, and Biographical and Critical Notes," *DA*, 17 (1957), 3014-15.

In addition to selections chosen for their intrinsic interest and representativeness of fin de siècle characteristics, includes a publication history based on numerous unpublished letters of Dowson, Symons, Mallarmé, Sharp and Crackanthorpe, a critical appraisal of the contents and biographical and critical sketches of contributors, again, based on unpublished letters and manuscripts.

188. Gaunt, William. *The Aesthetic Adventure*. London: Jonathan Cape, 1975. Rev. Ed. [First pub. 1945]

A popular ("Meanwhile Algernon Charles Swinburne was running riot") account of British aesthetic culture 1870-1900, emphasizing the visual arts and stressing the Continental origins of and influences upon aestheticism and decadence. Concentrates on Whistler and Wilde, and includes many anecdotes of other colorful figures: "In [Conder] and Dowson are to be seen the familiar symptoms, the lurking consumption, the savage need for squalor or excess, the self-abasement, linked with a delicate art."

189. Gekle, William F. *Arthur Machen: Weaver of Fantasy*. Milbrook, NY: Round Table Press, 1949.

A personal and highly partisan account of Machen's life and work. Insists that the best five books of the 1890s were not written by "the delicate decadents" but by Machen, whose work is pervaded by a quality of "ecstasy" -- in Machen's own words, "the sense of the eternal mysteries, the eternal beauty hidden beneath the crust of common and commonplace things: hidden and yet burning and glowing continuously if you care to look with purged eyes."

190. Gerber, Helmut, ed. *The English Short Story in Transition 1880-1920*. NY: Western, 1967. "Introduction," pp. xi-xv.

Suggests that *"mood, variable, contradictory, curiosity, visible world* and *possibility* are the key terms, if one must embalm a cultural period with labels." By his selections for this anthology, the editor has "tried to correct the fallacy that this is the decadent period, or that it is a period in which everyone tried to write

naturalistic, sociological, psychiatric or anatomical literature according to Zola's ridiculous credo in *The Experimental Novel* . . . .
It is only the Beardsley Period or the Yellow Nineties to those who
have read the poets very selectively and the prose writers hardly at
all. It is only the period of Bodley-headism to those who are un-
aware of the rise of such vigorous publishers as, say, T. Fisher Unwin and William Heinemann."

191. Gerber, Helmut E. "George Moore: An Annotated Bibliography of
    Writings About Him," *English Fiction in Transition*, 2, ii
    (1959), 1-91; Supplement I, 3, ii (1960), 34-46; Supplement
    II, 4, ii (1961), 30-42.

192. Gerber, Helmut E. "George Moore: From Pure Poetry to Pure
    Criticism," *JAAC*, 25 (1967), 281-291.

    GM's extraordinary variety of artistic activities and alle-
giances throughout his long career "all contributed to a constantly
evolving, often self-contradictory, complex, never systematized
philosophy of art" whose central motif was that "all art is autonomous and that the perfection of form is virtue."

193. Gerber, Helmut E. and Bruce E. Teets. *Joseph Conrad: An Anno-
    tated Bibliography of Writings About Him*. Dekalb, Ill.: North-
    ern Illinois Univ. Press, 1970.

194. Gerber, Helmut E. "The Nineties: Beginning, End, or Transi-
    tion?" *Edwardians and Late Victorians*, ed. Richard Ellmann.
    NY: Columbia Univ. Press, 1960, pp. 50-79. [English Insti-
    tute Essays, 1959]

    Transition. Includes summaries of the various interpretations
of the period written during 1893-1925 and longer accounts of more
recent work. Concludes that term "decadence" is of only very limited
use in discussing the period. Bibliographically rich. Indicates
areas future scholarship should pursue.

195. Gerber, Helmut E. and Edward S. Lauterbach. "Rudyard Kip-
    ling: An Annotated Bibliography of Writings About Him," *Eng-
    lish Fiction in Transition*, 3, iii-v (1960), 1-235.

196. Gerber, Helmut E. "Some Problems in Definition," *English
    Fiction in Transition*, 5, v (1962), 31-32.

    After urging that the specifically derogatory meanings of the
terms "aestheticism" and "decadence" be dropped from critical usage,
poses a series of questions meant to focus discussion of the use and
significance of the two terms in British literature 1870-1900.

45

197. Gerber, Helmut E. and W. Eugene Davis. *Thomas Hardy: An Annotated Bibliography of Writings About Him*. Dekalb, Ill.: Northern Illinois Univ. Press, 1973.

198. Gibbons, T.H. "The Reverend Stewart Headlam and the Emblematic
Dancer: 1877-1894," *BJA*, 5 (1965), 329-340.

An account of the career and influence of the man whose lifelong championing of the performing arts, the theater and, in particular, the music-hall ballet contributed largely to that general interest in the arts of performance found in the work of Symons, Wratislaw, Image, Horne and others.

199. Gibbons, Tom. *Rooms in the Darwin Hotel: Studies in English
Literary Criticism and Ideas 1880-1920*. Nedlands, Western
Australia: Univ. of Western Australia Press, 1973.

Studies the literary criticism of Symons, Ellis and Alfred
Orage whose shared beliefs -- in some form of mysticism, in the
desirability of a social elite and in transcendentalist and anti-
naturalist theories of art and literature -- "seem central to our
understanding of a complex, fascinating and seminal literary period
which continues to elude definition." Examines the source and
nourishment of these beliefs in the "Age of Evolutionism," which is
offered as the defining term for the period.

200. Gilcher, Edwin A. *A Bibliography of George Moore*. Dekalb,
Ill.: Northern Illinois Univ. Press, 1970.

201. Gilsoul, Robert. *La théorie de l'art pour l'art chez les
écrivans belges de 1830 à nos jours*. Liège: H. Vaillant-
Carmanne, 1936.

Views art for art's sake as the result of the romantic elevation of the artist and the reaction against a milieu whose attitude
toward art had moralizing, utilitarian intentions. Art for art's
sake attitude characterized by a belief in the unity of form and
content, a tendency to treat literature as music or as one of the
plastic arts, by impersonality, exoticism of time and place, originality and pessimism. Includes chapters on naturalism and symbolism;
pays particular attention to the role of the periodical *Jeune-Bel-
gique* during the Belgian aesthetic movement. [In French]

202. Goldberg, Gerald J. "The Artist-Novel in Transition," *English Fiction in Transition*, 4, iii (1961), 12-27.

Traces the development of the *künstlerroman* in England with
special emphasis on 1880-1914. "The new artist -- sensitive, intro-
spective, isolated -- [is seen] as essentially a twentieth-century

phenomenon and a figure born of the decadence." The new artist's characteristic etrangement from society takes four chief forms: bohemianism, isolation, exile, suicide. Considerable summary of plot.

203. Goldfarb, Russell M. "Arthur Symons' Decadent Poetry," *VP*, 1 (1963), 231-234.

Believes that every element of decadence present in late Victorian literature can be found in Symons' work -- artifice and artificiality, anti-nature bias, images, perverse and sordid experience, excluded moral sense. "An abundance of blatantly decadent material appears in *Silhouettes* and *London Nights*. Arthur Symons' volumes are entirely suitable for teaching the Victorian fin de siècle."

204. Goldfarb, Russell M. "Ernest Dowson Reconsidered," *TSL*, 14 (1969), 61-73.

Discusses sources, influences and characteristic themes in ED's work. Concludes "we should remember him not as a typical decadent, but as a lyric poet who had moments when he could sing exceptionally well."

205. Goldfarb, Russell M. "Late Victorian Decadence," *JAAC*, 20 (1962), 369-373.

After referring to the articles by Ryals [see #447] and Peters [see #398] and surveying the various definitions offered by fin de siècle and later writers, suggests there is a consensus as to the meaning of term "decadent." Concludes "we understand that late Victorian decadence refers to poetry and prose which does not emphasize philosophical, historical or intellectual concerns, but which does emphasize the value to be gained both from experience of all sorts and from indulgence in a life of sensations. Because of this emphasis, decadent literature is animated by the exploration of immoral and evil experience; never does it preach morality, nor does it strongly insist upon ethical responsibilities. Decadent literature is characterized by artistic concern for the morbid, the perverse, the sordid, the artificial, the beauty to be found in the unnatural, and the representation of cleanness in unclean things; it is characterized by a self-conscious and weary contempt for social conventions such as truth and marriage, by an acceptance of Beauty as a basis for life."

206. Goldfarb, Russell M. "Time for Aestheticism," *ELT*, 6, i (1963), 17-18.

See #176.

207. Gordon, Jan B. "The Danse Macabre of Symons' *London Nights*,"
      VP, 9 (1971), 429-443.

Agrees with other critics who have seen the nineties' interest
in dance as fascination with a mode of transcending individual isolation. Particularly concerned with the spectator of dance who, "unable to participate in such transcendence, can participate only
through voyeurism." Suggests that Symons in his poetry "is painfully
aware that the mere act of writing, because it involves the detachment of a non-participatory eye, is an imprisoning activity." Suggests that Symons used the dance "to structure the dialogue of 'inner' and 'outer' in a manner parallel to the more radical choices of
his personal life." Believes that dance "provides not only a frame
for a better understanding of *London Nights*, but a context for relating Symons' dilemma to the poetics of the late nineteenth century."

208. Gordon, Jan B. "The Dialogue of Life and Art in Arthur Symons'
      Spiritual Adventures," *ELT*, 12, iii (1969), 105-117.

Finds *Spiritual Adventures* full of AS's preoccupying concerns:
"the perpetual threat of imprisonment by the randomness of nature,
the necessity of a mediating mask; and ultimately, a progressive
loss of selfhood which characterizes the conversion to art." Traces
thematic and structural relations among stories and their connection
to the artistic concerns and motifs of the "decadents."

209. Gordon, Jan B. "The Imaginary Portrait: Fin de Siècle Icon,"
      UWR, 5 (1969), 81-104.

Attempts to study the ways in which a literary genre becomes an
imaginative mode. Discussions of Rossetti, Pater, Symons, Wilde,
Synge, Dowson, Le Gallienne and Joyce. Notes affinities of the imaginary portrait with period visual arts and confessional modes, and
with Freud. Concludes "all of the characteristics appropriate to the
Imaginary Portrait form -- the androgyne, mirrored surfaces which reflect a fictive, authorial 'self,' and the linguistic doubling of
language which sees its own genesis as an object in the aphorisms of
Wilde -- seem tangential to the larger aesthetic issues. In its justification for dehumanization, its attempt to confuse play, life and
art, and its emphasis upon stylization, the *fin de siècle* genre of
the Imaginary Portrait exists as the tormented icon of a tormented
era, for whom it was both an index of illness and an attempt at thera-
peusis."

210. Gordon, Jan B. "The *Imaginary Portraits*: Walter Pater's
      Aesthetic Pilgrimage," *UR*, 35 (1968-69), 29-39.

Sees in Pater's homeward-returning youths who leave a wider
world for confined space " a unique version of the romantic quest
which typically ends in apocalypse . . . .the fin de siècle journey
reaches its culmination in the sacrifice of selfhood."

211. Gordon, Jan B. "Poetic Pilgrimage of Dowson," *Renascence*, 20 (1967), 3-10; 55.

Suggests that "in detailing his quest for a landscape of innocence, Dowson may actually be giving us an allegory of the imaginative effort to order the world."

212. Gordon, Jan B. "'The Wilde Child': Structure and Origin in the *Fin de Siècle* Short Story," *ELT*, 15 (1972), 277-290.

Attempts to give a phenomenological interpretation of fictional space in Victorian and fin de siècle works; particularly interested in the connection between regressive narration and "the quest for Origins."

213. Gordon, Jan B. "William Morris' Destiny of Art," *JAAC*, 27 (1968-69), 271-279.

Perceives in WM's refusal of the Poetry Chair at Oxford in 1887 "another of those innumerable ironies of the nineties; Morris having taken over the Pre-Raphaelite desire for a medium of artistic expression that would encompass diverse modes within a 'total' art, ends by rejecting poetry as incommunicable -- precisely because it cannot be communally shared."

214. Gorman, Herbert S. *The Procession of Masks*. Boston: B.J. Brimmer, 1923.

Includes essays on Beerbohm, W.H. Hudson, Swinburne and Symons, who is portrayed as the "perfect product of the Yellow Nineties," a period whose characteristic writing is marked by "the demon of sensual love, the frantic desire for material beauties, the painful self-torture of the spirit."

215. Gourmont, Remy de. "Stéphane Mallarmé and the Idea of Decadence," *Decadence and Other Essays on the Culture of Ideas*, trans. W.A. Bradley. NY: Harcourt, 1921, pp. 139-155.

Maintains that the idea of literary decadence arose "abruptly, around 1885" because professors of literature needed a convenient way of understanding the new literature -- Huysmans' *A Rebours* provided the analogy of the Roman decadence. "Stripped of its mysticism, its necessity, all its historical genealogy, the idea of literary decadence is reduced to a purely negative notion -- to the simple idea of absence."

216. Graham, Kenneth. *English Criticism of the Novel, 1865-1900*. Oxford: Oxford Univ. Press, 1965.

An account of English criticism as represented by Victorian periodical reviewers. Sections on the status of fiction as instructor, entertainer and art-form, on realism and romance, on the place of morals and ideas in the novel, and on various novelistic techniques. Finds that late Victorian critics of the novel "were remarkably unaffected by the ideas of Aestheticism, and the moral-utilitarian strain in English thought still predominated."

217. Green, R.J. "Oscar Wilde's *Intentions*: An Early Modernist Manifesto," *BJA*, 13 (1973), 397-404.

Notes a contradiction in OW's *Reviews* between "a recognizably 'modern' theory of literature . . . and a style and stance that are basically Victorian." By *Intentions* Wilde had replaced a pellucid Arnoldian manner with an elusive and aphoristic style. "In its apparent lack of concern with either internal consistency or with the reader's immediate and total comprehension of what is being said, *Intentions* is as symptomatic of modernism as Pound's *Cantos*, Beckett's *Godot* or Joyce's *Finnegans Wake*.

218. Gribble, Francis. "The Pose of Mr. Arthur Symons," *Fortnightly Review*, 74 n.s. (July-Dec 1908), 127-136.

A not unsympathetic account of the influences on AS's work and the evolution of the movement whose spokesman he became. Particularly remarkable for its analysis of the role of Methodism in shaping AS's attitudes toward aesthetic or other kinds of intense experience and for its astonishing diagnosis of the breakdown Symons suffered just a few months later. "Methodism, and the hell fire which blazes around Methodism, and the madness which is akin to it, are themes to which Mr. Symons recurs as if they had a special fascination for him."

219. Gribble, Francis. *Seen in Passing.* London: Ernest Benn, 1929.

Chapters on Oxford in the 1880s, Fleet Street in the eighties and nineties, literary groups of the 1890s. Remarks on poetry of Rennell Rodd, J.W. Mackail, Herbert French, D.S. MacColl, on the rout of the aesthetes at the Oxford Union, on Teixeira de Mattos.

220. Grierson, H.J.C. *Lyrical Poetry of the Nineteenth Century.* NY: Harcourt Brace, 1929.

Includes chapters on Arnold and the Pre-Raphaelites and on the nineties. Believes that what truly distinguished the last decade of the nineteenth century was not Wilde's antics but the emergence of a series of young poets like Kipling, Henley, Yeats, Davidson, Ronald Campbell Macfie, Housman and Hardy. Unlike the decadents, this group cultivated colloquial language and popular rhythms.

221. Gross, Beverly. "Walter Pater and the Aesthetic Fallacy,"
     SAQ, 68 (1969), 220-230.

    Stresses the evolution of Pater's thought from the sensational
relativism of the early works to the "aesthetic moralism" of *Marius*.
Finds that for Pater participation in art "is not primarily an aesthetic experience at all, but psychic ministration: art is at the
service of the philosophical stances, the emotional needs, the quest
for self-discovery of the critic."

222. Gross, John. *The Rise and Fall of the Man of Letters: Aspects
     of English Literary Life Since 1800*. London: Weidenfeld and
     Nicolson, 1969.

    An engaging account with chapters on "bookmen" like Saintsbury,
Lang, Henley and Gosse, popular press critics like Gissing and Shorter, and on the rise of university English studies. Suggests that a
mood of faltering confidence prompted the late Victorian critical
withdrawal or retreat "into nostalgia, exoticism, fine writing,
belles lettres": "It can been seen, in the first place, as a
straightforward swing of the pendulum, the young reacting against the
sheer frumpishness of their elders; and in the second, as a watered-
down version of tendencies represented more vividly by, say, Swinburne and Art for Art's Sake. The bookman was a genteel first cousin
of the aesthete: he, too, had taken to heart the lessons of Pater,
though he drew less dramatic conclusions from them."

223. Grushow, Ira. "The Chastened Dandy: Beerbohm's 'Hilary Malt-
     by and Stephen Braxton'," *PLL*, 8 [Supplement] (1972), 149-164.

    A reading of Beerbohm's story that seeks to show a greater in-
terpenetration of writer's life and work, and clarify the story's
place in MB's literary career. Suggests that "almost all of Beerbohm's writing has as its central concern the effect of crystallized
'literary' postures or attitudes on the writer's response to life and
work."

224. Guérard, Albert. *Art for Art's Sake*. Boston: Lothrop, Lee
     and Shepard, 1936. [Rptd NY: Schocken, 1963]

    An account meant to show the recurrence in Europe and America
of the idea of art for art's sake from antiquity to contemporary
times. Prefers term "Symbolism" to describe "that queer state of
mind whose sole purpose was to be elusive" at the end of the nineteenth century, whose aim was "not to attain but to flee . . . .Hence
the pitiful chaos offered by the Symbolist movement: incomplete
geniuses, pretentious mediocrities, and dipsomaniacs. The best have
strange illuminations which, like the poems of their distant forerun-
ner Blake, give us sudden intolerable glimpses of a rival universe.
The average are histrionic bohemians. The worst barely manage to
elude the insane asylum . . . [Nordau] was painfully right."

225. Guillaume, André. *William Ernest Henley et son groupe: Néo-romanticisme et impérialisme à la fin du XIXe siècle.* Paris: C. Klincksieck, 1973.

A psycho-literary study of WEH's life, criticism, journalism and poetry, including discussions of specific works and various literary influences. Notes that Henley's aestheticist and anti-decadent poems sprang from the same source -- a resurgent and essentially egocentric romanticism. [In French]

226. Gunn, Peter. *Vernon Lee: Violet Paget, 1856-1935.* London: Oxford Univ. Press, 1964.

A critical biography of the sharp-tongued essayist, feminist, aesthetician and rival of Bernard Berenson. Of *Miss Brown* concludes: "Vernon Lee had set out to write a satire that would explore the 'sins', shams, insipidity and ridiculous artificialities of the so-called 'fleshly school'. What she in fact wrote was a very bad novel."

227. Gwynn, Frederick L. *Sturge Moore and the Life of Art.* Lawrence, Kan.: Univ. of Kansas Press, 1951.

Biographical and critical discussion of this disciple of Ricketts and lifelong friend of Yeats. Finds him unique "for an artist and poet trained in the nineties -- in insisting that esthetic activity is but one of three allied disciplines necessary to man's salvation."

228. Halloran, William F. "William Sharp as Bard and Craftsman," *VP*, 10 (1972), 57-78.

Despite the division Sharp himself imposed on his writings in 1894 by adopting the persona "Fiona Macleod," finds his poetry "unified by its concern with nature's beauty, the potential for human fulfillment, and the inevitability of loss, defeat, and death." Notes shift in Sharp's view of the poet from bardic recorder to poet-craftsman or seer and maker of verbal objects. "Sharp's experiments with impressionism in the eighties and early nineties deserve attention as a reaction against the precise detail and evocative diction of the Pre-Raphaelites and as an anticipation of Imagism, which came to fruition after the turn of the century when others attained the crisp, unembellished language that eluded Sharp."

229. Hamburger, Michael. "Art as Second Nature," *Romantic Mythologies*, ed. Ian Fletcher. London: Routledge and Kegan Paul, 1967, pp. 225-241.

Primarily concerned with Hugo von Hofmannsthal's interest in the dance and other forms of non-verbal expression as a manifestation of his "experience of the inadequacy of words . . . inseparable from his awareness of living in a civilization lacking in style, cohesion, and continuity."

230. Hamilton, Walter. *The Aesthetic Movement in England*. London: Reeves and Turner, 1882. [Rptd Folcroft Library, 1973]

The term "aesthetic movement" would be more correctly styled "a Renaissance of Medieval Art and Culture." The essence of the movement is "the union of persons of cultivated tastes to define, and to decide upon, what is to be admired, and their followers must aspire to that standard in their works and lives." Includes chapters on the Pre-Raphaelite Brotherhood, on Ruskin, on the Grosvenor Gallery, on aesthetic culture, on poets of the aesthetic school (Rossetti brothers, Woolner, Morris, Swinburne, O'Shaughnessy), on *Punch*'s satiric attacks, on Wilde and on Bedford Park. Predicts that while aestheticism has long been abused, "the poetry of the Aesthetic School will come to be regarded as a distinct growth typical of the later half of the nineteenth century, as the Lake School of Poetry was of the earlier portion."

231. Hanna, Susan J. "The Diction of English Poetry 1889-1900," *DA*, 31 (1971), 6609A. [Michigan]

Notes "a definite pattern" in the debate between traditionalist critics like Courthope and Paterian critics like Walter Raleigh, that is, between "those critics suspicious of over-concern with matters of language, and protective of the established poetic diction of the nineteenth century" and those who were "appreciative of obvious concern with language and willing to widen the diction of poetry." Analyzes *Verses, Ballads and Songs* and *London Nights*.

232. Harms, William A. "Impressionism as a Literary Style," *DA*, 31 (1971), 2090A. [Indiana]

Chiefly concerned with post-nineteenth-century fiction by Mirò, Mansfield, Woolf, Richardson, Ford. The impressionist will to style "originates (and results) in a denial of the significance of intellectual analysis and objective phenomena as usually interpreted by common sense, while attesting to an overwhelming belief that human existence is a continuous process of becoming, by means of which one comes into contact with the interpenetrating motions of sensation and apperceptive responses."

233. Harpham, Geoffrey. "The Incompleteness of Beardsley's *Venus and Tannhäuser*," *ELT*, 18 (1975), 24-32.

Sees AB's story as divided between a plot leading to papism and penitence, and a style tending towards aesthetic hedonism. "The very incompleteness of the story contributes to this sense of it as an allegory for the doomed solipsistic aestheticism of the generation, itself cut short by the Wilde trial and the early, tragic deaths of many of its most talented artists -- including Beardsley himself."

234. Harris, Wendell V. "Arnold, Pater, Wilde, and the Object as in Themselves They See It," *SEL*, 11 (1971), 733-747.

Argues that Pater's modification and Wilde's rebuttal of Arnold's doctrine that the object of criticism is to "see the object as in itself it really is" is the result of Arnold's failure to consider certain metaphysical assumptions, particularly the relativity of judgments. "If it cannot be shown that the object 'in itself' is a possible object of knowledge, we are left with only the effects or impressions of objects; if we only have impressions, we are seeing the object as 'in itself' it is not, but in the act of creativity which gives form to the impression which is the object as in itself it is not, we discover the range of qualities, powers, and desires which make up the race of man as in itself it really is."

235. Harris, Wendell V. "Beginnings of and for the True Short Story in England," *ELT*, 15 (1972), 269-276.

Offers Kipling as the originator of the true short story in England. Discusses his contributions to the form: compression, sense of a beginning, externality of narration. Distinguishes the "interactive stance" of the short story writer from the "immersive technique" of the novelist.

236. Harris, Wendell V. "A Bibliography of Writings About Hubert Crackanthorpe," *ELT*, 6 (1963), 85-91.

237. Harris, Wendell V. "English Short Fiction in the 19th Century," *SSF*, 6 (1968), 1-93.

Notes that the tradition of aesthetic short fiction, from Rossetti to Yeats and Fiona Macleod, centered in a "special kind of impressionism: the attempt to render the writer's intense impression not of the actual world he has experienced, but of a past age, a type of mind or a point of view that the writer cannot have directly or fully experienced." Though aesthetic fiction of the 1890s often combined fantasy, mannered style and playful use of historical or legendary settings, it made "relatively little use" of the resources of Symbolism. And, "rather interestingly, the most hectic and morbid stories of the 1890's [e.g. those by Machen and Stenbock] received little notice."

238. Harris, Wendell V. "Fiction in the English 'Experimental' Periodicals of the 1890's," *BB*, 25 (1968), 111-118.

Lists short stories and similar short fiction by author for the following: *Albemarle, Anglo-Saxon Review, Butterfly, Dome, Evergreen, Pageant, Quarto, Savoy, Venture* and *Yellow Book.*

239. Harris, Wendell V. "Hubert Crackanthorpe as Realist," *ELT*, 6 (1963), 76-84.

Maintains that the usual portrayal of HC as Maupassant's disciple does scant justice to the development of the English realistic short story in the 1890s. "I should like to suggest that Crackanthorpe's artistic vision, as distinct from that of Maupassant, derived from a sense of disillusionment lurking just off-stage, of sorrow waiting in the wings, during the most romantic and ideal scenes of life, that because of this sense even the earliest of his stories differ materially from those of the French writer, and that the techniques he developed to portray this disillusionment in his later stories remove almost all grounds of similarity."

240. Harris, Wendell V. "Identifying the Decadent Fiction of the Eighteen-Nineties," *English Fiction in Transition*, 5, v (1962), 1-13.

Suggests that Symons, who was responsible for the wide currency of the term "decadence," deliberately sought to profit from the broadness of meaning the term had already acquired in France. Urges that it is fruitless to continue adding to the string of definitions of "decadent" now extant; instead, scholars should devote themselves to describing the characteristics of the wide range of literary work produced in the period, most of which eludes previous definitions of "decadence."

241. Harris, Wendell V. "Innocent Decadence: The Poetry of the *Savoy*," *PMLA*, 77 (1962), 629-636.

Distinguishes the English syndrome of decadence from the French. Notes that even the English mode of decadence (ennui leads to quest for new sensations which leads to despair at the banality of all experience) inapplicable to the poetry appearing in the *Savoy*. Instead, "the lament for the probable unattainability and inevitable transience of the experience of the ideal, specifically the ideal love" is the central theme of the English decadents. Suggests that the difficulty of finding decadent poetry in what has been presumed to be the veritable organ of English decadence should alert scholars to the dangers "of misinterpreting the poetry of the decade whenever it is approached along the beaten paths of ruling preconceptions about the 'decadent spirit' of the 1890's."

242. Harris, Wendell V. "John Lane's Keynotes Series and the Fiction of the 1890's," *PMLA*, 83 (1968), 1407-13.

"The minor writers gathered around the Bodley Head were much more interested in experimenting with their craft than with their souls, and generally more interested in personal innovation than successful imitation. Describes the thematic and technical interests of the novelists and short fictionists of the Bodley Head's Keynotes series which "offers a significant sample from the heart of the 1890's . . . particularly illustrative of what happened to fiction at the time." Finds the series writers "not greatly devoted to the exploration of strange sins. Rather, most of them were absorbed in exploring new fictional techniques" and such new thematic concerns as "the marriage question."

243. Harris, Wendell V. "The Novels of Richard Whiteing," *ELT*, 8 (1965), 36-43.

Argues RW's highly successful novels merit our attention because they "provide an excellent example of what was regarded as realism by most critics and readers of the time" and illustrate the need to re-examine minor figures of the period.

244. Harris, Wendell V. "Pater as Prophet," *Criticism*, 6 (1964), 349-360.

Seeks to place in perspective the assumptions about WP's shaping influence on the generation of the nineties, reminding us that the themes of "l'art pour l'art" and the brevity of life date from the 1868 version of the "Conclusion" to *The Renaissance* as well as being current in FitzGerald and Swinburne works of the period. Asserts that "the more one knows about the lives of the members of the 'decadent' coterie, the less importance has Pater in determining either their art or their personal tragedies." Finds Pater's really significant literary influence on the writers of the twentieth century expresses itself in these characteristic emphases: the evanescence, complexity and aesthetic importance of the individual moment, the singularity of the individual person's experience and the primacy of the visual experience.

245. Harris, Wendell V. and Rebecca Larsen. "Richard Le Gallienne: A Bibliography of Writings About Him," *ELT*, 19 (1976), 111-132.

246. Harris, Wendell V. "Richard Whiteing: A Selective Annotated Bibliography of Writings About Him," *ELT*, 8 (1965), 44-48.

247. Harris, Wendell V. "Transitional Short Fiction in England during the 1890's," *DA*, 22 (1961), 1176. [Wisconsin]

Attempts to reconstruct "the various literary ideals toward which these writers looked" and the formal and technical means they employed in the process. Considers the "aesthetic" fiction of Wilde, Yeats, Beerbohm, John Gray and Richard Garnett, the "new realism" of Crackanthorpe (extensively) and Ella D'Arcy, George Gissing and John Buchan, and the sentimental romances of Harland, Dowson and Wedmore. "The meaninglessness of the term 'decadence' as applied to this fiction is insisted upon."

248. Harrison, Fraser, ed. *The Yellow Book, An Illustrated Quarterly: An Anthology*. NY: St. Martin's Press, 1974. "Introduction," pp. 3-48.

Seeks to strip away the myths and prejudices that have surrounded the *Yellow Book* and place the magazine in a new context, "a context prescribed by the social conditions in which it flourished and foundered." Notes that "the identity of woman, and, more specifically, her sexuality" were central issues in many *Yellow Book* stories, and further, that the female contributors were robust and energetic compared to the men who seemed "unnerved and unbalanced" and driven to 'seek comfort and oblivion in homosexuality, prostitution, addiction to alcohol and opiates, sterile relationships with children, and, in some cases, forlorn celibacy." Includes brief treatments of the magazine's founding and foundering, its contributors, editors and critics.

249. Harrison, Frederick. "Decadence in Modern Art," *Forum*, 15 (1893), 428-438.

Chiefly concerned with visual arts; attacks the descent to sordid chirurgical realism in contemporary art: "It boots little to be rid of the conventional in order to set up an idol in the brutal, the coarse, the odd, the accidental, and dull imitation of rank commonplace." Concludes that "Decadence in art is a sure sign of some organic change taking place in our moral sense."

250. Hauser, Nancy. "Arthur O'Shaughnessy and the Doomed Circle," *Columbia Library Columns*, 18, ii (Feb 1969), 17-24.

A brief biographical account of AO'S and the Pre-Raphaelite circle; both depicted as having been stalked by tragedy. Notes Columbia University holdings in AO'S; little critical comment: "His slender frame and spiritual expression recalled Chopin and his best poetry has the characteristics of Chopin's music -- dreamy and sometimes weird, with an original, delicious and inexhaustible melody."

251. Hawkey, Nancy J. "Olive Custance Douglas: An Annotated Bibliography of Writings About Her," *ELT*, 15 (1972), 49-56.

Includes an introduction.

252. Heath-Stubbs, John. *The Darkling Plain: A Study in the Later Fortunes of Romanticism in English Poetry from George Darley to W.B. Yeats*. London: Eyre and Spottiswode, 1950.

Includes chapters on Pre-Raphaelitism and reactions to aestheti-cism. Aestheticism viewed as a resumption of Pre-Raphaelitism, part of the aesthetic withdrawal characteristic of late Romanticism and necessary in the face of an uncompromising materialism. Discussions of Meredith, Bridges, Kipling, Doughty, Michael Field, Blunt and Yeats; the Rhymers' Club represents a "backwater."

253. Held, George. *"The Second Book of the Rhymers' Club,"* JRUL, 28, ii (June 1965), 15-21.

A brief account emphasizing the diversity of the Rhymers and the second collection of poetry they produced. Suggests that the reason for the group's dissolution was due to this very diversity and to their conflicting attitudes about the importance of ideas in poetry.

254. Hepburn, James G. "Transition, Decadence, and Estheticism: Some Notes," *ELT*, 6, i (1963), 16-17.

See #176.

255. Hicks, Granville. *Figures of Transition: A Study of British Literature at the End of the Nineteenth Century*. NY: Macmil-lan, 1939.

Chapters on Morris, Hardy, Butler, the novel, Wilde and the cult of art. Changing mood of the period brought about by failure of capitalism which increased the number of neurotic personalities. Decadence "the anarchism of the hopeless; unable to overcome their vices, they made virtues of them."

256. Hill, John E. "Dialectical Aestheticism: Essays on the Criti-cism of Swinburne, Pater, James, Shaw, and Yeats," *DAI*, 33 (1973), 3648-49A. [Virginia]

Argues that the aesthetic movement, "like socialism, developed out of the romantic spirit of revolution and adopted, for its own purposes, the Hegelian method as a mode of expression. Its charac-teristic form is the impressionist essay, which allows the greatest possible freedom of movement. . . .The direction of aestheticism is not escapist but inclusive, comprehending experience with a far broad-er perspective than any offered by ethical theories."

257. Holdsworth, R.V., ed. *Arthur Symons: Poetry and Prose*. Cheadle, Eng.: Carcenet, 1974. "Introduction," pp. 9-24.

Finds it "likely that he both practised and expounded the ideals of the Decadence more energetically than any of his contemporaries. . . . Symons' poetry also meets all the requirements of Decadence," that is, employs suggestion rather than statement, nuances rather than sharp edges, musicality. Stresses AS's contributions to modernist poetry.

258. Holmes, Ruth Van Zuyle. "Mary Duclaux (1856-1944): Primary and Secondary Checklists," *ELT*, 10 (1967), 27-46.

Includes an introduction to the life and works of this friend of George Moore and Violet Paget.

259. Hönnighausen, Lothar. *Präraphaeliten und Fin de Siècle: Symbolistische Tendenzen in der Englischen Spätromantik*. Munich: Wilhelm Fink, 1971.

A detailed study of the development of late Romantic ideas of the symbol with discussions of Pre-Raphaelite realism and allegory, the influence of interart analogies, the imaginary landscape, images of the ideal mistress, and late Romantic mysticism. Unusually wide reference to such writers as Allingham, Wratislaw, Douglas, Custance, Todhunter, O'Sullivan, Marston, Field, Hake, Payne and O'Shaughnessy, as well as their better known contemporaries. [In German]

260. Hosmon, Robert S. "Adventure in Bohemia: A Study of the Little Magazines of the Aesthetic Movement," *DA*, 30 (1970), 3907A. [Arizona State]

"Presents the materials and contributors published in [the *Germ, Oxford and Cambridge Magazine, Century Guild Hobby Horse,* and *Savoy*] as they reflect the philosophy of the group which formed the periodical, examines the common bonds which each magazine shared with another, and points out the effects of the publications upon history, art and literature."

261. Hough, Graham. "George Moore and the Nineties," *Edwardians and Late Victorians,* ed. Richard Ellmann. NY: Columbia Univ. Press, 1960, pp. 1-27. [English Institute Essays, 1959]

Finds three principal literary developments during the period 1880-1914: (1) increased range and freedom of choice in subject; (2) a confused set of tendencies clustering around the notion of art for art's sake and later passing over into symbolism ("Symbolism can be said to occur when the cult of the exquisite, particular sensation, embodied in the perfect form, begins to acquire transcendental overtones"); (3) the conscious reaction against English literary tradition. Treats Moore as typical figure of the 1890s; believes "the trouble about the actual achievements of the nineties in their most characteristic forms is that they are so minuscule."

262. Hough, Graham. *The Last Romantics*. NY: Barnes and Noble,
      1961. [First pub. 1947]

    Traces the aesthetic direction in thought and feeling from Rus-
king through Rossetti and Morris to the fin de siècle and Yeats; antiquarian, traditional and conservative, this line is portrayed as
the antithesis produced by Victorian materialism and positivism.
Notes that the artists and writers studied show less a cohesive program than a "common passion for the life of the imagination, conceived as an all-embracing activity, apart from the expression of it
in any one particular art. Hence a tendency to assimilate the different arts to each other, to allow their values to interpenetrate
each other, forming together a realm of transcendent importance, for
which a status has somehow to be found in an inhospitable world.
This endeavour becomes so absorbing that it leads to a gradual sever-
ance, increasingly apparent from Ruskin onwards, of art from the interests of common life, and a constant tendency to turn art itself into the highest value, to assimilate aesthetic to religious experience." Of the fin de siècle concludes: "from the thinnish trickle
of original work and the fragmentary medley of personal reminiscence
that go to make up our picture of the nineties, it is hard to extract
any consistent impression; and from the *Yellow Book* and the *Savoy* it
is hard to extract anything but a faint and unanalysable period fla-
vour. It was an age of minor successes and minor failures, where
fragments of delicate distinction emerge from a jumble of tasteless
trivialities. Its ultimate importance in literary history is likely
to be that it nourished the genius of Yeats."

263. Houghton, Walter E. and G. Robert Stange. "The Aesthetic
      Movement: Introduction," *Victorian Poetry and Poetics*.
      Boston: Houghton Mifflin, 1959, pp. 724-730.

    A brief survey of sources and influences with special emphasis
on Wilde, Johnson and Dowson. Could it ever be defined, the term
décadence "would be the most satisfactory label for the whole period
[1885-1900]." Concludes that the aesthetes' primary contribution
was negative: "they cleared the way for one of the periodic renewals
of the English poetic idiom . . . . Both their practice and their emphasis on a serious dedication to poetry . . . underlie the new classicism, the formalism, the concentration on precise technique, which
characterize the important poetry of our century."

264. Housman, Laurence. "Pre-Raphaelitism in Art and Poetry,"
      *Essays by Divers Hands: Being the Transactions of the Royal
      Society of Literature of the United Kingdom*, ed. R.W. Macan,
      Vol 12, n.s. London: Oxford Univ. Press, 1933, pp. 1-29.

    Pre-Raphaelitism defined as "an endeavour to express romance in
terms of nature, with a great intensity of feeling, and with a strong
sense of character . . . . Rejecting rhetorical movement and conventional gesture for the pictorial rendering of passion, it gave emphasis
to the eloquence of quiet attitudes and the interchange of the human

glance." The central interest of most Pre-Raphaelite art "consists in the exchanged regards of friends and lovers, or in strong re- strained pose from which all gesticulation is banished, or even in the deeply divined expression of a single glance." This "dramatic portraiture" characterized by its strange blend of detailed external- ity and intense inwardness of feeling.

265. Hunt, John Dixon. *The Pre-Raphaelite Imagination 1848-1900*. Lincoln, Nebr.: Univ. of Nebraska Press, 1968.

A study of the "continuity of admiration" of Pre-Raphaelite inspirations and principles from the members of the Brotherhood it- self to what is found "the most vocal, blatant, yet complex moment of that art -- the 1890's." Stresses the primacy of Pre-Raphaelite over French influences to the generation of the nineties. Subsequent chapters discuss various modes of Pre-Raphaelite imagination: medie- valism, subjective experience, symbolism, the Pre-Raphaelite woman, and realism.

266. Hunt, Lorraine R.L. "*The Century Guild Hobby Horse*: A Study of a Magazine," *DA*, 26 (1966), 3954. [North Carolina]

Finds that "in protesting so much about its own time, the *Hob- by Horse* aligns itself with Arnold, Ruskin, Morris, and other impor- tant Victorians who objected to many of the attitudes that are con- sidered 'typically Victorian'." Decides the magazine does not, how- ever, "subscribe to the Pateristic art for art's sake aesthetic, which represents another kind of anti-Victorian reaction."

267. Hutchins, Patricia. "Elkin Mathews, Poets' Publisher," *Ariel*, 1 (1970), 77-95.

Drawing upon the collection of Mathews papers at the University of Reading, outlines Mathews' relationships with his authors and with his ambitious and occasionally unscrupulous partner, John Lane.

268. Hutchinson, Horace G. *Portraits of the Eighties*. NY: Scrib- ner's, 1920.

Impressionistic essays and reminiscences by a contemporary. Includes chapters on Morris, Swinburne and Meredith, on artists like Watts, Millais, Burne-Jones, Sickert, on the aesthetes and Wilde, on "the Souls."

269. Inglish, Ida. "The English Decadence and the Satirists," *DA*, 28 (1967), 1051A. [Arizona State]

A survey of the satires, burlesques and parodies of aestheti- cism and decadence, from Mallock's *New Republic* to Max's "Enoch Soames."

270. Ireland, Kenneth R. "The Late Nineteenth-Century Revival of
     Interest in Rococo," *DAI*, 34 (1974), 6644A. [Princeton]

     Attempts to trace "an overall pattern" in several arts of
France, England, Austria and Germany 1850-1910, while noting the shifting ideals and modes of rococo during this period. Believes the
years 1890-1910 "can be viewed as the most international and inter-
artistic display of the neo-Rococo, emphasizing a general revival of
interest rather than the accidental coincidence of merely local, isolated and episodic phenomena."

271. Ireland, Kenneth R. *"Sight and Song*: A Study of the Inter-
     relations between Painting and Poetry," *VP*, 15 (1977), 9-20.

     Believes that this collection of poems by "Michael Field"
based on paintings raises three important critical questions about
the picture-poem: its structure, its authorial objectivity and its
value.

272. Jackson, Holbrook. *The Eighteen Nineties: A Review of Art
     and Ideas at the Close of the Nineteenth Century*. NY: G.P.
     Putnam's Sons, 1966. [First pub. 1913]

     The classic study, stressing the liveliness, diversity and re-
awakened energies of the period. Chapters on fin de siècle characteristics and personalities, decadence, the Wilde debacle, Beardsley,
the new dandyism, Beerbohm, the art of shocking people, literary
stylism, the Celtic Renaissance, the minor poet, Francis Thompson,
Davidson, Shaw, the higher drama, the new realism and romantic fiction, Kipling, the Arts and Crafts Movement, the revival of printing,
British impressionists, and black-and-white artists. Decadence characterized by four qualities: perversity, artificiality, egoism and
curiosity. Believes "all so-called decadence is civilisation rejecting through certain specialised persons, the accumulated experiences
and sensations of the race. . . . If you will, it is a form of imperialism of the spirit, ambitious, arrogant, aggressive, waving the
flag of human power over an ever wider and wider territory." Concludes that "all the cynicisms and petulances and flippancies of the
decadence, the febrile self-assertion, the voluptuousness, the perversity were, consciously or unconsciously, efforts towards the re-
habilitation of spiritual power . . . . the transmutation of vision
into personal power."

273. Jackson, Holbrook. "A Note on the Period," *Fin de Siècle:
     A Selection of Late Nineteenth-Century Literature and Art,*
     ed. Nevile Wallis. London: Allan Wingate, 1947, pp. 11-14.

     Its legend intensified by circumstances, the fin de siècle now
seems "a lost paradise of peace" to the post-bellum young. Period
characterized by revolt, a growing irritation with conventional hab-
its and ideas, and disapproval of the "obvious" in art.

274. Jackson, Thomas H. *The Early Poetry of Ezra Pound*. Cambridge,
     Mass.: Harvard Univ. Press, 1968.

     Includes consideration of those elements of the decadent aes-
thetic that particularly appealed and were useful to Pound: "what
the Decadents could offer to attract Pound's attention . . . were a
desperate kind of professionalism, an uncompromising insistence that
art was important, a belief in its power to hypostatize important experiences and to allow the exercise of various human spiritual energies, and, from a more technical point of view, a cluster of models
for handling moments of unusually intense emotional experience."

275. Jean-Aubry, Georges. "Paul Verlaine et l'Angleterre: 1872-
     1893," *Revue de Paris*, 6 (Dec 1918), 600-620.

     Chiefly concerned with PV's trip to London, Oxford and Manchest-
er in 1893-94 and his friendly reception by the advanced young writers of the day. [In French]

276. Jepson, Edgar. *Memories of a Victorian*. London: Gollancz,
     1933.

     Interesting memoirs by a friend of Dowson and Horne. Anecdotes
about various Rhymers, Beardsley, Teixeira de Mattos. Remarks on the
favorite gathering places, the cult of the music-hall. "When in the
nineties we talked of the decadent poets we did not mean what the
journalists of to-day mean when they write with shocked pens of the
decadent poets of the nineties. We were speaking of a French school
of poets, of whom Verlaine was the chief, in whose verse there was a
certain fall, a *décadence*, which you find in the best verse of Mr.
Arthur Symons and in some of the poems of Ernest Dowson."

277. Joad, C.E.M. *Decadence: A Philosophical Inquiry*. London:
     Faber and Faber, 1948.

     After examining and rejecting other definitions, suggests that
the meaning of decadence is "to be found in the view that experience
is valuable or is at least to be valued for its own sake, irrespec-
tive of the quality or kind of the experience." Associated with decadence are scepticism of belief, epicureanism and hedonism, and subjectivism; common to all is "the dropping of the object." Second
part of treatise illustrates general definition in literature, art
and society.

278. Johnson, Alan P. "The Italian Renaissance and Some Late
     Victorians," *VN*, No. 36 (Fall 1969), 23-26.

     By including Wilde's *The Duchess of Padua* and *A Florentine
Tragedy*, is able to trace a late Victorian shift in response away
from the religious pietism of Ruskin through the conventional morality

of Symonds to Pater's amoral aestheticism and, finally, to Wilde's "ethic of personal power and self-satisfaction," identified with the "Nietzschean position implicit in the humanistic appreciation of the Renaissance."

279. Johnson, Diane C. "A Contribution to the 90's [*The Studio*]," *Apollo*, 91 (1970), 198-203.

Examines the four topics discussed in the first issue of the *Studio* (Apr 1893), the monthly that "presented the views of a small group of people who were reacting against the industrial ugliness of nineteenth-century England and whose objective was to raise the overall standard of aesthetic sensibility by utilizing art in all phases of life." Notes that these four topics -- poster art, Beardsley, photography and Eastern art -- were all important constituting elements of art nouveau.

280. Johnson, E.D.H. "The Eighteen Nineties: Perspectives," *Wilde and the Nineties: An Essay and an Exhibition*, ed. Charles Ryskamp. Princeton, N.J.: Princeton Univ. Press, 1966, pp. 25-30.

Believes the decade "stands in relation to the Aesthetic Movement of the 1870's and 1880's in somewhat the same relation as the Rococo to the Baroque. Its effort was less to develop new expressive forms than to refine and embellish received motifs. It is perhaps best described as a final efflorescence of the romantic sensibility, ignited by the example of the French symbolists and naturalists with whom their English compeers had so many and such close ties." Cites as characteristic of the "strange uniformity within heterogeneity that sets the achievement of the *fin de siècle* apart from anything that came before or after" the rage for experience, the obsession with mutability, the insistence on formal perfection, the wedding of literature to the sister arts, the astonishing proliferation of little magazines.

281. Johnson, Lionel. "The Cultured Faun," *Anti-Jacobin*, No.7 (March 1891), 156-157.

Satiric program for the aspiring "decadent": "a reassuring sobriety of habit, with just a dash of the dandy," "exquisite appreciation of pain, exquisite thrills of anguish, exquisite adoration of suffering," "a tender patronage of Catholicism," "a scientific profession of materialist dogmas, coupled -- for you should forswear consistency -- with gloomy chatter about 'The Will to Live'," "Impressions! exquisite, dainty fantasies; fiery-colored visions; and impertinence straggling into epigram, for 'the true' criticism," "occasional doses of 'Hellenism' . . . . together with the elegant languors and favorite vices of (let us parade our 'decadent' learning) the *Stratonis Epigrammata*." "*Fin de siècle! Fin de siècle!* Literature is a thing of beauty, blood, and nerves."

282. Johnson, Lionel. "A Note Upon the Practice and Theory of
     Verse at the Present Time Obtaining in France," *Century
     Guild Hobby Horse*, 6 (1891), 61-66.

     An approving if somewhat tentative notice of French decadent
and symbolist schools of poetry. "In English, *décadence* and the literature thereof, mean this: the period, at which passion, or romance, or tragedy, or sorrow, or any other form of activity of emotion, must be refined upon, and curiously considered, for literary
treatment: an age of afterthought, of reflection . . . . In English,
symbolisme, and its literature, mean this: a recognition, in things,
of a double existence: their existence in nature, and their existence in mind."

283. Johnson, R.V. *Aestheticism*. London: Methuen, 1969. [Vol.
     3 of Critical Idiom Series]

     A somewhat disapproving account of aestheticism as a view of
art ("aestheticism represents a drastic attempt to separate art from
life"), as a view of life ("taking life 'in the spirit of art', as
something to be appreciated for its beauty, its variety, its dramatic spectacle") and as a practical tendency in literature and the
arts ("a movement away from didacticism . . . . corresponding to the
principle of art for art's sake'). Chapters on sources and influences, on literary exponents and on critical spokesmen. Aestheticism
seen as becoming increasingly histrionic in the 1890s: "The link between aestheticism and decadence is perhaps a matter for speculation.
It may be that aestheticism, like vulgar hedonism, comes up against
the law of diminishing returns -- that beauty, like happiness, evades
us when too persistently and self-consciously pursued, and that the
lover of beauty is, sooner or later, impelled to seek it in things
not commonly considered beautiful."

284. Johnson, R.V. "Pater and the Victorian Anti-Romantics,"
     EIC, 4 (1954), 42-57.

     Notes that the critics of the *Quarterly Review* led the move-
ment toward classicism and Augustan standards usually associated
with Arnold; the critics failed to appreciate the conditions in
society which were producing the self-culture and virtual segregation
of the cultivated minority. "An assiduous cultivation of private
sensibility seemed to give life the only sort of meaning it could now
have, a meaning to be found, not in remote and problematical objec-
tives, but in immediate experience. 'Aestheticism' was the extreme
development of this tendency."

285. Jose, Arthur W. *The Romantic Nineties*. Sydney: Angus and
     Robertson, 1933.

     Referring the the "decadence" of Beardsley and Conder, declares
"nothing could be more alien from the romanticism of the Australian

Nineties. Here we were experiencing rather a naissance than a renaissance; we had no decadents to combat (or to fondle), but only
the upward rush of youthful emotion, youth trying out in all manner
of awkward ways the wings it had just begun to sprout."

286. Jullian, Philippe. *Dreamers of Decadence: Symbolist Painters
      of the 1890s*, trans. Robert Baldick. NY: Praeger, 1972.

      An enthusiastic study of the visual arts 1880-1910 that con-
centrates upon the various ruling "myths" which shaped aesthetic consciousness. Includes chapters on the "new beauty," on mystical, erotic and macabre imagery, on Byzantium, on other exotic places favored
by "decadents" and appends an anthology of symbolist terms. Believes
that decadence was above all the revolt against a materialist society.

287. Karl, Frederick R. "Joseph Conrad: A *fin de siècle* Novelist --
      A Study in Style and Method," *LitR*, 2 (1958-59), 565-576.

      Argues that critics have failed to see the continuity between
the poetic language of the 1890s and Conrad's early work; discussions of *Almayer's Folly* and *An Outcast of the Islands*.

288. Kennedy, John M. *English Literature 1880-1905*. London:
      Stephen Swift, 1912.

      Essays from a convinced Catholic, Tory, classicist point of
view. Chapters on Pater, Wilde, the *Yellow Book* group, Beardsley
and Whistler, Shaw, Wells, Gissing, Yeats and the Celtic Renaissance.
Melancholy found to be the keynote of a generation caught in the web
of materialism, atheism, idealism, romanticism. "The whole atmosphere of the time is yellow, jaundiced. Weakness of will is a prominent characteristic of those who, had they been stronger in this res-
pect, might have rescued the literature of the age from the mire into
which it was gradually sinking."

289. Kermode, Frank. "Modernisms," *Continuities*. London: Rout-
      ledge and Kegan Paul, 1968, pp. 1-32.

      Argues against the notion of "post-modernism," recognizing in-
stead "palaeo" and "neo-modernism" and pointing out the similarities
between the two phases so distinguished: "the modernism of the 'Nineties has a recognisable touch of [an apocalyptic world-view], if decadence, hope of renovation, the sense of transition, the sense of an
ending or the trembling of the veil, are accepted as its signs. At
such times there is a notable urgency in the proclamation of a break
with the immediate past, a stimulating sense of crisis, of an historical license for the New. And there appears to be a genuine continuity here, for all modernist art and literature between the 'Nineties
and now is associated with similar assumptions in some form or other."

290. Kermode, Frank. "Poet and Dancer Before Diaghilev," *Puzzles and Epiphanies*. London: Routledge and Kegan Paul, 1962, 1-28.

Studies the dancer as image in symbolist and early modernist art, particularly as embodied by Loie Fuller whose increasingly abstract compositions of motion depended upon the swirling, diaphanous effects achieved by illuminating her draperies with colored lights. Notes her impersonal artistic style paralleled and perhaps suggested a similar tendency in modernism.

291. Kermode, Frank. *Romantic Image*. London: Routledge and Kegan Paul, 1957.

A luminous and influential study of the origins and influence of the Romantic-Symbolist beliefs in the "Image as a radiant truth out of space and time, and in the necessary isolation or estrangement of men who can perceive it." Centrally concerned with Yeats, but includes highly suggestive remarks on Pater, Wilde, the "tragic generation." Includes chapters on the isolation of the artist, on the image of the dancer, and on Symons' role as transmitter of the Symbolist aesthetic to modernist poetry.

292. Kilmer, Joyce. "Lionel Johnson, Ernest Dowson, Aubrey Beardsley," *The Circus and Other Essays and Fugitive Pieces*. NY: George H. Doran, 1921, pp. 237-252.

Insists that the beauty all three sought was found when they submitted to the Catholic Church. Wishes Beardsley's every drawing had been destroyed. Finds the "one real value of the cult of peacocks and green carnations, of artificial paganism and sophisticated loveliness, is that it furnishes a splendid contrasting background for the white genius of Lionel Johnson," who, as a Catholic poet, is surpassed only by Francis Thompson.

293. Klingopulos, G.D. "The Literary Scene," *From Dickens to Hardy*, ed. Boris Ford. Harmondsworth, Eng. and Baltimore: Penguin, 1958, pp. 59-116. [Vol. 6 of *The Pelican Guide to English Literature*]

Brief remarks about the "decadent" strain in Victorian writing. Contends that "the nineties" was not a discrete phenomenon; rather, fin de siècle elements -- elements that "stand for something unsatisfactory about the inner life of the period" -- are to be found in the Oxford Movement, Pre-Raphaelitism, Ritualism, etc.

294. Kopp, Karl C. "The Origin and Characteristics of 'Decadence' in British Literature of the 1890's," *DA*, 24 (1963), 1604. [Berkeley]

British literary decadence defined as a decline from art for

art's sake assumptions. Examines *Dorian Gray, Under the Hill* and
Dowson's poems, finding the decadent parody of aestheticism "strikingly present" in Wilde and Beardsley, though not in Dowson. "The
decadents called attention to the immorality of their lives and of
their art. In this way they not only undermined the aesthetic principles of harmony and amorality that they had learned to cherish, but
also they failed to produce an art capable of containing and direct-
ting the aesthetic responses of their audience."

295. Krishnamurti, G. *The Eighteen-Nineties: A Literary Exhibition,*
      September, 1973. London: National Book League, 1973. "Pre-
      face," pp. 7-10.

      An annotated bibliography of 861 items including anthologies
of nineties works, works by individual nineties authors, illustrated
books, literary periodicals and books about the period. "The selection of material for this exhibition is based on the belief that the
character of 'Nineties literature did not die with the century or
with the great Queen. It was only the war of 1914 that inflicted the
final blow and the change was quick and merciless. In the same way
the character of the 'Nineties did not begin on New Year's Day,
eighteen hundred and ninety."

296. Krishnamurti, G. *The Eighteen-Nineties: A Literary Exhibition,*
      Sept. 1973: Supplement to the Catalogue. London: Francis Thomp-
      son Society and Enitharmon Press, 1974.

      Lists 39 items not included in the original catalogue.

297. Lang, Andrew. "Decadence," *Critic*, 37 (1900), 171-173.

      Contemptuous dismissal of Symons' obituary account of Ernest
Dowson's life and works. "I am apt to believe that [a "decadent"]
is an unwholesome young person, who has read about 'ages of decadence'
in histories of literature, likes what he is told about them, and
tries to die down to it, with more or less success."

298. Langbaum, Robert. "Max and Dandyism," *VP*, 5 (1966), 121-126.

      [Review of David Cecil's *Max*] Dandyism is "like the monastic
rule a ritual for achieving control," "a way of being in the world
without being of it." "It is the self-parody in the dandy posture
that makes it unassailable."

299. Laurent, Emile. *La poésie décadent devant la science*
      psychiatrique. Paris: Maloine, 1897.

      Believes that in the work of decadent poets, good and bad alike,
one may read "les signes incontestables, les stigmates indélébiles de

68

la déséquilibration cérébrale," a nervous disorder expressed in the poetic use of outlandish comparisons, excessive images, incoherent ideas, color audition, neologism, mysticism and eroticism; concludes with a description of the decadent physiognomy. [In French]

300. Larsen, Rebecca and Wendell V. Harris. "Richard Le Gallienne: A Bibliography of Writings About Him," *ELT*, 19 (1976), 111-132.

301. Lauterbach, Edward S. "An Annotated Bibliography of Writings About Rudyard Kipling: First Supplement," *ELT*, 8 (1965), (Part I), 136-202; (Part II), 203-241.

302. Lauterbach, Edward S. and W. Eugene Davis. *The Transitional Age, British Literature, 1880-1920.* Troy: Whitston, 1973.

Part I considers important trends in genres of fiction (novel, short story and "entertainment"), poetry, drama and prose with brief discussions of representative figures. In general the period viewed as one of reaction against Victorian standards, pursuing new subject matter and formal techniques. Part II gives selective primary and secondary bibliographies for more than 170 British authors of the period as well as providing definitions of such literary terms as aestheticism, decadence, fin de siècle, etc.

303. Lavers, Annette. "Aubrey Beardsley, Man of Letters," *Romantic Mythologies*, ed. Ian Fletcher. London: Routledge and Kegan Paul, 1967, pp. 243-270.

Believes that Beardsley's few literary remains suggest he was "the epitome of 'decadence' in literature as well as art." Studies psychological dimensions of his literary work, paying particular attention to *The Story of Venus and Tannhäuser*, a fiction which "can be viewed as an attempt to reach a satisfactory synthesis of his various tendencies."

304. Lavrin, Janko. *Aspects of Modernism: From Wilde to Pirandello.* London: Stanley Nott, 1935. [Rptd Books for Libraries Press, 1968]

Fin de siècle decadence perceived as romanticism without convictions, an exaggerated hysterical egoism. "The more passive 'decadents' hoped to get out of the *cul-de-sac* . . . through a second-hand mysticism, or even through a timely surrender to the authority of the Roman Catholic Church. Others again thought they would find salvation in a new return to the 'fundamentals' of life, or in the mysteries of sex."

305. Le Gallienne, Richard. *Retrospective Reviews: A Literary Log*. 2 Vols. London: John Lane, 1896.

Literary journalism written 1891-95 with essays on Watson, Meredith, Henley, Kipling, Stevenson, Pater, Symons, John Gray, Symonds, Crackanthorpe, Yeats, Moore, Davidson, Thompson, O'Shaughnessy. Famous remarks on decadence occur in essays on Churton Collins' *Illustrations of Tennyson* and on Gray's *Silverpoints*; defines it as "the euphuistic expression of isolated observations. Thus disease, which is the favorite theme of the décadents, does not in itself make for decadence: it is only when, as often it is, studied apart from its relations to health, to the great vital centre of things, that it does so. Any point of view, seriously taken, which ignores the complete view, approaches decadence."

306. Le Gallienne, Richard. *The Romantic 90's*. NY: Doubleday, Page, 1925.

Literary gossip about virtually everyone in the period, drawn from LeG's column in the *Star*. Sees "the will to romance" as the operative force in the period, expressive of "the modern determination to escape from the deadening thraldom of materialism and outworn conventions, and to live life significantly -- keenly and beautifully, personally and, if need be, daringly."

307. Le Gallienne, Richard. "What's Wrong with the Eighteen Nineties?" *Bookman (NY)*, 54 (1921), 1-7.

Denounces the "feminine ferocity" of the contemporary reaction against the nineties, pointing out the debt owed to the earlier period. "Generally speaking, the world we live in at the moment has been created by three men: Aubrey Beardsley, Oscar Wilde, and Bernard Shaw."

308. Legouis, Emile and Louis Cazamian. "New Divergences," *A History of English Literature*, trans. H.D. Irvine, W.D. MacInnes and L. Cazamian. NY: Macmillan, 1935, pp. 1218-1365.

See #88.

309. Lehmann, A.G. "Pierrot and Fin de Siècle," *Romantic Mythologies*, ed. Ian Fletcher. London: Routledge and Kegan Paul, 1967, pp. 209-223.

Believes Pierrot especially appealed "to the idle and crestfallen poets of a police-state Empire" because he was "the figure most akin themselves." Studies the role of Pierrot in works of Laforgue and Verlaine. Concludes both poets resist "the sentimental or clownish embroidery of Pierrot, and instead take the image to the limit beyond which the name and associations of the traditional part are on the point of disappearing."

310. Lehmann, A.G. *The Symbolist Aesthetic in France 1885-1895*. Oxford: Basil Blackwell, 1950.

A detailed study of the development and the manifold aspects of French symbolist theories of poetic knowledge, language, analogous arts, the Idea and the Symbol. Emphasizes the diversity of theoretical views and poetic practice. Notes "the terms 'literary symbol' and 'symbolist' are terms which, introduced and fortified by a series of mischances, should never have been allowed to remain in usage; after all, Verlaine's 'décadence' was permitted to lapse after the brief outburst which gave it point; and between these two terms there is little to choose for inappropriateness."

311. LeRoy, Gaylord C. *Perplexed Prophets: Six Nineteenth-Century British Authors*. Philadelphia: Univ. of Pennsylvania Press, 1953.

Studies Carlyle, Arnold, Ruskin, Rossetti, James Thomson and Wilde to elucidate the adjustments made between individual personality and the demands of the new society. Sees the aestheticism of the 1870s through 1890s "as a response to a civilization that to many appeared so drab and dishonest that they saw no alternative except to escape from it and look elsewhere for patterns of meaning, beauty and passion."

312. Lester, John A., Jr. "John Davidson: A Grub-Street Bibliography," *Bibliographical Society of the University of Virginia*, No.40 (Sept 1958), 3-8.

Brief introduction to a bibliography of JD's journalistic writings stresses the involvement of London newspapers 1890-1905 in contemporary creative literature.

313. Lester, John A., Jr. *Journey Through Despair, 1880-1914: Transformations in British Literary Culture*. Princeton, N.J.: Princeton Univ. Press, 1968.

A richly documented study that discerns a trend in 1880-1914 literary culture moving "from a suspicion that the old bases of significant imaginative life were indefensible" to "a widespread if not dominant conviction that they had altogether collapsed." Believes "the unity among myriad moods and motives of the period may best be found by viewing them as varied responses evoked by a single challenge which was posed to man's imaginative life at that time." Chapters describe the challenge posed by the "new cosmology" of late nineteenth-century science, and the characteristic responses made by the heart (pessimism, activism, hedonism, socialism), the mind (reinterpretation of Darwinism, skepticism about the empirical inductive intellect, interest in the unconscious and in psychical research) and the imagination (the aesthetic search for beauty, realism, impressionism, symbolism, exploitation of myth). Concludes with a study of three characteristic themes in period literature: the mask, ecstasy and the will to believe.

314. Lester, John A., Jr. "Prose-Poetry Transmutation in the Poetry of John Davidson," *MP*, 56 (1956), 38-44.

Studies the prose sources, particularly the grub-street journalism, underlying many of JD's poems. Includes catalogue of prose sources, identifying poems drawn from them.

315. Levitt, Paul M. "The Well-Made Problem Play: A Selective Bibliography," *ELT*, 11 (1968), 190-194.

Includes a brief introduction.

316. Lhombreaud, Roger. *Arthur Symons: A Critical Biography*. London: Unicorn, 1963.

Seeks to clarify AS's role in the "decadent movement"; it was much more detached and reportorial than is generally recognized: "There was nothing of the launcher of manifestoes, still less of the *chef d'école*." Points out that one may search in vain through the pages of the *Yellow Book* "for the unity and quality of a movement called decadence. Either they were of a savage realism (for many of the writers of the stories were disciples of Maupassant and Zola) or they evoked hackneyed 'amorism,' too stereotyped to recall anything of the themes of the French Decadents. The word 'decadent' had therefore a different meaning on each side of the Channel. Yet Symons himself and a small number of the young people of his generation were on the eve of a change of attitude: they wished to dissociate themselves from the realist school represented by George Moore, Ella D'Arcy, Hubert Crackanthorpe, Henry Harland, and from the erotic patterns which seemed to them, rightly, as threadbare as they were useless . . . .If it be true that there was not in England a 'school,' in the French sense, there can be detected the existence of a group of artists and writers who shared in the same revolt on the same grounds of understanding, and who were attacked, discredited, and ridiculed."

317. Lindsay, Maurice, ed. *John Davidson: A Selection of his Poems*. Preface by T.S. Eliot. With an essay by Hugh MacDiarmid. London: Hutchinson, 1961.

Eliot and MacDiarmid discuss their debt to JD's poetry, particularly his urban subject matter and colloquial language. Lindsay's introductory essay mainly biographical with comments on the poetry and quotation from the critical works.

318. Lock, D.R. "John Davidson and the Poetry of the 'Nineties," *LQHR*, 161 (1936), 338-352.

A biographical appreciation stressing JD's membership in the "tragic generation." Feels that despite bodily ills, poets of the nineties were trenchant versifiers.

319. Lombardo, Agostino. *La poesia inglese dall'estetismo al simbolismo*. Rome: Edizioni di Storia e Letteratura, 1950.

Not seen.

320. Long, Richard A. and Iva G. Jones. "Towards a Definition of the 'Decadent Novel'," *CE*, 22 (1961), 245-249.

Finds that the "literature of decadence" involves "the transference of the artistic focus from the larger and more general concerns of life, the subject and starting point of art, to special and rarified ones." Most salient of general characteristics of decadent literature: "the attentuation of emotion and the detailed analysis of it," ennui, frustration and moral confusion, all themes of disintegration and alienation. "Its general temper is static; there is not sensation of movement; time acquires in this type of novel a spatial quality . . . of necessity it treats the leisured classes, and in a highly mannered fashion." Concludes that conscious form in structure and especially in language a "hallmark" of the form, as are the "specialization of situation and emotion beyond the probabilities of daily life, and consequently the imposition of values which relate negatively to the stated values of the culture."

321. Longaker, Mark. *Ernest Dowson*. Philadelphia: Univ. of Pennsylvania Press, 1944. [Third Edition, 1967]

Attempts to separate Dowson from the "Ariel-in-Limehouse" myth publicized by Symons, Yeats and others. Traces the role of Adelaide Foltinowicz and dissipation in ED's work; examines his literary influences and companions. Insists that "to identify the Rhymers' Club with the esthetic movement of the 'nineties, or the with decadence, or with any other so-called movement is a convenience for literary historians, but of dubious critical worth."

322. Looker, Samuel J. "A Neglected Poet -- John Barlas," *Socialist Review*, 19 (1922), 28-34; 78-82.

A brief but enthusiastic account of Barlas' life and poetry. His finest work judged to be *Love Sonnets* (1889) which "convey ethical sentiments and humanitarian principles in such a manner that they pass out of the region of propaganda and into the domain of high art."

323. Lovett, Robert M. and Helen S. Hughes. *The History of the Novel in England*. Boston: Houghton Mifflin, 1932.

Discussions of James, Stevenson, the Kailyard School, Kipling, Hewlett, Hudson, Gissing, Moore. Finds the period strikingly self-conscious, marked by shifting and contrary currents, with a serious interest in the plight of the lower classes plus a conscious reaction against seriousness and decorum.

324. Lowe, David. *John Barlas: Sweet Singer and Socialist.* Cupar-Fife, Scotland: Craigwood House, 1915.

Not seen.

325. Lucas, F.L. *The Decline and Fall of the Romantic Ideal.* Cambridge: Cambridge Univ. Press, 1936. [2nd Ed., 1948]

Romanticism, "a liberation of the less conscious levels of the mind," died of old age in England: "Rossetti with his chloral, Swinburne with his half-adult eccentricities, Francis Thompson with his opium, the poets of the nineties with their liqueurs and languors."

326. MacBeth, George. "Lee-Hamilton and the Romantic Agony," *CritQ*, 4 (1962), 141-150.

Views Lee-Hamilton as one of the most important English classical poets of nineteenth century, an essential link between Arnold and Housman. Explores connection between disease and literary skill, concluding "the career of Lee-Hamilton provides us with a classic case of a poet made by misfortune and unmade by the return to normal life."

327. McCormack, M. Jerusha. "The Person in Question: John Gray, A Critical and Biographical Study," *DAI*, 34 (1974), 4211A-12A. [Brandeis]

Assuming a "continuous relationship between the life and the work," and concentrating on *Silverpoints*, "The Person in Question," and *Park*, finds that Gray's work "is more interesting and more important in the definition of late Victorian literature than the standard accounts imply."

328. Madden, William A. "The Divided Tradition of English Criticism," *PMLA*, 73 (1958), 69-80.

Considers the conflicting elements in Arnold's criticism and their effects upon four "moments" in subsequent criticism: (1) Pater, Yeats and the Celtic Twilight; (2) T.E. Hulme and neoclassicism; (3) I.A. Richards and objectless faith; (4) T.S. Eliot, Herbert Read and the divided tradition. Finds Pater's role crucial in converting the aspiration to an ideal life into the intense moment of aesthetic passion; influence of decadence in literature and criticism negligible. In Yeats "the break between Christianity and romanticism, implicit in

Arnold, is rendered explicit, complete, and all-determining, and the relevance of poetry henceforth derives, in a world without a prevailing set of values, from the tensions in the personality of the artist appealing to similar tensions in value-hunting readers."

329. Madden, William A. "The Victorian Sensiblity," *VS*, 7 (1963-64), 67-97.

Traces the shift from romantic to modern sensibilities in terms of the interplay between "public" and "private" voices. Like the mid-Victorian private voice, the late Victorian's was pessimistic, subjective, relativist and detached. Unlike the mid-Victorians, the late Victorians lacked a public voice; instead there was the "anti-public" voice of Morris, Butler, etc.

330. Marandon, Sylvaine. *L'image de la France dans l'Angleterre Victorienne, 1848-1900*. Paris: Armand Colin, 1968.

Notes that while France's more philosophical romanticism was a barrier to English understanding of French romantic works, the Celtic Renaissance diminished the racially pure character of Victorian literature at the same time as the absence of great figures in fin de siècle literature encouraged an interest in foreign authors; points out that the delay between French publication and translation into English of French works grew less and less toward the end of the century. [In French]

331. Marcus, Phillip L. *Yeats and the Beginning of the Irish Renaissance*. Ithaca, NY: Cornell Univ. Press, 1970.

Treats WBY's literary activities 1885-1897 with chapters on his ideals for Irish literature, his prose fiction, his relations with other Irish writers, on the uses of Irish myth.

332. Mariani, Paul L. "Hopkins' 'Andromeda' and the New Aestheticism," *VP*, 11 (1973), 39-54.

Believes the Victorian dimension of GMH is overlooked: "'Andromeda" is Hopkins' own attraction and repulsion -- for the most part unconscious -- for a sensuousness and freedom manifested in the predominant art movement of his time -- the New Aestheticism. Hopkins' ambivalence, which shows up in his nostalgia for a moral order combined with a manneristic style (an unmistakable sign of aesthetic decadence), is a touchstone of most Victorian writers."

333. Markgraf, Carl. "John Addington Symonds: An Annotated Bibliography of Writings About Him," *ELT*, 18 (1975), 79-138.

Includes a brief introduction.

334. Mason, Stuart. *Oscar Wilde and the Aesthetic Movement*.
Dublin: Townley Searle, 1920.

Collects the numerous extra-*Punch* and *Patience* satires and
parodies of Wilde in the early 1880s.

335. May, J. Lewis. *John Lane and the Nineties*. London: John
Lane, 1936.

A partisan biography by a younger colleague that reflects Lane's
views of such events as Beardsley's departure from the *Yellow Book*.
Chapters on that magazine, on the poets, on the prose writers, on
contemporary parodies of these three topics. "Decadence" found merely a pose; the nineties movement in art and literature defined and
delimited by Lane: "when one of these writers, or artists, came into
the charmèd circle, he at once became 'a Ninety'; when he departed
beyond its circumference, he ceased to be 'a Ninety.'"

336. Mégroz, Rodolphe L. *Modern English Poetry 1882-1932*. London:
Ivor Nicholson and Watson, 1933.

Includes chapters on decadence and anti-decadence. Decadence
not limited to the 1890s; instead it is a temperamental inclination
to self-centeredness, ennui, preciosity found in all periods. Traces
Swinburne's influence on poets of 1880s and 1890s, notes decadent
characteristics of Housman and Meynell. Decadent impulse survives in
work of Phillips, Middleton and Edmund John; especially evident in
post-war poetry of Huxley, Osbert Sitwell and Eliot. "As the Wilde
school did with the movement inspired by Rossetti, and as some youthful and self-conscious admirers of T.S. Eliot are doing in our own
day, they often screen an inherent aimlessness with enthusiasm for
some kind of first-rate work which provides easy possiblities of imitation on a lower level of creative energy."

337. Melchiori, Giorgio. *The Tightrope Walkers: Studies of Mannerism in Modern English Literature*. London: Routledge and Kegan
Paul, 1956.

Essays on James, Hopkins, Joyce, Eliot, Woolf et al. Rejects
notion of progress or decline in literary history in favor of a theory
of alternating periods of doubt and certainty expressing themselves
in alternations of styles. Thus, "from the clear line of development
followed in the narrative of Dickens or Thackeray, or in the poetry
of Tennyson or Matthew Arnold, [James and Hopkins] pass to more tor-
tuous and tormented forms; to the effects of straightforwardness and
harmony they prefer those of nicety in details and preciosity in con-
struction." Suggests that the mannerist phase of the moderns may be
giving way to a new Baroque, as suggested by some of the later poems
of Auden.

338. Merivale, Patricia. *Pan the Goat-God: His Myth in Modern Times.* Cambridge, Mass.: Harvard Univ. Press, 1969.

Studies the "astonishing resurgence of interest" in the Pan myth between 1890 and 1926. Notes that in early modern literature Pan "provided a powerful and necessary expression of the nonrational, at a time when the mainstream of literature was realistic, socially oriented, and, in some matters, inhibited."

339. Merritt, Travis R. "Taste, Opinion, and Theory in the Rise of Victorian Prose Stylism," *The Art of Victorian Prose*, ed. George Levine and William Madden. NY: Oxford Univ. Press, 1968, pp. 3-38.

Includes consideration of the role of aestheticism in the development of high Victorian stylism with special reference to the contributions of Pater, Saintsbury and Stevenson. "During the last fifteen years of the century, prose stylism fully flowered and withered almost simultaneously . . . . The cult of prose style could not have survived for long, even under the most favorable conditions. Its inevitable if undeserved association with weakness and decadence was damaging enough, but the final disintegration came from a hopeless internal warring of the several main ideas which had been intrinsic to it, exotically compounded, from the start."

340. Michelson, Peter. *The Aesthetics of Pornography.* NY: Herder and Herder, 1971.

Includes consideration of Beardsley's *Story of Venus and Tannhäuser*, whose exhaustion of the aestheticist devotion to beauty is seen as pointing the way to the modernist rejection of "Beauty," the dadaist-surrealist cult of the banal and Burrough's affection for the repellent. "Beardsley's pornography carried the grand decadence as far as it could go in creating a cosmos where morality was non-existent, sentiment was merely an ironic rhetorical device, and classical artifice was the nature of being."

341. Miles, Josephine. *Eras and Modes in English Poetry.* Berkeley, Calif.: Univ. of California Press, 1957.

Includes chapters on the "classical mode" in the late nineteenth century and in Yeats. By a quantitative analysis of three kinds of "modes" -- phrasal, clausal and balanced -- notes a characteristic shift during the fin de siècle in four centuries of English poetry from extreme modes to the balanced mode, described as "a leveling, composing, classicizing of what had gone before, an enriching by sensuous and presentative vocabulary, a filling in and loading of metrical line, a stabilizing of action for the sake of reception." Between the elaborated or Pindaric extremes of Wilde and Henley, and the understated extremes of Hardy and Housman, locates the "classical mode" of Bridges, Hopkins, Patmore, Thompson and Phillips. "The

poetry of the late nineteenth century, often called decadent, was
structurally not only a falling off from old sublimities, but also a
building up, a return from romantic extremes to poise and equilibrium
with the renewed aid of classical models."

342. Miles, Josephine. *Pathetic Fallacy in the Nineteenth
Century: A Study of a Changing Relation Between Object
and Emotion*. Berkeley and Los Angeles: Univ. of California
Press, 1942. [*University of California Publications in English*
12, ii, 183-304]

Intended as a correction of modernist critiques of nineteenth-
century Romantic assumptions about poetry, essay traces the decline
in poetic usage of the pathetic fallacy and the corresponding growth
in the "power of qualitative comparison between object and object in
terms of senses," a comparison chiefly expressed by "the adjective of
quality, the bright, dim, and sweet which made the new bonds of connection between feeling and object." Why do the concrete and the
vague appear so often together in Victorian poetry? Because "an increasingly precise way of seeing natural objects" involved "an increasingly uncertain and nebulous way of interpreting the large
amount of new detail acquired."

343. Miller, John R. "Dante Gabriel Rossetti, From the Grotesque to
the *Fin de Siècle*: Sources, Characteristics and Influences of
the Femme Fatale," *DAI*, 35 (1975), 5355A. [Georgia]

"Since she is so compelling a figure, certain aspects of Rossetti's creation live on, apotheosized into that eighteen-nineties
phenomenon, the 'Pre-Raphaelite woman.'" But in the hands of Aubrey
Beardsley and Alphonse Mucha the image declined in power: "What began full of the power of both an archetypical being and a vibrant
creation of Rossetti's mind, ends as a deflated, two-dimensional image in the service of the world of business."

344. Milner, John. *Symbolists and Decadents*. NY: Dutton Pictureback, 1971.

Summary treatment of symbolism and decadence as movements in
the visual arts in England, France, Belgium, Holland, Austria and
Germany. Finds that "the 'Decadents' were primarily a French mani-
festation of a malaise in evidence throughout Europe. They viewed
with grave misgivings and pessimism the vigorous optimism and deadening comforts of materialism. They did not see their own age as in
decline -- indeed they were only too aware of its robust health . . .
. The Symbolist was perhaps more dynamic in his reaction against materialism than was his pessimistic contemporary. He sought escape
from the banal in an art that was expressive of ideas and emotions."

345. Mix, Katherine L. *A Study in Yellow: The Yellow Book and Its Contributors*. Lawrence, Kansas: Univ. of Kansas Press, 1960.

An anecdotal and detailed account with chapters on the late Victorian artistic milieu, Continental and American literary relations with England during the nineties, on the various literary coteries, on John Lane, Beardsley and Harland, and on the critical reception of the *Yellow Book*.

346. Miyoshi, Masao. *The Divided Self: A Perspective on the Literature of the Victorians*. NY: New York Univ. Press, 1969.

Includes a chapter on the 1890s with discussions of the relevant works by Stevenson, Wilde and Hardy, and mentions of the Rhymers' Club, Gosse, Butler and Shaw. "Whether it is the 'metaphysical' double of Hardy's novels of the 'aesthetic' double of Wilde, the writers of the nineties take the insufficiency of the mere ur-self, the born identity, as axiomatic."

347. Mizener, Arthur. "The Romanticism of W.B. Yeats," *SoR*, 7 (1941-42), 601-623.

"Yeats was, to the end of his career, a poet of the romantic '90's and . . . the greatness of the later poetry is a kind of greatness inherent in the '90's attitude."

348. Moers, Ellen. *The Dandy: Brummel to Beerbohm*. NY: Viking, 1960.

Finds that between 1878 and 1895 "the weakening of Victorian values and vitality, the strengthening of continental influences, the revival of Regency attitudes, all combined to produce a favorable atmosphere" for the "New Dandyism" of Wilde, Beardsley, Beerbohm and the Rhymers' Club poets, who "built a literature around themes from the dandy tradition: worship of the town and the artificial; grace, elegance, the art of the pose, sophistication and the mask." Believes that "as we come further off in time from the literary and artistic movements of the 'nineties, there is less and less to be seen of Yeats's 'tragic generation,' wasted by poverty, disease and public neglect, or Holbrook Jackson's age of experiment, vitality, curiosity and high spirits -- both images elaborated in the first quarter of this century. Instead, the dominant note of the decade appears to be its commercialism : the *tragic* spectacle of literature and personality thrown open on the market place, the great *experiment* of selling talent by advertising, publicity and showmanship. Little of the posing of the time makes sense unless we remember the enormous public before which it was performed." Traces the demise of the dandy in the fin de siècle to the rise of the "New Woman": Whatever was genuine in the English decadence of the 'nineties rested on a fear of the decay of one sex beside the looming dominance of the other."

349. Monro, Harold. *Some Contemporary Poets*. London: Leonard
      Parsons, 1920.

      Includes a section on "elder" poets like Yeats, Kipling, Dough-
ty, Meynell. Along with with Rhymers' Club group, poets like Henley
and Watson "filled the transition period of the 1890's with dignity
but no great distinction." The chief poets who spanned the change
of century were Bridges, Hardy, Yeats, Thompson, "Michael Field,"
Symons and Davidson.

350. Monsman, Gerald. "Pater and His Younger Contemporaries,"
      VN, No. 48 (Fall 1975), 1-9.

      Citing specific works and passages, discusses Pater's influence
on younger writers from Dowson, Johnson and Yeats to Pound, Stevens,
James, Conrad, Woolf, Proust and Joyce. Concludes that if Pater
stands as a kind of *Ur*-modern, "he is a modern whose greatest contributions often lie beyond the range or compass of sources either peri-
pheral or direct; rather, he exists as a 'praeter-source' in unac-
knowledged, subliminal associations which have combined with other
influences and emphases not exclusively his own."

351. Monsman, Gerald. "Pater's Aesthetic Hero," *UTQ*, 40 (1970-71),
      136-151.

      "In Pater rather than in Wilde do we find the best description
of the aesthetic hero who makes life a work of art," an attempt "to
define the moral temperament possible in a strongly rationalistic
age."

352. More, Paul Elmer. *The Drift of Romanticism*. Boston: Houghton
      Mifflin, 1913. [Shelburne Essays, Eighth Series]

      Includes anti-romantic essays on Pater, whom he condemns for his
relativism and egoism, and "Fiona Macleod," whose supernatural visions he puts down to "loose vaporings."

353. More, Paul Elmer. "A Naughty Decade," *Nation (NY)*, 98
      (1914), 566-568.

      [Review of Jackson's *The Eighteen Nineties*] "The disease from
which [the fin de siècle] sprang was no jest, and beneath the antic
contortions of their wit these men were suffering the very real pangs
of physical disorganization."

354. More, Paul Elmer. *Shelburne Essays: First Series*. London
      and NY: Putnam, 1906.

      Includes essays on Symons, Yeats and Johnson. Finds AS's poems "the first full and sincere expression of decadence in English, with their light and fair illusion passing gradually into the terror of disillusion." Prefers the "sternly idealised sorrow of Lionel Johnson" to the "wistfulness, I had almost said the sickliness, of Mr. Yeats."

355. Morland, M.A. "Nietzsche and the Nineties," *ContempR*, 193 (1958), 209-212.

More than 60 articles on N. published during the decade with Davidson, Ellis and Seth his most assiduous commentators and popularizers.

356. Morrisette, Bruce A. "The Early English and American Critics of French Symbolism," *Studies in Honor of Frederick W. Shipley*. St. Louis: Washington Univ. Press, 1942, pp. 159-180.

Aside from Symons, who made a career out of symbolism, and Moore, whose comments are superficial, finds no real understanding or interest in symbolism among English writers and critics, particularly among major figures. "The conclusion is unavoidable that by 1890 English estheticism was formulated, cut and dried, conservative." Blames this failure on the English inability to understand French symbolist texts.

357. Moult, Thomas. "The Taint in Literature," *English Review*, 31 (1920), 278-281.

[Review of Muddiman's *Men of the Nineties*] Stresses the "antagonistic" schools during the 1890s: "The sense of an absolutely satisfying value of beautiful workmanship, the recognition of the primary importance of the sensuous element in art, the love of art for art's sake . . . were shared, and far more vitally, by that whole populace of 'outsiders,' with W.E. Henley popularly regarded as the chief, who in the intervening years have come to such artistic fruition that to-day we have to regard the 'eighteen-ninety group' as the outsiders."

358. Muddiman, Bernard. *The Men of the Nineties*. London: Henry Danielson, 1920.

Survey of the period drawing heavily on earlier studies, particularly Murdoch's *Renaissance of the Nineties*. Chapters on Beardsley, the *Yellow Book* and the *Savoy*, fiction writers, poets, essayists and dramatists, exotic and abnormal artists. Sees period as a "distinct secession." "The majority of the work of the movement, in fact, can be described as impressionism of the abnormal by a group of individualists."

359. Munro, John M. *Arthur Symons*. NY: Twayne, 1969. [TEAS 76]

A sympathetic critical study that seeks to establish AS's importance as an influence as it places him in the fin de siècle and
modernist literary contexts. Studies AS's development from Victorian
through decadent to symbolist phases with discussions of individual
works. Concludes that "Symons' literary career, perhaps more clearly than that of any of his contemporaries, show us that the artistic
sensibility did not go into hibernation at the end of the nineteenth
century to reawaken somewhere around the time of World War I; it
was, in fact, very much alive all the time."

360. Munro, John M. "Arthur Symons and W.B. Yeats: The Quest
       for Compromise," *Dalhousie Review*, 45 (1965), 137-152.

Studies the literary aspect of their friendship and its importance to the work of each. Distinguishes their different understand-
ings of symbolism, unity.

361. Munro, John M. "Arthur Symons as Poet: Theory and Practice,"
       ELT, 6, iv (1963), 212-222.

Attempts to gain for AS's poetry the same sympathetic attention
increasingly given his critical prose. Acknowledges that "decadent"
eludes firm definition; nonetheless AS had his own definition which
he tried to fulfill in his poetry.

362. Munro, John M. *The Decadent Poetry of the Eighteen-Nineties*.
       Beirut: American Univ. of Beirut Press, 1970.

Section I surveys various fin de siècle opinions and definitions
of "decadence." Concludes use of the term partially justified in
describing the character of the period though "only in general terms
may we speak of a 'Decadent Movement.'" Section II sketches the cultural background of the period, emphasizing decadent poetry as "a rejection of established values, a conscious inversion of the way of
life associated with the respectable middle class." Section III details the early literary sources and influences on Decadence, stressing the importance of Pater's misinterpretation by his disciples.
Section IV follows the later influences on decadence, particularly
those from France: "it may be argued that the English Decadence was
not so much a new departure as an intensification of existing practices." Notes that French decadence or symbolism pursued the ideal,
while few English decadents were interested in ideal values. Section
V concludes "for all their enthusiasm for contemporary French literature, the English Decadents failed almost completely to appreciate
its ultimate intentions . . . a very feeble echo of the plaintive cry
across the Channel . . . . prompted merely by a spirit of revolt."
Section VI discusses decadent poets, their lack of coherent identity,
their withdrawal from life, their publishers. Section VII concludes
that "ultimately, a split personality seems to characterize the late

nineteenth-century Decadent more than any other quality." Believes
the decadents, by virtue of their technical innovations and their re-
affirmation of the primacy of individual feeling in poetry, deserve
more sympathetic attention.

363. Munro, John M. "The Double Vision of the Decadents," *ELT*,
      9 (1966), 174-176.

      [Review of Charlesworth's *Dark Passages*] Faults Charlesworth's
definition of "decadent" as the triumph of subjective over objective
vision. "If we must use 'Decadent' to characterize a particular kind
of literature, we must use it more broadly. Assuming that artistic
perception tends either to emphasize the individual perceiver or to
lay stress on objective reality, only the greatest artists being capable of achieving a meaningful compromise between the two, it would
seem that Decadent literature ought to be that which reveals an exaggerated stress on the imaginative sensitivity of the perceiver or an
excessive preoccupation with external reality, both being valued simply for their own sake rather than media through which one may discover order." Suggests abandoning the use of the term altogether in
literary discussions.

364. Munro, John M., ed. *English Poetry in Transition: 1880-1920*,
      NY: Pegasus, 1968. "Introduction," pp. 19-34.

      Warns that terms like "decadent" and "counter-decadent" may
give "a general indication of boundaries, but they may hardly be used
to specify the terrain." Both groups shared "the desire to find new
and interesting ways of expressing themselves." Experimentation the
dominant impulse in poetry during the fin de siecle. Points out that
the "intellectual" poetry usually associated with Eliot and modernism
was anticipated by the fin de siècle interest in metaphysical poetry
and the symbolist dislocation of language.

365. Murdock, W.G. Blaikie. *The Renaissance of the Nineties*.
      London: Alexander Moring, 1911.

      An enthusiastic defense of the period, seen as "a distinct se-
cession from the art of the previous age," a revolutionary reaction
begun in the transitional decade of the eighteen-eighties and led by
men who were French or Celtic in background. The new writers of the
nineties preferred "Life" and, largely due to the marked increase
during the eighties of agnosticism, "Freedom" to mere "Beauty," and
dealt with the actual circumstances of their lives in their art.
"The movement of the nineties made for greater subtlety, greater deli-
cacy . . . . an art of nerves." Traces sources, finds Wilde's work
slightly influential but not typical of the nineties movement. Concludes that "the superb virility which marked our art of fifteen
years ago seems to be largely gone."

366. Murtagh, S.C.S.L., Sister Anne Hygina. *"The New Review*: Mirror of a Literary Culture 1889-1897," *DAI*, 35 (1974), 2949A. [St. Louis]

The *New Review* studied as an index of the counter-decadent or activist movement. Finds the "new conservatives" like Henley who represented it were "intellectually keen, artistically open to newness and some experimentation, but emotionally and morally Victorian." Examines the magazine's fiction and criticism in detail.

367. Nadelhaft, Janice R. "Punch Among the Aesthetes: A Chapter in Victorian Criticism," *DAI*, 31 (1971), 6019A. [UCLA]

Previous critics have mistakenly dismissed the *Punch* campaign as good-natured spoof. "Rather, *Punch* offered serious criticism of the cultivated classes -- a criticism that stressed the narcissistic unproductiveness of a life devoted exclusively to self-cultivation . . . . *Punch*'s lampoons during the nineties of the Decadents and Realists suggest that basic assumptions linked these schools that on the surface seem so widely divergent."

368. Nadelhaft, Janice R. *"Punch* and the Syncretics: An Early Victorian Prologue to the Aesthetic Movement," *SEL*, 15 (1975), 627-640.

Argues *"Punch*'s use of 'aesthetic,' particularly in its squibs against the Syncretics . . . offers evidence that a group of characteristics later associated with the Aesthetic Movement had been attacked by *Punch* as early as the 1840's and was in fact part of the intellectual milieu that gave rise to aestheticism." Stresses the importance of German influences on early English aestheticism, particularly with regard to the notion of self-perfection through art.

369. Nagy, N. Christophe De. *The Poetry of Ezra Pound: The Pre-Imagist Stage*. Basel: Francke Verlag Bern, 1960.

"The 'Nineties do not mean simply ornate language, or impressionism, or symbolism, nor is the French impact -- suggested by Burdett in his "The Beardsley Period" -- a sufficiently comprehensive criterion." The only satisfactory applicable definition of the nineties is as the last phase of the second wave of romanticism begun by the Pre-Raphaelites. Notes the means are subtillized in nineties verse, there is a shift away from Parnassian decoration and a tendency toward the disappearance of content and a corresponding emphasis on form. Distinguishes four stages: (1) a continuation of a highly decorative technique, inherited from the Pre-Raphaelites, but strongly modified; (2) impressionistic poetry in the narrower sense of the word -- reordering the *effects* of the outer world; (3) registration of fugitive psychic states; (4) symbolist poetry, in many shades, from a rather facile handling of symbols to generate certain moods to the "poésie pure" of Yeats.

370. Nassaar, Christopher. *Into the Demon Universe: A Literary Exploration of Oscar Wilde*. New Haven: Yale Univ. Press, 1974.

A critical interpretation of OW's major works stressing the centrality of homosexual experience to Wilde's ideas of evil and innocence. Sees decadent art characterized by its pleasurable portrayal of the soul as evil. Doubts the "modernity" of the 1890s; would shift emphasis to Victorian aspects of decadence. Includes many remarks on and readings of related figures.

371. Nathan, Leonard P. "W.B. Yeats's Experiments with an Influence," *VS*, 6 (1962-63), 66-74.

The influence is Pater's. Finds Yeats remarkable in his ability "to discover what in any influence suited his own artistic needs," and this capacity is "one of the things that mark him off from all other poets of the 'nineties, from that melancholy tribe that failed, unlike him, to get the nineteenth to the twentieth century without disastrous consequences."

372. Nelson, James G. *The Early Nineties: A View from the Bodley Head*. Cambridge, Mass.: Harvard Univ. Press, 1971.

An extremely detailed study of virtually every aspect of the publishing house during the years 1887-1894, with special emphasis on the artistic and literary relations inspired by the Bodley Head's publishers, authors, artists and books. Includes chapters on the origin of the house, the typical Bodley Head book, the artistic, literary and financial aspects of its book production, and the break-up of the partnership of Lane and Mathews; in addition gives valuable critical and biographical accounts of the many poets, essayists, dramatists and fictionists published by the house. Emphasizes the diversity and complexity of literary activity during the nineties, "a many-sided, often paradoxical period of artistic creativity."

373. Nelson, James G. "The Nature of Aesthetic Experience in the Poetry of the Nineties: Ernest Dowson, Lionel Johnson, and John Gray," *ELT*, 17 (1974), 201-232.

Sees the attitudes of Pater and Rossetti toward aesthetic experience as central to the development of the fin de siècle point of view: "the nineties poets, attentive to the life styles of such figures as Rossetti and Pater as well as to the aesthetic views conveyed in their writings, retreated into a realm of art and personal emotions which served as the sole source of intensity and life." Studies this central experience of coming to life through an encounter with beauty in several poems by Dowson, Johnson and Gray.

374. Nelson, James G. *Sir William Watson*. NY: Twayne, 1966.
[TEAS 45]

Biographical and critical account of the near-Laureate and
poetic traditionalist whose disastrous decline in reputation after
1900 suggests something about "the momentous revolution in taste" at
the end of the Victorian period. "The last decade of Victoria's
reign was in no frivolous or superficial sense *fin de siècle*. It
was in the broadest significance of that popular phrase a decadent
age, an era of decline" in which the posturings of Wilde and his
followers must be seen as "the hectic flashes of feverish discontent
on the surface of the late Victorian scene."

375. Nevinson, Henry W. *Changes and Chances*. London: Nisbet,
1923.

Memoirs of a newspaperman and husband of *Yellow Book* author
Evelyn Sharp. The years 1891-1897 were "a period of strangely vivid
interests and strangely diverse pursuits. We were simultaneously,
and almost equally, attracted by the soldier, enthusiastic for the
rebel, clamorous for the poor, and devoted to the beautiful . . . .
The apparent contradictions were reconciled in a renewed passion --
a glowing intensity -- of life as we issued from the rather chilly
rationalism and moralising of former years." The spirit of decadence,
which never spread beyond the well-to-do, fell with Wilde "and both
before and after the hideous event, we regarded our life in that
epoch rather as a Renaissance."

376. Nicoll, Allardyce. *A History of Late Nineteenth-Century
Drama: 1850-1900*. Vol. 1 Cambridge: Cambridge Univ. Press,
1945.

Includes chapters on the plays of the 1880s and 1890s, a period
that saw "the growing power of naturalism in the theatre."

377. Nordau, Max. *Degeneration*. Translated from the 2nd edition
of the German work. NY: Howard Fertig, 1968. [First pub. in
English 1895]

The famous fulmination against international avant-gardism.
Applies Lombroso's theories of degeneration to fin de siècle authors
and artists, and finds that the "nervous excitement" characteristic
of industrialized urban life has produced in this small but dangerous-
ly influential class the symptoms of unbounded egoism, impulsiveness,
emotionalism, pessimism, languor, lack of will and mysticism: "the
ego-mania of decadentism, its love of the artificial, its aversion to
nature, and to all forms of activity and movement, its megalomanical
contempt for men and its exaggeration of the importance of art, have
found their English representative among the 'Aesthetes,' the chief
of whom is Oscar Wilde." Chapters on fin-de-sièclism, mysticism, symbolism, the Pre-Raphaelites, the Wagner cult, the Parnassians,

Ibsenism and Nietzsche. Concludes that degenerate authors and artists "dream only of the satisfaction of their basest instincts, and
are pernicious -- through the example they set as drones, as well as
through the confusion they cause in minds insufficiently forewarned,
by their abuse of the word 'art' to mean demoralization and childish-
ness. Ego-maniacs, Decadents and Aesthetes have completely gathered
under their banner this refuse of civilized peoples, and march at
their head."

378. O'Connor, William Van. "The Poet as Esthetician," *QRL*,
     4 (1948), 311-318.

     Concludes "the bulk of Victorian poets had versified the stale
thoughts of an intellectual climate that no longer served to give
hope. Poets had lost their place as innovators or as investigators of
new areas of discovery. The Symbolists saw themselves at a point
where they had little, if any, faith in the sentiments of their predecessors. Lacking a set of universal values in relation with which
their sensibilities might play, these poets fell back, for artistic
purposes, upon the chief reality they knew: momentary states of
being."

379. Ojala, Aatos. *Aestheticism and Oscar Wilde. Part I: Life
     and Letters.* Helsinki: Finnish Academy of Science and Let-
     ters, 1954.

     In this study "the unity of the man and his art is sought in
aestheticism." Includes consideration of the historical setting
and psychological characteristics of aestheticism: "when all is said
and done, aestheticism makes up a peculiar intellectual enterprise.
By its formal restraint it reminds one of classicism. The spirit,
however, which inhabits the quasi-classic abode, possesses such characteristics as prove it the offspring of romanticism. Finally realism is also an important shareholder in this enterprise as attested
by the eagerness to apply the technique and methods of Science to
Art." Decadence must be regarded "as an ultimate consequence of
practical aestheticism. The difference between both is that of quan-
tity rather than quality: they represent, as it were, different
stages of the same process."

380. Ojala, Aatos. *Aestheticism and Oscar Wilde. Part II:
     Literary Style.* Helsinki: Finnish Academy of Science
     and Letters, 1955.

     Includes a section on the literary style of aestheticism,
stressing the aesthetes' "vivid consciousness of language as a concrete resistant material." Also notes their "word-consciousness,"
their fondness for technical, learned and exotic nomenclatures, their
considerable use of adjectival images, comparisons, synaesthesia.
"In their nostalgias the artists of aestheticism created a verbal
world, where they stored what is rare, exquisite, and corruscating"

as well as what was hideous or bizarre for "the naturalist element ran parallel with the decorative one."

381. Orel, Harold and Paul L. Wiley, eds. *British Poetry 1880-1920: Edwardian Voices*. NY: Appleton-Century-Crofts, 1969. "Introduction," pp. xxix-xliii.

See #566.

382. Orel, Harold. *The Development of William Butler Yeats: 1885-1900*. Lawrence, Kan.: Univ. of Kansas Press, 1968.

Argues that "the years between 1885 and 1899 should be looked at through Yeats's eyes," i.e. by examining the letters, essays and literary journalism written at the time rather than by depending upon the later autobiographical writings "which subtly distort and often 'recreate' the condition of Yeats's formative period." Includes chapters on the playlets and *Wind Among the Reeds*, on WBY's role as anthologist and newspaper correspondent, and on his relationships with Madame Blavatsky, Ellis, the Rhymers, George Russell (AE), Symons and Maude Gonne. Concludes that "all the evidence suggests that during the 1890's he avoided committing himself to a long-range program . . . and that he tested and turned away from theosophy, the aesthetic creed of the Decadents, and Blake's vision, keeping only what he needed and found valuable for his craft."

383. O'Sullivan, Vincent. "On the Kind of Fiction Called Morbid," *Savoy*, 2 (Apr 1896), 167-170.

"Nowadays we seem to nourish our morals with the thinnest milk and water, with a good dose of sugar added, and not a suspicion of lemon at all."

384. O'Sullivan, Vincent. *Opinions*. London: Unicorn, 1959.

Essays on George Moore, "Ouida," Frank Harris, "John Oliver Hobbes," Rolfe, Wilde and the 1890s which include personal recollections as well as critical comment. Disputes A.J. Farmer's [see #159] view of the nineties; it was instead a timid movement, puffed by Symons whose influence was nonetheless slight.

385. Palmer, Herbert. *Post-Victorian Poetry*. London: Dent, 1938.

Primarily concerned with Georgian poets, but includes chapters on Watson and Newbolt, on Kipling, with commentary on Yeats, Davidson, Bridges and Thompson. Believes that the end of the Victorian age, "though it saw no wide reactions against its characteristic poets, Tennyson and Robert Browning, was marked by the rise of verse rhetoricians and rhapsodists, as well as the less popular poets of the aesthetic school who were affected by the philosophy of Walter Pater" and whose work was characterized by pessimism, despair and "a crude contemplation of sex . . . coupled with exceptionally strong sympathy for harlots and women of easy virtue."

386. Parrott, T.M. and W. Thorp, eds. *Poetry of the Transition, 1850-1914.* NY: Oxford Univ. Press, 1932. "Introduction," pp. xxi-xli.

Finds the period particularly concerned with technical problems in poetry; its predominant trait -- individualism; its common center -- the disintegration of faith under the challenge of science.

387. Paterson, Gary H. "The Place of the Roman Catholic Church in the Literature of the Decadence in England," *DA*, 32 (1971), 928A. [Toronto]

Examines the motives of conversion of and the influence of the Church on Dowson, Johnson, Wilde, Douglas, John Gray, Beardsley, Rolfe.

388. Paterson, Gary H. "The Religious Thought of Lionel Johnson," *AntigR*, 13 (1973), 95-109.

Traces the influence of Arnold, Pater and Newman on the formation of LJ's religious thought. Concludes "of all the aesthetes who dallied with religion in the 'nineties, Johnson was -- with the possible exception of John Gray -- the most intellectually precise in his religious attitudes. It is ironical that such a mind could produce some of the most emotionally expressive religious poetry of the decade."

389. Patnode, Jack. "English and American Literary Relations in the 1890's: The Cosmopolitan Impressionists," *DA*, 29 (1969), 2721A. [Minnesota]

Though they never considered themselves a group, writers like Edgar Saltus, Percival Pollard, Walter Blackburn Harte and Ambrose Bierce "may be studied as an un-organized decadent movement," one which had, however, "small effect" on twentieth-century American literature. Includes some account of American little magazines of the 1890s.

390. Patrick, Arthur W. *Lionel Johnson (1867-1902) poète et critique.* Paris: L. Rodstein, 1939.

Detailed and informative account of LJ's art and life, including many valuable excerpts from Johnson's unpublished letters. Part I treats Johnson's life with a chapter on his personality; Part II deals with the works, with chapters on *The Art of Thomas Hardy*, on the critical articles and reviews, on the prose style and on the poetry. Concludes LJ can be claimed by no movement of the period, whether it be neo-Catholic, Celticist or decadent: "Il a trop de foi, de culture générale, pour se soumettre aux limites imposées par une Ecole étroite." [In French]

391. Peckham, Morse. "Aestheticism to Modernism: Fulfillment
     or Revolution?" *Mundus Artium*, 1 (1967), 36-55.

     Fulfillment. Believes that "the program of the original Romantics and the revised Romantic program of the Stylists [i.e. aesthetic poets]" were "logically necessary strategies for encompassing that breakthrough into comprehension of the very principle of self-transformation which is Modernism." Argues that if modernism is a realization rather than a departure from Romanticism, then our usual conceptions of aestheticism, decadence and art nouveau must be overhauled.

392. Peckham, Morse. *Beyond the Tragic Vision: The Quest for
     Identity in the Nineteenth Century*. NY: George Braziller,
     1962.

     Sees the central problem of nineteenth-century art "the creation of an aesthetic world which the Philistine could not enter without ceasing to be a Philistine," a problem whose solution is found in the "stylism" of Mallarmé, Cézanne and Debussy. Locates the first phase of stylism in Swinburne and his followers, the decadents "who likewise created works of art characterized by great beauty of surface and style with an exploration of the most profoundly concealed and erotically sinister aspects of the personality. Their style was exquisite; the subject was sexual transgression and what the Philistine called perversion. The strategy of the attacks on the decadents was, of course, always to ascribe the creation of such works to the depravity of their personalities. The truth of the matter is that sometimes the transgressions of the decadents were imaginative and sometimes they themselves were transgressors. In either case their explorations into the horrors of personality were sustained by style. In art they were aesthetes or, to use the term of this book, stylists; in life they were dandies."

393. Peden, William. "Hubert Crackanthorpe: Forgotten Pioneer,"
     SSF, 7 (1970), 539-548.

     Biographical survey of Crackanthorpe's "doomed" life; plot summaries and scattered critical references to HC's collections of stories and sketches. Attempts to place HC in literary milieu of the period. Suggests that "if Crackanthorpe prayed to any literary god, it was most probably Henry James rather than Maupassant or Flaubert and Balzac."

394. Perkins, David. *A History of Modern Poetry: From the 1890s to the High Modernist Mode.* Cambridge, Mass.: Harvard Univ. Press, 1976.

An informative account of the development of poetic modernism, a mode which may be considered "in some respects a revival of the premises and intentions that had also shaped the avant-garde poetry of England in the eighties and nineties, though 'revival' does not seem the right word for a poetry that in genius and boldness went so much further." Distinguishes in the 1890s a "poetry of *Ars Victrix*" which includes "diverse, shifting, and vague groupings, since it refers generally to the aesthetic-decadent-symbolist-formalist poetry of the period." Views this poetry as an anti-Victorian revolt that in turn provoked reactions to itself by contemporary narrative poets and later by the Georgians. Includes chapters on the poets of the Victorian tradition (Watson, Phillips, "Michael Field") and the Celtic Twilight (Yeats and Sharp), on avant-garde poets of aestheticism (Dowson), decadence (Wratislaw, Barlas, Wilde), symbolism (Yeats) and impressionism (Symons and Pater), on the protest of narrative poets (Kipling, Davidson, Chesterton, Noyes, Masefield).

395. Perosa, Sergio. "The Fiction of Frederick Rolfe, 'Baron Corvo'" *Mosaic*, 4, iii (1971), 111-123.

Suggests that "if Rolfe's autobiographical fiction is often a direct expression of the defenceless and alienated self, it shows on the other hand revealing links and coincidences with the historical experience of the Decadent Movement . . . . The main characteristics of his historical or pseudo-historical fiction can often be related to the ideals and the forms of Decadent literature and reveal striking experimental aspects which foreshadow some important trends of twentieth century fiction." Among those aspects discussed: the "affectation of mock simplicity . . . the worldly taste for fairytales, the insistence on exotic or surrealistic effects and on a kind of hedonistic and aesthetic Christianity with pagan undertones . . . the adoption of fluid and 'open' narrative forms, of artificial structures and frames, the use of a precious, elaborate, overly refined type of language."

396. Peters, Robert L. "Athens and Troy: Notes on John Addington Symonds' Aestheticism," *ELT*, 5, iii (1962), 14-26.

Argues that JAS's understanding of the Renaissance was vitiated by the faults of British aestheticism. "Symonds' specialized interest in Whitman, his absorption in Greek and Renaissance literature and art, and his dedication generally to sexual-aesthetic fusions in all art reflect a serious narrowing of artistic view, a refinement of taste and an exclusiveness of interest which we might term 'aesthetic.'" Notes that though JAS kept up with most artistic developments, he remained aloof from French symbolism, an influence which might have invigorated his work.

397.   Peters, Robert L.   "The Salomé of Arthur Symons and Aubrey
       Beardsley," *Criticism*, 2 (1960), 150-163.

       Taking Symons' *Studies in Strange Sins* and Beardsley's illus-
trations for *Salomé*, examines the interrelations among the arts in
the fin de siècle. Sees in Symons' tendency to overlook "the pro-
nounced sardonic elements in Beardsley, and [to emphasize] the more
overtly 'decadent' strain," an attempt "to purify evil by intensity,
an anticipation of the modernist view of art which holds any subject
matter appropriate." Though believes Symons was "rarely able to sub-
ordinate his borrowings to a controlled personal statement or to in-
form his raw material with a superior artistic wisdom," concludes
that he was able to "explore more fully the nature of a specialized
'sin' -- a topic of primary concern to the decadents; and an imple-
mentation for his view, one he shared with the other modernists of
his day, that the arts are appropriate stimuli for each other and
can provide material as suitable for shaping by creative imagination
as the untried matter of life itself."

398.   Peters, Robert L.   "Toward an 'Un-Definition' of Decadent
       As Applied to British Literature of the Nineteenth Century,"
       JAAC, 18 (1959-60), 258-264.

       Points out four significant failures of Ryals' [see #447] pro-
posed definition of decadence and indicates the issues which must be
dealt with before any useful or adequate definition of decadence is
achieved: the would-be definer "should concede the vast complexity
of late Victorian art, of which decadence is but one important mani-
festation; and he should have the perspicacity to see that the final
years were years of connection and prediction as well as culmination.
Further he should seek to distinguish carefully between the artist's
personality and his art . . . . He should also guard against treating
all decadent art as if of equal worth."

399.   Peters, Robert L.   "Whistler and the English Poets of the
       1890's," *MLQ*, 18 (1957), 251-261.

       Argues that the characteristic stylistic emphases of Whistler's
art -- anti-anecdotal, highly selective, interested in transitory effects, nuance, harmony of color and shape -- had a pervasive influence on poets like Wilde, Symons and Henley. Finds most Whistlerian
poems of the period "represent an objective seeing and feeling, and
do assert . . . that poets and painters should not be anecdotal,
should record life itself, directly, no matter how refined or pallid
their chosen areas of life appear to be."

400.   Petersen, Karl M.   "Arthur Machen and the Celtic Renaissance
       in Wales," *DAI*, 34 (1973), 3426A-27A. [Louisiana State]

       Studies AM's use of Welsh material as vehicle for expression of
fin de siècle sensibility. "The solitary and imaginative escape into

the dream world which characterizes all Machen's heroes is a Celtic quality, but is also common to the heroes of Aestheticism. Although Machen denied any explicit contact with the disciples of Aestheticism, his work exhibits the same concern with the cultivation of sensation, and the dedication to beauty, and their reconstruction by the imagination."

401. Peterson, Carroll V. *John Davidson*. NY: Twayne, 1972. [TEAS 143]

Critical account of JD with some biographical comment. JD seen as early exemplar of twentieth-century responses to materialism, hero-worship and imperialism. Central themes in his work: (1) the problem of belief and (2) hero-worship and heroic vitalism. Sees Davidson moving through a Carlylean crisis of faith with the nineties as the center of indifference. "In an age of decadence, an age of minor writers and minor poetry, Davidson tried very hard to be not a minor writer but a major prophet." Finds the ironic Davidson still readable but the writings of the later hero-worshipper are dead.

402. Peterson, William S. *"The Light That Failed*: Kipling's Version of Decadence," *ELT*, 9 (1966), 153-155.

Viewing the work as "yet another late nineteenth century novel about art and artists," finds that "the grouping of events and characters . . . suggests that in additon to Dick's two artistic styles of compromise and boldness, there is a third possibility of decadence -- a passionate intensity of vision, linked with violence and sex, which destroys the artist just as surely as does pleasing a Philistine public."

403. Pick, John. "Divergent Disciples of Walter Pater," *Thought* 23 (1948), 114-128.

Studies Pater's movement away from the Heraclitan doctrine of flux and suggests that Pater thus passed beyond his own disciples, Moore, Wilde and Symons. Finds that only Lionel Johnson could grow with Pater for perhaps only Johnson understood the monastic, ascetic side of WP. Most of the writers of the nineties listened to the early not the contemporaneous Pater.

404. Pinto, Vivian de Sola. *Crisis in English Poetry, 1880-1940*. London: Hutchinson, 1955. 2nd Ed.

Argues that the balance in Victorian poetry between inner and outer "voyages" failed around 1880, precipitating the "crisis." Believes decadent poets like Yeats, Wilde, Symons, Dowson, Johnson and Wratislaw cut themselves off from life of the common man in order to dedicate themselves to a purely aesthetic ideal and, on the whole, were "too timid, too cloistered, too pedantic and too self-consciously

Bohemian to make that thorough exploration of the inner life which was the necessary prelude to any rebuilding of English poetry." Comments upon Blunt, Henley, Kipling and Davidson. Includes chapters on Hardy and Housman, Hopkins and Bridges, Yeats and Synge.

405. Pitts, Gordon. "Lord de Tabley: Poet of Frustration," *West Virginia University Philological Papers*, 14 (1963), 57-73.

Urges publication of a selective anthology for this author of 14 volumes of poetry whose major themes include frustrated desire, nature as wasteland and God-abandoned man.

406. Plarr, Victor. *Ernest Dowson 1888-1897: Reminiscences, Unpublished Letters and Marginalia.* London: Elkin Mathews, 1914.

A self-justifying account by Pound's "M. Verog" that tries to rescue Dowson from his double, "the vexed and torn spirit of the biographers," in order to present the "intimate and perhaps essential Dowson" -- diffident, beautiful, boyish and well-bred.

407. Plowman, Thomas F. "The Aesthetes: The Story of a Nineteenth-Century Cult," *Pall Mall Magazine*, 5 (Jan 1895), 27-44.

Now that the aesthetic movement of the 1870s "has lain long enough in the limbo of forgetfulness for the haziest notions to prevail concerning it," undertakes to rehearse its actual history from the Gothic Revival to *Patience*. Finds the movement chiefly valuable for having assisted the effort "to throw off the old trammels of conventionalism and to live in an atmosphere of greater freedom."

408. Poggioli, Renato. *"Qualis Artifex Pereo!* or Barbarism and Decadence," *HLB*, 13 (1959), 135-159.

An interpretative reading of a series of poems -- including Yeats's "Byzantium" poems -- focussing upon the psychological and aesthetic aspects of decadence as it contronts its destroyer and liberator, barbarism. Believes that decadence "may well be another name for civilization's self-betrayal," noting that the decadent humanist, instead of openly defending the integrity of culture, "will patiently and painfully collect the broken pieces of its monuments and artifacts and hide them from the sight of the authors of such a ruin."

409. Poggioli, Renato. *The Theory of the Avant-Garde*, trans. Gerald Fitzgerald. Cambridge, Mass.: Havard Univ. Press, 1968.

Suggests that although decadence is absorbed by its "appeal to defunct civilizations, to predecessor and ancient decadences," and is thus frequently hostile to contemporary civilization, nonetheless it and avant-gardism "are related if not identical." For while the futurist mentality "tremulously awaits an artistic palingenesis, preparing for its coming practically and mystically, the decadent mentality resigns itself to awaiting passively, with anguished fatality and inert anxiety." Believes there is no great difference "between the decadent's dream of a new infancy (dear to old age) and the futurist's dream of a new maturity or youth, of a more virginal and stronger world. Degeneration and immaturity equally aspire to transcend the self in a subsequent flourishing; thus the generations that feel themselves decrepit, like those that feel themselves adolescent, are both lost generations, par excellence. If agonistic tendencies triumph in avant-garde futurism, a passive agonism dominates the decadent mentality, the pure and simple sense of agony. Decadence means no more than a morbid complacency in feeling oneself passé: a sentiment that also, unconsciously, inspires the burnt offerings of the avant-garde to the cultural future."

410. Ponrom, Cyrena N. "A Note on the Little Magazines of the English Decadence," *VPN*, No.1 (Jan 1968), 30-31.

Finds that although the *Yellow Book* fully deserves its reputation as the leading periodical of the English decadence, its fame has obscured both earlier and more "decadent" periodicals. The *Dial*, for example, was earlier in directing attention to the literary and artistic elements, especially French elements, that went into decadence, while the *Spirit Lamp* and the *Chameleon* sought more daring themes.

411. Pope, Myrtle P. "A Critical Bibliography of Works by and about Francis Thompson," *BNYPL*, 62, xi (Nov 1958); 63, i (Jan 1959); 63, iii (March 1959); 63, iv (Apr 1959).

412. Pound, Ezra, ed. *The Poetical Works of Lionel Johnson*. London: Elkin Mathews, 1915. "Preface," pp. v-xix.

[Preface was later cancelled by Mathews, according to EP, "due to pressure from the howly or howlink cawfliks . . . .They scared Mathews; threatening non sale of vol to all the pious who had boomed Lionel on acc/ his RRRRomanism so called"] In an appreciative description of LJ's poetry, notes that "the 'nineties' have chiefly gone out because of their muzziness, because of a softness derived, I think, not from books but from impressionist painting. They riot with half decayed fruit."

413. Powell, James Kerry. "Theatre of the Mind in Late Victorian Literature: Swinburne, Pater, Wilde, Beardsley and Symons," *DAI*, 35 (1974), 2238A. [Kentucky]

Believes aesthetic or decadent writers reverse the traditional meaning of the world-as-stage metaphor: "Emblemizing life as an attempt to transcend the worldly theatre by creating in art a more elegant and meaningful drama in which they can imaginatively participate." This redramatization of life "functions as the primary [strategy]in literature as diverse as Swinburne's *Thallasius* and *Lesbia Brandon*, Pater's *Marius the Epicurean*, Wilde's *The Picture of Dorian Gray*, Beardsley's fragmentary *Venus and Tannhäuser*, and Symons' *London Nights*."

414. Praz, Mario. *The Romantic Agony*, trans. Angus Davidson. London: Oxford Univ. Press, 1951. 2nd Ed.

"A study of Romantic literature (of which the Decadent Movement of the end of the last century is only a development) under one of its most characteristic aspects, that of erotic sensibility . . . . Looked at from this point of view, the literature of the nineteenth century appears as a unique, clearly distinct whole, which the various formulas such as 'romanticism,' 'realism,' 'decadence' &c., tend to disrupt. In no other period, I think, has sex been so obviously the mainspring of works of imagination." Chapters on the idea of tainted beauty, the fatal man, the early influence of Sadism, la belle dame sans merci, and the decadence of civilization. Includes copious quotation from representative works of English, French and Italian literatures. Relatively brief mention of Pater, Wilde and the English decadents.

415. Prince, Jeffrey R. "Havens of Intensity: Aestheticism in the Poetry of Keats, Tennyson, and Yeats," *DA*, 32 (1971), 4629A. [Virginia]

Contends that aestheticism cannot be satisfactorily assessed "until we examine its themes and style in the works of the greatest who handled them." Derives an operational model of aestheticism or aesthetic poetry from the works of D.G. Rossetti with these characteristics: (1) an ambivalent attitude towards aesthetic experience; (2) an intense preoccupation with plastic arts whose static qualities can be borrowed to describe the moment of aesthetic penetration of the aesthetic object by the imagination; (3) sensuous experience primary, rational experience secondary, while didactic or discursive statements are avoided.

416. Quilter, Harry. "The Gospel of Intensity," *ContempR*, 67 (June 1895), 761-782.

Notes with some satisfaction that one month after the Wilde conviction there has been a distinct shift in tone towards the innovative art in the periodicals that had earlier puffed it. Predicts a renewed faith in God and a return to the old ways will succeed the "morbid extravagances of hysterically neurotic and erotic imaginations."

417. Ramsey, Jonathan. "Ernest Dowson: An Annotated Bibliography of Writings About Him," *ELT*, 14 (1971), 17-42.

418. Ray, Laura K. "Kenneth Grahame and the Literature of Childhood," *ELT*, 20 (1977), 3-12.

Discusses KG's use of Wordsworthian and Dickensian motifs in *The Golden Age* (1895). "A participant in the Neo-Pagan movement of the nineties, Grahame saw in nature not so much a source of emotional enrichment and self-awareness as an escape from the artificial structures and standards of English society."

419. Raymond, Ernest T. *Portraits of the Nineties*. London: T. Fisher Unwin, 1921.

Considers the 1890s "essentially a time of transition" characterized by two main attitudes: imperialistic and decadent, the latter "revolt without a standard, a rebellion without object or hope," an assault "on Victorian console tables and antimacassars by men and women who had grown too soft in Victorian easy chairs." Beardsley the typical figure of the period "in his unenjoying luxuriousness, his invalid decorum, his untrammelled originality, and his pert pessimism." Includes chapters on Meredith, Wilde, Beardsley, Hardy and the nineties.

420. Raymond, Jean Paul and Charles Ricketts. *Oscar Wilde: Recollections*. London: Nonesuch, 1932.

Reminiscences and a ringing defense of Wilde in the form of a dialogue and letters between the pseudonymous Raymond and Ricketts himself.

421. Read, Herbert. "The Symptoms of Decadence," *To Hell With Culture*. NY: Schocken, 1963, pp. 86-92.

"The symptoms of decadence as they reveal themselves in the art of a country are indifference, vanity and servitude."

422. Reade, Brian, ed. *Sexual Heretics: Male Homosexuality in English Literature from 1850-1900: An Anthology*. NY: Coward-McCann, 1971. "Introduction," pp. 1-56.

Traces the rise of homosexual literary effusions of a high level of artistic expression from 1850 onwards, with brief discussions of the role played in that development by such writers as Tennyson, Hopkins, Swinburne, Simeon Solomon, Pater, Symonds, Carpenter, Wilde and many minor figures. Notes that by the 1880s the encouragement to homosexual literary expression provided by the Oxford Movement and the muscular Christianity of Dr. Arnold was augmented by "the arrival of

younger generations of literary men accepting homosexual sentiment
as part of the whole range of feeling which waited to be explored.
The next stage was when the admission of such sentiments, albeit only
among a few people who were haunted by them, grew into a belief that
the more acute sensibility of the 'artistic temperament' was often
allied to the frustrated senses of the homosexual. To be homosexual-
ly inclined thus became one of the secondary qualifications for declaring oneself a 'artist.'"

423. Reckitt, Maurice B. "When Did 'Victorianism' End?" *VS*,
      1 (1957-58), 268-271.

      1887. "The *fin de siècle* does not tranquilly wind up the cen-
tury; it inaugurates a new one." "The writers of the nineties, with
all their vivid variety of outlook, were in few cases characteristi-
cally Victorian either in their manner or their interests."

424. Reed, John R. "Bedlamite and Pierrot: Ernest Dowson's
      Esthetic of Futility," *ELH*, 35 (1968), 94-113.

      Finds that the characteristic search for isolation or sanctuary
in Dowson's poems and stories is more than simple escapism: "it is
the consequence of a painful idealism." Art, for Dowson, is "an attempt to incarnate the imperishable Idea through the medium of the
artist's egoistic expression, thereby phenomenologizing and destroying it as well." Believes that ED's aesthetic of futility consists
in this: "the artist *is* the sensations that he has, and he must con-
vert them into art; yet his art can never be the sensations, and the
artist's procedure is the end of art."

425. Reed, John R. "Mixing Memory and Desire in Late Victorian
      Literature," *ELT*, 14 (1971), 1-15.

      Examines the connection "between the fashioned nostalgia for
the past, the wistful hope for an altered future, and the esthetic
self-consciousness of the writers of the late nineteenth century."

426. Reid, John C. *Francis Thompson: Man and Poet*. London:
      Routledge and Kegan Paul, 1959.

      Argues against the tendency to isolate FT from other period
writers: "Thompson is a typical decadent poet in the literary sense--
his language is artificial and affected, sensation concerns him more
than emotion, his images, in their bookishness, operate at a couple
of removes from life; and the general tone of his early poetry is
morbid, spiritually inert, in the minor key."

427. Reynolds, Aidan and William Charlton. *Arthur Machen: A Short
      Account of His Life and Work*. London: John Baker, 1963.

428. Rhys, Ernest. *Everyman Remembers*. NY: Cosmopolitan, 1931.

Vivid though frequently unreliable memoirs of the 1890s and chief characters. In his later *Wales England Wed* [NY: Dutton, 1941], Rhys retells many of the same incidents, giving names of participants he had suppressed before.

429. Rhys, Ernest. *Letters from Limbo*. London: Dent, 1936.

Includes letters from Herbert Horne, Johnson, Selwyn Image, Vincent O'Sullivan, Sharp, Dobson, Stenbock and others of the period; provides brief explanatory notes.

430. Richard, Noël. *Le mouvement décadent: dandys, esthètes et quintessents*. Paris: Nizet, 1968.

Traces the brief career of French decadence as a precursor to symbolism. "Si le mouvement poétique que nous avons analysé se caractérise par l'engouement pour les néologismes, par la recherche de la singularité et de l'exceptionnel, par le désir de la subtilité et d'un certain byzantinisme, parfois même par un soupçon de bravade et de mystification . . . . peut-être que le phénomène de la Décadence a-t-il été surtout un crise d'adolescence esthétique." [In French]

431. Richardson, Dorothy. "Saintsbury and Art for Art's Sake in England," *PMLA*, 59 (1944), 243-260.

Saintsbury seen as "a consistent advocate of aestheticism" whose separation of form and content -- encouraged by aestheticism's emphasis on form -- and stress on the critic's appreciative role had some harmful effects on the the development of modern criticism. Though Saintsbury denied art had a didactic or moral function, he did not sympathize with the decadents either; he demanded sincerity.

432. Ricketts, Charles and Jean Paul Raymond. *Oscar Wilde: Recollections*. London: Nonesuch, 1932.

See #420.

433. Riewald, J.G. *Sir Max Beerbohm, Man And Writer: A Critical Analysis with a Brief Life and a Bibliography*. The Hague: M. Nijhoff, 1953.

Believes "the vexed and much eschewed question of Beerbohm's place in the so-called 'Decadent' movement practically resolves itself into the alternative problem of his literary relationship to Oscar Wilde," a relationship that began with parody and ended in imitation. Most striking similarity between the two -- their ideas of individuality. Includes discussion of period ideas of the mask, dandyism, intellectual hedonism, the allure of the past, moods.

434.   Roberts, S.C. "At the Heart of the Nineties," *E&S*,
       27 (1941), 66-75.

       Objects to the exclusive rights literary historians have given the Rhymers' Club writers to the period. Surveys the "fertile and varied output" during the decade with special attention to popular tastes in literature in 1894; insists that any view of the 1890s "should also reveal a varied picture of gaiety, humour, satire, and romance."

435.   Robinson, James K. "Austin Dobson and the Rondeliers,"
       MLQ, 14 (1953), 31-42.

       Notes Dobson took up the French fixed form in the early 1870s, hoping to extend the range of the *vers de société* poet; despite the efforts of Dobson, Lang, Gosse and others, the vogue of the French forms was never really thorough-going -- Dobson himself began to tire of them as early as 1878. According to Saintsbury, the chief reason for their decline in popularity was that "no poet had cared or dared, save in a very few cases, to ease the syllabic rigidity into that equivalence which is the soul of English verse."

436.   Robinson, James K.   "A Neglected Phase of the Aesthetic
       Movement: English Parnassianism," *PMLA*, 68 (1953), 733-754.

       Discusses the origins and characteristics of French Parnassianism and studies its most important English followers. Sees in the work of Dobson, Monkhouse, Gosse, O'Shaughnessy, Marzials and Payne a reaction against the Spasmodic School in favor of marmoreal form and impersonal craft. The English Parnassians' modest aims -- "honestly regarding themselves as minor poets, they set out to cultivate competently a carefully limited sort of poetry" -- included no dogmatic or theoretical ambitions and ignored their French predecessors' subversive transvaluation of art and life.

437.   Robinson, Lennox. "Yeats: The Early Poems," *REL*,
       6 (1965), 22-33.

       Insists "it is stupid to ignore the early Yeats, as stupid as to talk in that connection about Pre-Raphaelitism and over-decoration. There was a decorated period -- which he recognized himself very soon and deliberately rejected -- but it was not his earliest period and some of the first lyrics have a simplicity, a clarity of thought and expression, a 'beauty like a tightened bow' which makes them take their places beside the best of his latest work."

438. Rodway, A.E. "The Last Phase," *From Dickens to Hardy*, ed.
Boris Ford. Harmondsworth, Eng. and Baltimore: Penguin,
1958, pp. 385-405. [Vol 6 of *The Pelican Guide to English
Literature*]

Believes that the point of view usually associated with the
1890s probably more characteristic of 1880s. Sees "decadence" as
a quality shared by both major groups of period -- the aesthetes
pursued a decadence of language, the "Patriots" a decadence of in-
telligence. Studies Wilde and Kipling as chief representative figures of two groups, noting their considerable similarities. Includes
discussion of Johnson, Dowson, Housman, Henley, Thompson, Davidson.
Concludes "if there is one thing common to all writers of the last
phase, whatever their political or psychological complexion, it is
the tendency to strike a pose and adopt a manner."

439. Ronsley, Joseph. *Yeats's Autobiography: Life as Symbolic
Pattern*. Cambridge, Mass.: Harvard Univ. Press, 1968.

A brief critical study that makes "no attempt to annotate the
book or to correct it for the sake of factual accuracy, but rather
to discover the design underlying Yeats's presentation of events,
people and ideas." Aim is accomplished chiefly by applying the lunar
phases of *A Vision* to the various persons and periods treated in the
Autobiography. Stresses WBY's subordination of event to pattern:
"Yeats had formulated his life into an evolving pattern, and his
friends of the nineties had a vital role to play in representing its
most subjective phases. Their brief lives, only slightly altered and
simplified, readily lent themselves to filling out his design."

440. Rose, Alan M. "Joseph Conrad and the Sirens of Decadence,"
TSLL, 11 (1969-70), 795-810.

Finds JC's early work combines "many of the interests of the
nineties, especially of the Decadence: realistic detail is rendered
in highly wrought prose; ethical problems are presented in the essentially visual manner of impressionism; attention to narrative
interest is overridden by the symbolist's concern with form. Although Conrad listened only momentarily to the call of the more extreme expressions of art for art's sake, the period of 1896-97 shows
him to have, indeed, belonged to Arthur Symons' Decadence."

441. Rosenblatt, Louise. *L'idée de l'art pour l'art dans la
littérature anglaise pendant la période victorienne*. Paris:
Champion, 1931.

Treats the period 1850-1900 with chapters on Ruskin and the
Pre-Raphaelite defense of beauty, the aesthetic revolt of Swinburne,
the aesthetic mysticism of Pater, the art for art's sake and realism
of Wilde and his contemporaries. "On ne peut pas comprendre Wilde,
ni les hommes de 1890-1900, si l'on n'apprécie pas la valeur qu'ils

trouvaient à ce ton de légèreté intellectuelle, en réaction contre le sérieux si lourd des bourgeois." [In French]

442. Rothenstein, John. *The Artists of the 1890's*. London: Routledge, 1928.

An introductory essay attempts to show that the spirit of the 1890s "was in its entirety one of revolt" against industrialism and classicism. A lengthy historical survey of the growth and decline of both indicates that the nineties were the natural and inevitable outcome of historical process "and not the unique manifestation its publicists claim." Includes chapters on Whistler, Greaves, Steer, Sickert, Conder, Beardsley, Ricketts and Shannon, the author's father Will Rothenstein, and Beerbohm.

443. Rothenstein, William. *Men and Memories*. Vol.1, *Recollections, 1872-1900*. NY: Coward-McCann, 1931.

Thoughtful, novelistically detailed memoirs of just about everybody in the artistic and literary circles of Paris and London.

444. Rutenberg, Daniel. "A New Date for the Rhymers' Club," *ELT*, 12 (1969), 155-157.

Suggests 1890 for its beginning. [See #33 and #521]

445. Ryals, Clyde de L. "Decadence in British Literature Before the *Fin de Siècle*," *DA*, 17 (1957), 3004. [Pennsylvania]

After a survey of Keats, Tennyson, Rossetti, Swinburne and Pater, concludes that "far from being a mere English importation, the decadence was conceived on English soil and was as old as romanticism itself."

446. Ryals, Clyde de L. "The Nineteenth-Century Cult of Inaction," *TSL*, 4 (1959), 51-60.

Concludes that the Victorian poets' preoccupation with the conflict between action and speculation is traceable to "(1) the Romantic overemphasis on the individual and the individual imagination, which sought to create a world of make-believe and fancy and, in turn, tended to undermine the will and the ability to act; and (2) a commercial society's overemphasis on practical values, causing the sensitive writer of the period to invert those values into a mode of philosophy which stressed the life of contemplation as opposed to the life of action."

447. Ryals, Clyde de L. "Towards a Definition of *Decadent* as
     Applied to British Literature of the Nineteenth Century,"
     JAAC, 17 (1958), 85-92.

     Argues that "decadence" ought to be revived as a critical term
in order to differentiate further between "classical" and "romantic."
Considers decadence a "subphase" of romanticism, but where "romanticism expressed itself by maintaining an equilibrium between the natural and the grotesque, decadence found expression in distorting
this balance and placing value on the grotesque at the expense of the
natural." Decadence "marked the virescence of a more feminine sensibility, characterized by a withdrawal from masculine reality. The
decadent poet no longer writes about life, but rather about his withdrawal from life." Decadence is romanticism without its humanitarian
ideals. [See #398]

448. Ryskamp, Charles, ed. *Wilde and the Nineties: An Essay
     and an Exhibition*. Princeton, N.J.: Princeton Univ.
     Press, 1966.

     Includes essays on Wilde and his times by Richard Ellmann and
E.D.H. Johnson. [See #148 and #280]

449. Saddlemyer, Ann. "The Cult of the Celt: Pan-Celticism in
     the Nineties," *The World of W.B. Yeats*, ed. Robin Skelton
     and Ann Saddlemyer. Seattle: Univ. of Washington Press,
     1965. Rev. Ed. pp. 3-5.

     A brief account of the sources and characteristics of the
Celticist movement: "it was essentially a re-naming and re-ordering
of a familiar trait, the 'folk spirit,' marked by the heightened
passions and superstitions common to all literature rising from the
people, and given new life by the recent scientific studies of folklore and myth culminating in Sir James Frazer's *The Golden Bough* in
1890. In addition, it possessed a strong tendency towards melancholy
which attracted mystics of Maeterlinck's school. But the new element in the 'celtic revival' was a sense of *place*, as opposed to a
vague atmosphere."

450. Sahai, Surendra. *English Drama 1865-1900*. New Delhi and
     Bombay: Orient Longman, 1971.

     Includes discussion of Gilbert, Pinero, Jones, Ibsen and the
development of the problem play, Shaw and Wilde. Concludes "the rejuvenation of English drama toward the close of the nineteenth century was the work of English dramatists. Ibsen's abrupt appearance
and short-lived influence on contemporary dramatists showed the depth
of native talent. It was through the efforts of Gilbert, Pinero,
Jones, Shaw and Wilde that the nineties saw a rejuvenation of drama."

451. Salt, Henry S. "The Poetry of John Barlas," *Yellow Book*,
      9 (Oct 1896), 80-90.

      Conceding that it takes longer for the "democratic" poet to
gain recognition, predicts that JB's *Love Sonnets* (1889) will one
day be ranked with the greatest.

452. Savage, D.S. "The Aestheticism of W.B. Yeats," *KR*,
      7 (1945), 118-134.

      Notes that English aesthetes differed from French symbolists
by being dilettantes "interested less in the ardors of artistic
creation than in the uses to which artistic precepts could be put
in the alleviation of living." Concludes "there is something in-
human, or soulless, about Yeats all the way through."

453. Scanlon, Leone. "Essays on the Effect of Feminism and
      Socialism Upon Literature of 1880-1914," *DAI*, 34 (1974),
      4218A. [Brandeis]

      Three essays on the New Woman, the cash nexus and the emergence
of the socialist hero in late Victorian literature. Concludes that
"feminism and socialism influenced the development of a new hero and
heroine in the literature of the period, and socialism enabled writers such as Shaw and Wells to view social unrest with less fear than
the non-socialist Gissing and to look with more hope for the reformation of society."

454. Schiff, Hilda. "Notes Towards an Inquiry into Late Nineteenth
      Century Literary Decadence," *Anglo-Welsh Review*, 19 (1971),
      91-96.

      Argues against simplistic definitions of decadence (e.g. over-
self-consciousness, insincerity, attitudinizing, fascination with
vice), pointing out that most uses of the term depend on private or
conventional evaluations. "If the salient feature of twentieth century literature has been one of disillusionment, cynicism, negation,
then we must look for its origins here; and if for no other reason
than fully to possess ourselves of our inheritance we must examine
this 'decadence' of the eighties and nineties, and revaluate the new
spirit which prompted it."

455. Schuetz, Laurence F. "The Suppressed 'Conclusion' to
      The Renaissance and Walter Pater's Modern Image," *ELT*,
      17 (1974), 251-258.

      Argues that WP withdrew the "Conclusion" for ethical rather
than -- as is usually assumed by modern critics -- for narrowly prudential reasons; Pater's primary concern was that his principles had
been misinterpreted. [See #73, #469 and #527]

456. Segnitz, Barbara J. "Narcissus and the Quest for Beauty: the Decay of Romantic Idealism," *DAI*, 31 (1971), 4733A. [Iowa]

Finds the Narcissus myth the "symbolic key" to understanding the shift away from Romantic idealism; notes a shift away from a woman figure to an androgynous form and an increasingly cynical, pessimistic tone. Discusses Keats, Rossetti, Swinburne, Pater, Wilde, Dowson, Moore.

457. Seitz, Margaret L. "Catholic Symbol and Ritual in Minor British Poetry of the Later Nineteenth Century," *DAI*, 35 (1974), 1634A. [Arizona State]

Studies Blunt, Johnson, Dowson and "Michael Field." "Although the strength of their faiths is enormously varied and in fact vacillates even within their individual lives and poetry, this only indicates the profound sense of insecurity that the age pressed upon them."

458. Sewell, Brocard and Cecil Woolf, eds. *Corvo, 1869-1960: A Collection of Essays by Various Hands to Commemorate the Centenary of the Birth of Fr. Rolfe, Baron Corvo.* Aylesford, Eng.: St. Albert's Press, 1961.

See #582.

459. Sewell, Brocard. *Olive Custance: Her Life and Work.* London: Eighteen Nineties Society, 1975. [Makers of the Nineties Series, ed. G. Krishnamurti]

A short biographical and appreciative essay with special emphasis on Custance's relationships with John Gray and Lord Alfred Douglas. Prints and comments upon several poems. Concludes "Olive Custance made a small but highly individual contribution to ["deca- dent" writing]: she had caught the mood, and was powerfully affected by it. But it *was* a mood, and a mood that she cultivated for a time only."

460. Sewell, Brocard, ed. *Two Friends: John Gray and André Raffalovich.* Aylesford, Eng.: St. Albert's Press, 1963.

Collects essays by various scholars and friends of the two poets and collaborators. In addition to reminiscences, includes treatments of Gray's prose works, poetry and his relationship with Pierre Louÿs. [For Ian Fletcher's essay on Gray's poetry see #172]

461. Sharp, Evelyn. *Unfinished Adventure: Selected Reminiscences from an Englishwoman's Life.* London: John Lane, 1933.

Autobiography including two chapters on the *Yellow Book* circle, Henry Harland and John Lane in particular. "I arrived on the crest of the wave that was sweeping away the Victorian tradition, and I see now that what kept our delirious iconoclasm sane, and preserved a sense of beauty in the most decadent among us, was the high standard of taste bequeathed to my generation by the great Victorians."

462. Sheridan, Daniel P. "Later Victorian Ghosts: Supernatural Fiction and Social Attitudes, 1870-1900," *DAI*, 35 (1974), 3770A. [Northwestern]

Describes "the range and complexity of later Victorian supernatural fiction, traces its origins and the sources of its popularity, and examines the attitudes toward religious belief, science, and nature which are reflected in the works themselves." Works include LeFanu's *In a Glass Darkly*, Oliphant's "The Open Door," Stevenson's "Dr. Jekyll and Mr. Hyde," Machen's "Great God Pan," Stoker's *Dracula*, Conan Doyle's *Hound of the Baskervilles*.

463. Shmiefsky, Marvel. *Sense at War with Soul: English Poetics (1865-1900)*. The Hague: Mouton, 1972.

Discusses the "questions at issue" between the expressionist and aesthetic schools of criticism. Aesthetic critics tended to stress form over expression, genius as technical virtuosity, suggestion over statement, revelation over interpretation -- though differences between the two emphases are found to be less between critics of stature. Includes explication of 9 critical texts by Swinburne, Hopkins, Arnold, Pater, Patmore, Wilde, Bridges, Yeats and A.C. Bradley.

464. Shmiefsky, Marvel. "Swinburne's Anti-Establishment Poetics," *VP*, 9 (1971), 261-276.

Argues Swinburne's "affinity with other late-century aesthetes has a broader basis than the issue of art for art's sake . . . . [In] his concepts of truth and nature in poetry, in his spiritualized doctrine of Beauty, in his reaction to the norm established by Wordsworth," ACS is the true antithesis of Arnold, the leading conceptualist critic of the period.

465. Sims, George. "Leonard Smithers: A Publisher of the Nineties," *London Magazine*, 3, ix (1956), 33-40.

Sympathetic account of the nineties publisher who "issued some of the most beautiful books of the period" but whose dealings with Dowson and Beardsley have confirmed his own saying that "if a publisher is remembered at all, he is never remembered well." Clears LS of the heaviest of the pornographer-degenerate-debaucher charges.

466. Singer, Irving. "The Aesthetics of 'Art for Art's Sake',"
     JAAC, 12 (1953-54), 343-359.

     Distinguishes four major premises in aestheticism: (1) the art-
ist is different from other men in having a predominance of sensuous
intuition or creative imagination; (2) the artist is a specialist in
the techniques of his own art; (3) great art is not necessarily
created by men of high moral character; (4) artistic creation is the
highest end of life.

467. Singh, Briraj. "A Study of the Concepts of Art, Life
     and Morality in the Criticism of Five Writers from
     Pater to Yeats," *DAI*, 32 (1971), 3331A-32A. [Yale]

     Detects two strains -- the "decadent" and the "humanist" -- in
Pater's criticism that influenced the work of later critics like
Johnson, Symons, James and Yeats.

468. Sisson, C.H. *English Poetry 1900-1950: An Assessment.*
     London: Rupert Hart-Davis, 1971.

     Argues that while some of the technical innovations of the
Rhymers' Club poets were important, "the vague and notorious aura of
the period matters less . . . [and is] little more than a side-effect
of the disintegration of Victorian morality and, to an extent which
cannot easily be judged, of the beginnings of an era to be dominated,
to an unprecedented extent, by the vulgar press." Finds the really
serious element in nineties poetry its subjectivism; its philosophy
of exquisite moments is a refined version of the sensationalism of
the press. With their interest in conversational tone and rhythm,
Johnson, Dowson, and Davidson all contributed to later poets; Wilde
and Symons, however, possess merely a "period charm."

469. Small, Ian and Lawrence F. Schuetz. "Pater and the Suppressed
     'Conclusion' to *The Renaissance*: Comment and Reply," *ELT*, 19
     (1976), 313-321.

     Small suggests that WP's reasons for withdrawing the "Conclu-
sion" were not "ethical" ones as Schuetz [see #455] had argued, but
prudential ones adopted in the face of local and national criticism
of him as an advocate of "paganism": "Surely men less sensitive to
criticism than Pater would have done the same, especially since most
of the hostility implied accusations of sexual perversion." Schuetz's
reply questions Small's assumptions and interpretations of contemporary criticism of Pater. "Small's attitude toward Pater reflects
precisely the type of negative image that my earlier article sought
to counter." [See also #73 and #527]

470. Small, Ian. "Plato and Pater: Fin-de-Siècle Aesthetics,"
     BJA, 12 (1972), 369-383.

Discusses Pater's special emphases in his interpretation of
Plato which influenced aestheticism. Finds WP's descriptions of
Plato, Parmenides and Heraclitus were in fact "masks by which con-
temporary moral positions could be explored."

471. Smerdon, Geoffrey and Richard Whittington-Egan. *The Quest
of the Golden Boy: The Life and Letters of Richard LeGal-
lienne*. London: Unicorn, 1960.

See #562.

472. Smith, James M. "Concepts of Decadence in Nineteenth Century
French Literature," *SP*, 50 (1953), 640-651.

Studies those elements most frequently noted as characteristic
of literary decadence, and advances this "composite concept which em-
braces the whole": "Decadent literature is characterized by non-
creative imitation of a preceding and superior literary expression.
The decadent writer, whose creative faculties have been impaired
through hyperanalysis and sterile erudition, lacks the ability to
create a really new literary expression. In an attempt to achieve
novelty he exaggerates certain elements in the established pattern,
especially vocabulary and syntax, upsetting, in the process, the
classical balance between form and content. Over-attention to form
implies a cult of artifice, and, indeed, decadent taste for the artificial is reflected not only in form but in content, the decadent
writer often rejecting nature as model in favor of the anti-natural
and the unnatural. In the pursuit of novelty, strange and unusual
subjects are treated, and exquisite and rare sensations are described,
often through devices like synaesthesia and the transposition of art
techniques. Beauty itself is transfigured by the decadents to include elements deriving from the ugly and the morbid. Such a literary expression, often obscure in its over-subtle refinement, reflects
an aging civilization, itself dying amidst the unquiet splendors of
refined corruption, just as Rome and Byzantium had expired."

473. Snodgrass, Chris G. "The Aesthetic Criminal: The Metaphysics
of Victorian Decadent Consciousness," *DAI*, 35 (1975), 4560A.
[SUNY-Buffalo]

Examines critical writings and fiction of Pater, Wilde, Symons
and the earlier poetry of Swinburne. "The Decadents' collapsing of
the distinction between ethics and aesthetics troubled not only a
Victorian society unusually preoccupied by moral questions, but also
the Decadents themselves . . . . As underlying currents in their work
clearly demonstrate, the Decadents feared that they might well be not
only saints of a new 'Religion of Art,' but also (if not simultaneously) irresponsible and criminally subversive perpetrators of cultural
decay."

474. Sontag, Susan. "Notes on 'Camp'," *PR*, 21 (1964), 515-530.

56 notes on this "certain mode of estheticism." Camp is "dandyism in an age of mass culture," "a glorification of character." Camp taste possible only in cultures or societies capable of experiencing "the psychopathology of affluence." Sees Wilde as a transitional figure between the older dandyism and Camp in urging the equivalency of aesthetic objects.

475. Southworth, James G. "Laurence Binyon," *SR*, 43 (1935), 341-355.

Contrasts T.S. Eliot's poetry, "a balm to the contemporary who lacks the strength to combat the anti-cultural forces of the present day," with Binyon's, "a constant challenge to a fuller life." Concludes "it is clear, I think, that Mr. Binyon is the poet of completion as contrasted to Mr. Eliot, the poet of frustration."

476. Spencer, Robin. *The Aesthetic Movement: Theory and Practice*. NY: Dutton Pictureback, 1972.

An illustrated study of the aesthetic movement primarily devoted to new developments in the fine and applied arts: "The theory behind the art of the Aesthetic Movement was that it could be enjoyed for its own sake, and need impart nothing more than its own decorative existence to the beholder. This idea, breaking down the barriers between graphic art and painting, also helped design to climb from its long-held position of inferiority to challenge the fine arts of painting, scupture and architecture, and attempt to co-operate with them on mutual terms." Chapters on origins, the fashion for japonaiserie and the Queen Anne style, on Whistler's role, on the arts and crafts movement and art nouveau.

477. Squire, J.C. "Preface," *The Book of Bodley Head Verse*, ed. J.B. Priestley. London: John Lane, 1926, pp. vii-xiv.

"Whatever taint or tincture of what used to be called 'decadence' and 'fin-de-siècle' (to which term, thank God, 1901 put an end) might have been sporadically present in Lane's list, as it was certainly present in British civilisation, it was a hasty and unjust opinion that made this ruddy-cheeked Devonian a principal propagandist of nihilism, cosmetics, and 'audacity'."

478. Stanford, Derek. "Arthur Symons and Modern Poetics," *SoR*, 2 n.s. (1966), 347-353.

Doubts AS's contribution to modern poetic theory as clear as Kermode [see #291] has claimed; though once in the van of the nineties, Symons today would prove a conservative influence.

479. Stanford, Derek, ed. *Critics of the 'Nineties.*
London: John Baker, 1970. "Introduction," pp. 11-64.

Believes "an extension of the sense of style and of sex" are
clear characteristics of the period. Employs an anecdotal, "ideo-
graphic" method to sketch, not without errors, the sensibility of
the nineties. Finds Baudelaire and Pre-Raphaelitism the crucial de-
terminants of fin de siècle cultural themes.

480. Stanford, Derek, ed. *Poets of the Nineties: A Biographical
Anthology.* London: John Baker, 1965. "Poets of the Nineties," pp. 17-45.

Adopting Yeats's view of the "tragic generation," suggests
that one aspect of decadence is "a pursuit of intensity beyond the
strength of the organism." Nineties movement in poetry should be
seen as a reaction to Victorian seriousness, eloquence; stresses
the influence of Verlaine, who taught the English poets to seek "a
new reconciliation between the written and the spoken word."

481. Stanford, Derek. "The Pre-Raphaelite Cult of Women:
From Damozel to Demon," *ContempR*, 217 (1970), 26-33.

Notes sociological factors contributing to the continuing interest in Pre-Raphaelite images of women. "The essence of the Pre-
Raphaelite appeal . . . lay in the nourishment it offered to the
forces of feminism." Considerable quotation from other secondary
sources. Brief remarks on Salome and Ella D'Arcy.

482. Stanford, Derek, ed. *Short Stories of the 'Nineties:
A Biographical Anthology.* London: John Baker, 1968.
"Introduction," pp. 13-47.

Nineties fiction distinguished by "greater artistic stringency"
and "broader moral permissiveness." Notes three recurrent themes:
"the life of sex, the life of art and bohemian and declassé existence."
English short story writers learn most from the French, though Stevenson and Pater are influences.

483. Stanford, Derek, ed. *Three Poets of the Rhymers' Club:
Ernest Dowson, Lionel Johnson, John Davidson.* Cheadle,
Eng.: Carcenet, 1974. "Introduction," pp. 11-37.

Brief biographical and critical sketches drawing upon various
critical estimates of the three. Davidson seen as the most influential, particularly in his colloquialism and urban imagery; Dowson's
influence on posterity due to his "cult of passion, languor and despair, expressed not so much in any distinctive technique as present,
generally, in a mood or a theme; and secondly, a vogue for 'la mu-
sique avant toutes choses' --- speech approximating as closely as

possible to music"; Johnson, "a learned reactionary, consciously harked back to the past, and has been the least influential of the trio."

484. Stanford, Derek, ed. *Writing of the Nineties*. London: Dent, 1971. "Introduction," pp. xvii-xxii.

A brief, popular survey of the more important characters and characteristics of the decade. Nineties writing known by its "tone of dedication, [its] persiflage, and [its] transvaluation of bourgeois values." Love of beauty and care for art are seen as the two poles between which most of the characteristic writing of the decade finds a place.

485. Stange, G. Robert. "The Victorian City and the Frightened Poets," *VS*, 11 [Supplement] (1968), 627-640.

Includes brief consideration of some nineties poets. Suggests it is "clear that the seemingly frivolous and amoral movement of the 'nineties made it possible for the late-Victorian poets to free themselves from the conventional antithesis of nature and city, and to find in London a significance and beauty that their predecessors could not perceive."

486. Stange, G. Robert and Walter E. Houghton. "The Aesthetic Movement: Introduction," *Victorian Poetry and Poetics*. Boston: Houghton Mifflin, 1959, pp. 724-730.

See #263.

487. Starkie, Enid. *From Gautier to Eliot: The Influence of France on English Literature, 1851-1939*. London: Hutchinson, 1960. [Rptd Scholarly Press, 1971]

A rapid overview of French literary influence, with chapters on art for art's sake, on Swinburne and Pater, on realism, on symbolism, on the "yellow nineties." Concludes decadence was dead by 1897; thereafter English poetry turned patriotic and conservative. "At the end of the nineteenth century literature in England no longer possessed its fundamentally English character . . . . probably due to the emergence of the Irish-born writers, and the manner of their emergence . . . . more ready than the indigenous English for new changes . . . and they found in French Symbolism the ideal atmosphere in which to merge, without losing their own characteristics."

488. Stavros, George. "Pater, Wilde and the Victorian Critics of the Romantics," *DA*, 33 (1972), 2344A. [Wisconsin]

Pater and Wilde viewed as figures mediating between the aesthetic emphasis on form and the ethical insistence on content. Both eventually approved of the ethical, meditative elements in Wordsworth, anticipating the twentieth-century revaluation of the Romantics.

489.   Stead, C.K. *The New Poetic*. NY: Harper and Row, 1966.

Believes that by the end of the nineteenth century the Romantic movement was split into two opposed impulses -- the purely aesthetic (Wilde) and the purely rhetorical (Kipling). Sees the major effort of twentieth-century poetry as an attempt to reunite them.

490.   Stein, Joseph. "The New Woman and the Decadent Dandy," *Dalhousie Review*, 55 (1975), 54-62.

Examines the "decadent" writings of Beerbohm, Beardsley and Wilde for signs of the decline of dandyism and the rise of feminism or female domination. Concludes that in these authors' view the dandy "was not suffered to survive, or rather he was hounded off the stage and into his grave by the dynamism of the 'new woman' . . . . The common man of the 'nineties saw his legal, social, and political supremacy undermined; the dandy lost his art."

491.   Stern, Carol S. "Arthur Symons's Literary Relationships, 1882-1900: Some Origins of the Symbolist Movement," *DA*, 29 (1969), 2282A-83A. [Northwestern]

Attempts to free Symons from the labels of impressionist and decadent; emphasizes instead the diversity of his poetic modes and techniques.

492.   Stern, Carol S. "Arthur Symons: An Annotated Bibliography of Writings About Him," *ELT*, 17 (1974), 77-133.

493.   Stevenson, Lionel. "George du Maurier and the Romantic Novel," *EDH*, 30 (1960), 36-54.

Emphasizes GDM's role in the literary world. Sees him drawing upon both "decadent" and "activist" qualities in *Trilby*. Finds du Maurier adapting the traditions of romantic fiction to suit mood of the new epoch. Notes that though GDM has failed to win modern critical approval, his romantic fiction was defended and enjoyed by such late Victorian men of letters as Stevenson, Wilde, Haggard, Hope, Quiller-Couch.

494.   Stevenson, Lionel. "The Short Story in Embryo," *ELT*, 15 (1972), 261-268.

"When the fragmentation of sensibility set in, about 1880, the short story was . . . the most appropriate medium for representing it."

495. Stokes, John. *Resistible Theatres: Enterprise and Experiment in the Late Nineteenth Century*. London: Elek, 1972.

An informative study of late Victorian non-commercial theatrical experiments emphasizing the social and artistic context of various efforts at reform and innovation. Chapters on the careers of E.W. Godwin, Herbert von Herkomer and the Independent Theatre.

496. Stone, Donald D. *Novelists in a Changing World: Meredith, James, and the Transformation of English Fiction in the 1880's*. Cambridge, Mass.: Harvard Univ. Press, 1972.

Views 1880s as the watershed decade for the battle between old and new, Victorian and modern -- a battle of which the "warfare" between romantic and realist ideas of the novel is part. Includes discussion of Pater, Mrs. Ward, Olive Schreiner, Richard Jefferies, Moore, Gissing and Hardy.

497. Strehler, Marguerite. *Der Dekadenzgedanke in "Yellow Book" und "Savoy"*. Turbenthal: Rob. Furrers Erben, 1932.

Not seen.

498. Stutfield, Hugh E.M. "Tommyrotics," *Blackwood's Magazine*, 157 (June 1895), 833-845.

Writing a month after the Wilde conviction, declares society's greatest danger is from "'neurotics' and hysteria in their manifold forms." "The predilection for the foul and repulsive, the puling emotionalism and the sickly sensuousness of the French decadents, are also the leading characteristics of the nescent English schools." Denounces "new woman" fiction and related political demands for equality. "Much of the modern spirit of revolt has its origin in the craving for novelty and notoriety that is such a prominent feature of our day. A contempt for conventionalities and a feverish desire to be abreast of the times may be reckoned among the first-fruits of decadentism."

499. Sudrann, Jean. "Victorian Compromise and Modern Revolution," *ELH*, 26 (1959), 425-444.

Sees *Marius the Epicurean* as the truly transitional work. Viewed from its "Victorian" side, Eliot sees a Pater who fails to reconcile all the faiths; viewed from its "modernist" side, Yeats sees an artist who sought definition of his vision through symbols. Traces work's metaphoric structure.

500. Sussman, Herbert. "Criticism as Art: Form in Oscar Wilde's Critical Writings," *SP*, 70 (1973), 108-122,

Argues that "Wilde is consciously working to create new forms of critical discourse through which he can adequately express his 'new views'." Among these forms is "the dialogue as performance . . . a Paterian *tour de force*, a form suggesting that intellectual formulation is itself a type of artistic creation which, for a moment, fixes in the form of language the complex of mental sensations or, in Wilde's terms, 'gives reality to every mood'."

501. Sutton, Denys. "Editorial: A Fresh Look at the Fin de Siècle," *Apollo*, 83 (1966), 2-9.

Surveys the changed critical attitudes towards the period, a shifting away from a "theological" view of nineteenth-century art history that read it as the battle between proto-modernist genius and regressive devilry. Stresses the cross-currents and interanimating influences in art and literature. Notes that English appreciation of Impressionist and Post-Impressionist painting was delayed by the continuing popularity of the Pre-Raphaelite mode. "The Anglo-Saxon delight in 'the Decadents', as we like to term so many of the *fin de siècle* artists and writers, must always be remembered. This trend had a prime inspirer in Whistler and, at a less exalted level, Arthur Symons, who wrote about Redon in 1890."

502. Swann, Thomas B. *Ernest Dowson*. NY: Twayne, 1964. [TEAS 15]

Includes chapters on literary background, on ED's love poems, on "The Hollow Land" (author's term for ED poems about nature, death, religion and escape), on the verse play, on the stories and sketches, on Dowson's translations and on the novels written in collaboration with Arthur Moore. Views the 1890s as "the decade of artful sighs and elegant sins," dominated by decadence which is seen as the "final phase" of aestheticism. "While Dowson is sometimes called an Aesthete instead of a Decadent, the second term -- the term to be used in this study -- is much more descriptive of his art, with its air of decay and finality and its morbid concern with death." [Contains a number of peculiar errors, e.g. "It was even rumored -- and this time with truth -- that Beardsley had drawn a sexually aroused bull for the cover of the first *Savoy*."]

503. Swart, Koenraad W. *The Sense of Decadence in Nineteenth-Century France*. The Hague: M. Nijhoff, 1964.

"Literary decadence in its purest form was the creed of a number of esthetes who believed that by giving an artistic expression to the evil which haunted them they would be able to deliver themselves from their obsessions. Although they lacked any desire or hope to reform society, they were still longing for a regeneration of their own soul. In their search for overcoming their anxieties, most of the prominent authors of the Decadent movement (Huysmans, Verlaine, Oscar Wilde, D'Annunzio) sooner or later renounced their nihilistic ideas and embraced Catholicism or a secular creed like nationalism. But this conversion, even if sincere, was seldom complete and traces of their original decadent individualism can still be detected in the later political or religious views of these writers."

504. Sweetser, Wesley D. *Arthur Machen*. NY: Twayne, 1964. [TEAS 8]

A critical and biographical study of Machen tracing his literary influences to the Romantics, Poe, Stevenson and Pater, and noting that though he held himself aloof from contemporary literary groups, Machen did share in the conscious rejection of the didactic in literature during the nineties: "Despite the general disparity of mediums, styles, and ways of life, the larger elements of decadence -- intent to shock, emphasis on sensation, and fascination with evil -- are common bonds . . . . The evidence is conclusive that, no matter how independent he felt himself to be, he was still somewhat a product of his age."

505. Sweetser, Wesley D. "Arthur Machen: A Bibliography of Writings About Him," *ELT*, 11 (1968), 1-33.

506. Symons, A.J.A., ed. *An Anthology of 'Nineties' Verse*. London: Mathews and Marrot, 1928. "Introduction," pp. xvii-xxi.

Brief remarks upon the sources (Pater, the religion of art) and contributions ("the elaboration of technique, the enlargement of subject matter") of 1890s verse. Noting the low reputation of nineties poets, suggests that "in this unanimity of disapproval lies the best hope of their future fame."

507. Symons, Arthur. "Editorial Note," *Savoy*, 1 (Jan 1896), 5.

"We have no formulas, and we desire no false unity of form or matter. We have not invented a new point of view. We are not Realists, or Romanticists, or Decadents."

508. Symons, Arthur. "The Decadent Movement in Literature," *Harper's New Monthly Magazine*, 87 (Nov 1893), 866-867.

Argues that given a decadent civilization, literary decadence is one way "of being true to nature." Notes the new movement shares with the Greek and Latin decadence the qualities that mark the end of great periods: "an intense self-consciousness, a restless curiosity in research, an over-subtillizing refinement upon refinement, a spiritual and moral perversity." Impressionism and symbolism are

seen as the two main branches of the movement: both seek "not general truth merely, but *la verité vraie*, the very essence of truth --
the truth of appearances to the senses, of the visible world to the
eyes that see it; and the truth of spiritual things to the spiritual vision." Discusses the contribution of the Goncourts, Mallarmé,
Maeterlinck, Huysmans and Verlaine -- "To fix the last fine shade,
the quintessence of things; to fix it fleetingly; to be a disem-
bodied voice and yet the voice of a human soul: that is the ideal of
Decadence, and it is what Paul Verlaine has achieved." Brief remarks
on decadence in Spain, Holland and Italy; mentions work of Pater and
Henley, a poet who has "come nearer than any other English singer to
what I have called the achievement of Verlaine and the ideal of the
Decadence."

509.   Symons, Arthur. "Modernity in Verse," *Studies in Two
       Literatures*. London: Leonard Smithers, 1897, pp. 186-
       203.

       [Review of Henley's *London Voluntaries* (1893)] "It is one of
the modern discoveries that 'the dignity of the subject' is a mere
figure of speech, and a misleading one." Praises Henley's "poetry
of the disagreeable" for its "eloquence without adjectives"; warns
against loosening the bonds of rhyme as suggested by WEH's experiment with free verse.

510.   Symons, Arthur. "Preface to the Second Edition of
       Silhouettes: Being a Word on Behalf of Patchouli,"
       Studies in Prose and Verse. London: Dent, 1904,
       pp. 279-282. [First pub. Feb 1896]

       "I do not wish to assert that the kind of verse which happened
to reflect certain moods of mine at a certain period of my life is
the best kind of verse in itself, or is likely to seem to me, in
other years, when other moods may have made me their own, the best
kind of verse for my own expression of myself. Nor do I affect to
doubt that the creation of the supreme emotion is a higher form of
art than the reflection of the most exquisite sensation, the evocation of the most magical impression. I claim only an equal liberty
for the rendering of every mood of that valuable and inexplicable
and contradictory creature which we call ourself, of every aspect
under which we are gifted or condemned to apprehend the beauty and
strangeness and curiosity of the visible world."

511.   Symons, Arthur. *The Symbolist Movement in Literature*.
       NY: Dutton, 1958. [First pub. 1899]

       The original edition contained essays on Nerval, Villiers, Rim-
baud, Verlaine, Laforgue, Mallarmé, Huysmans, Maeterlinck and an
introduction in which AS revised his earlier views of symbolism and
decadence: "It pleased some young men in various countries to call
themselves Decadents, with all the thrill of unsatisfied virtue

masquerading as uncomprehended vice. As a matter of fact, the term is in its place only when applied to style . . . . But a movement which in this sense might be called Decadent could but have been a straying aside from the main road of literature . . . . The interlude, of Decadence, diverted the attention of the critics while something more serious was in preparation. That something more has crystallised, for the time, under the form of Symbolism, in which art returns to the one pathway, leading through beautiful things to the eternal beauty." Symbolism is further defined as "an attempt to spiritualise literature, to evade the old bondage of rhetoric, the old bondage of exteriority. Description is banished that beautiful things may be evoked, magically." Concludes by suggesting that symbolist literature may become "itself a kind of religion, with all the duties and responsibilities of the sacred ritual."

512. Symons, Arthur. "Walter Pater: Some Characteristics," *Savoy*, 8 (Dec 1896), 33-41.

"Pater did more than anyone of our time to bring about a more intimate sympathy with some of the subtler aspects of art . . . his influence did much to rescue us from the dangerous moralities, the uncritical enthusiasms and prejudices, of Mr. Ruskin."

513. Sypher, Wylie. *Rococo to Cubism in Art and Literature*. NY: Random House, 1960.

Includes a chapter on art nouveau whose "decadent mannerisms," "loss of weight," neo-rococo lightness, economy of line and "*cloisonnisme*," it is argued, may be found in the work of such writers as Huysmans, Pater, Wilde, Yeats and Housman ("Housman's verse has neatly beaten contours, a stripped and lapidary statement that seems to be functional"). Believes the acceptance of artifice in literature and painting "is from one point of view decadent but from another it is the new formalism toward which all the main streams of the time were flowing."

514. Taylor, John Russell. *The Art Nouveau Book in Britain*. Cambridge, Mass.: MIT Press, 1966.

"British art nouveau is a reaction in favour of spareness and simplicity after the intricacy of what had gone before, while Continental art nouveau is a further elaboration . . . . If Continental art nouveau, like Continental late-Gothic styles of Rococo, can be seen in certain respects a decadent style, British art nouveau is more a reformation, carried out at times, especially on its Arts and Crafts fringes, with almost crusading fervour."

515. Teets, Bruce E. and Helmut E. Gerber, *Joseph Conrad: An Annotated Bibliography of Writings About Him*. Dekalb, Ill.: Northern Illinois Univ. Press, 1970.

516. Temple, Ruth Z. *The Critic's Alchemy: A Study of the Introduction of French Symbolism into England.* NY: Twayne, 1953.

Discussions of Arnold, Swinburne, Symons, Gosse, Moore and others. Urges a revaluation of the standard estimate of decadence, a movement whose role in preparing the way for modernism is emphasized: "If the Decadence helped to shape the genius of the two greatest modern British poets, it also helped to prepare their audience."

517. Temple, Ruth Z. "The Ivory Tower as Lighthouse," *Edwardians and Late Victorians*, ed. Richard Ellmann. NY: Columbia Univ. Press, 1960, pp. 28-49. [English Institute Essays, 1959]

Traces the development of the characteristic emphases of aesthetic criticism -- the ideas of impressionism and the autonomy of art in particular -- and their legacy left to twentieth-century "New Criticism." Stresses the importance of impressionism to the criticism of Pater, Wilde, Moore and Symons: "I think a rather good case might be made out for impressionism as the general label of the new arts and of criticism from the 1870's on."

518. Temple, Ruth Z. "Truth in Labelling: Pre-Raphaelitism, Aestheticism, Decadence, Fin de Siècle," *ELT*, 17 (1974), 201-222.

Declares the "general misuse and misapprehension [of the four terms above] constitutes a scandal in literary history." Citing the "rich chaos" of conflicting meanings, gives trenchant critiques of various attempts at definition, going on to offer "my own view of the distinctions that should properly be made and the historical design that should be drawn." Distinguishes two phases in Pre-Raphaelitism whose later phase had three issues: "(1) the elements of design in painting, stained glass, and book illustration which on one hand affected Beardsley and merged in Art Nouveau; (2) the imaginative handling of mythological subjects which appealed to French Symbolist poets and painters; and (3) in the poetry and painting of Rossetti, especially, and Morris, the strange union of sharp concrete detail with dreamy emblematic vision which is the essence of this late flowering of medievalism, had some influence on Wilde and the fin-de-siècle, and has the best claim to be called Pre-Raphaelite." Believes "fin de siècle" should be restricted to the last decade of the nineteenth century and to certain tendencies in tone, choice of diction and theme. Recommends "aesthetic" be discarded as a label for a literary movement. Finds "decadence" useful as a literary term, believes it should have the same status as symbolism or impressionism: "Decadence exhibits preferences in subject matter -- which reflect the artist's situation and his beliefs -- the city, the man-made, the artificial in preference to the natural (*le fard*, patchouli), what is sordid or trivial rather than what is obviously beautiful or good. Preferences in theme, such as boredom raised to the intensity of spleen . . . disorientation in an alien world, *homo duplex*."

519. Thatcher, David S. *Nietzsche in England 1890-1914:*
The Growth of a Reputation. Toronto: Univ. of Toronto
Press, 1970.

Concerned less with specific instances of "influence" than with
"the way Nietzsche affected English literary and social conscience."
Chapters on English translations, Davidson, Ellis, Yeats, Shaw. N's
influence greatest among artists; his view of life as a dance, aris-
tocratic emphasis, transvaluation of values, revolutionary role of
artist in society, irony, aphorisms and apparent lack of system
especially appealed to writers of the nineties.

520. Thompson, Paul Van Kuykendall. *Francis Thompson: A*
Critical Biography. NY: Gordian, 1973.

Argues that "a concern and conflict over the relation between
religion and poetry form an essential part of the course of his life
and thought." Believes FT felt a tension in himself between aestheticism and the demands of a deeply religious outlook; FT at once despised the "school of form" and was deeply attracted by its delight
in sensory words and images.

521. Thornton, R.K.R. "Dates for the Rhymers' Club, *ELT*,
14 (1971), 49-53.

A response to Beckson and Rutenberg [see #33 and #444] meant to
confirm and to qualify the 1890 dating. Notes the Jan 1891 meeting
described by Horne, Dowson and Johnson represents the "reconstituted"
Rhymers' Club; the group had previously been Celtic in emphasis
(Yeats, Todhunter, Greene, Rolleston, Rhys). "It is probably fairest
to allow the long-accepted dates 1891-1894 to stand as representing
the period when the club had some meaning and importance."

522. Thornton, R.K.R., ed. *Poetry of the 'Nineties.* Harmondsworth, Eng. and Baltimore: Penguin, 1970. "Introduction,"
pp. 15-33.

Without discarding the myth of the nineties, qualifies the
generalizations usually made about the period -- its sensational
"decadents," its muscular "counter-decadents," etc. Notes that
"though it is a critical commonplace to insist on qualifications
of the picture, the simplifications persist," and suggests these
are useful in summarizing elements of nineties history and criticism. Finds common ground for decadents and counter-decadents in
their search for novelty, their determination to catch the exact
nature of the thing described and their belief in the musicality
of verse.

523. Thorp, W. and T.M. Parrott, eds. *Poetry of the Transition, 1850-1914.* NY: Oxford Univ. Press, 1932. "Introduction," pp. xxi-xli.

See #386.

524. Tierney, Frank M. "The Causes of the Revival of the Rondeau in Nineteenth Century England," *Revue de l'Université d'Ottawa,* 43 (1973), 96-113.

Argues that the "heavy moral overtones in the poetry and prose produced by many English writers and the dominance of blank verse in English poetry caused a reaction which produced the aesthetic movement: English parnassianism." Discussions of Dobson and Gosse.

525. Tierney, Frank M. "Sir Edmund Gosse and the Revival of the French Fixed Forms in the Age of Transition," *ELT,* 14 (1971), 191-199.

Considers EG as a major influence on the revival and includes and analysis of Gosse's "manifesto," "A Plea for Certain Exotic Forms of Verse" (1877). Believes EG's intention was to check the excesses of the blank verse imitators of Tennyson and Browning.

526. Tillotson, Geoffrey. "Ernest Dowson," *Essays in Criticism and Research.* Cambridge: Cambridge Univ. Press, 1942, pp. 153-156.

"Like all good poets he epitomizes signficant developments in the poetical history." Dowson's loosening of poetic rhythm by means of the alexandrine influenced Yeats and Eliot.

527. Tillotson, Geoffrey. "Pater, Mr. Rose, and the 'Conclusion' of *The Renaissance,*" *E&S,* 32 (1946), 44-60.

Suggests that Mallock's satiric portrait of Pater as Mr. Rose in *The New Republic* influenced WP's decision to withdraw the "Conclusion" from the second edition. [See also #73, #455 and #469]

528. Tindall, William York. *Forces in Modern British Literature, 1885-1956.* NY: Vintage, 1956. Rev. Ed.

Believes there "is reason to call contemporary literature the literature of romantic decadence . . . . The allusiveness of Eliot, the artificiality of Edith Sitwell, the transcendentalism of Huxley, the complexity of Joyce and Dylan Thomas, the deliquescence of Virginia Woolf, are not only romantic but, compared with customary strangeness, strange." The decadents of the nineties merely "differ from their successors in being aware of their condition and proud of it." Includes chapters on the effects of reactionary philosophies on

literature, on disenchantment and fantasy, on the influence of French
naturalism, on the search for unity and religious authority, on the
influence of symbolism.

529. Townsend, J. Benjamin. *John Davidson: Poet of Armageddon.*
New Haven: Yale Univ. Press, 1961.

Sees Davidson as having "bridged all these movements [i.e.
activism, imperialism, impressionism, social realism, symbolism] and
yet emerged with a philosophy and style that are his own."

530. Townsend, J. Benjamin. "The Yellow Book," *PLC*, 16 (1955),
101-103.

A series of telegrams acquired by the Princeton University Library relating to Beardsley's forced departure from the *Yellow Book*
makes it "clear that [Lane, then in America] was inadequately in-
formed of the facts and that he acted on the advice of a nervous sub-
ordinate and under pressure from several of his leading authors with
a misguided sense of righteousness."

531. Turner, Paul. "John Davidson: The Novels of a Poet,"
Cambridge Journal, 5 (1952), 499-504.

Argues that JD's novels and stories "deserve more attention
than either the poet or his public were willing to give them; first
because their unique blend of wit and fantasy gives them an intrinsic value; secondly, because they express a vital component of Davidson's personality which was essential to the proper operation of his
poetic faculty." Believes that the fiction, with its wit and humanity, was an antidote to JD's tendencies towards the humorlessness and
megalomania that surfaced so disastrously in his life and work after
1900.

532. Turquet-Milnes, G. *The Influence of Baudelaire in France
and England.* London: Constable, 1913.

Chapters on Swinburne, O'Shaughnessy, Wilde and "contemporary
writers" (e.g. Machen, Yeats, Moore and Lord Alfred Douglas).

533. Tye, J.R. *"Malleus Maleficorum:* The Reverend W.F. Barry,
D.D., 1849-1930," *ELT*, 16 (1973), 43-56.

Studies the critical views of this vituperative foe of decadence and French literary influence. Concludes that "the rigour of
his dogmatic position was a wholesome corrective to the criticism of
the more flaccid adherents of Walter Pater and Oscar Wilde, and
passed as an inheritance to . . . G.K. Chesterton, Charles Williams
and C.S. Lewis."

534. Tye, J.R. *Periodicals of the Nineties: A Checklist of Literary Periodicals Published in the British Isles at Longer than Fortnightly Intervals, 1890-1899.* Oxford: Oxford Bibliographical Society, 1974.

The main criteria for inclusion in this list of 138 periodicals were two: "a serious interest in literature *per se*, if only occasional, and, secondly, the presence of original writing of some value or literary significance." Also includes lists of publishers, printers and editors.

535. Tynan, Katharine. "A Catholic Poet," *Dublin Review*, 141 (1907), 327-344.

A worshipful account by a co-religionist the great value of which resides in its publication of Johnson's notes on some contemporary poets: Watson, Davidson, Le Gallienne, Symons, Thompson, John Gray among others.

536. Tynan, Katharine. *Memories.* London: Nash and Grayson, 1924.

Includes a brief hagiography of "our Saint Lionel." "The little Revival of the Nineties comprised a great many people who aimed at being French; but they did it heavily, reminding one of the respectable English one has seen rollicking at a French watering place. Only the Celt and the Latin can be wicked without being self-conscious."

537. Tytell, John. "Frederick Rolfe and His Age: A Study in Literary Eccentricity," *Studies in the Twentieth Century*, No. 10 (Fall 1972), 69-89.

Urges a more disinterested criticism of FR than he has yet received. The facts of his life "serve to separate him from the aesthetic, "decadent," *Yellow Book* tradition." Examines FR's fiction from the point of view of style, the characteristics of his typical hero and the relation between Rolfe's psychological needs and the romances he wrote. Concludes FR anticipates "the major motivation for the novel in our time. His use of his own life and personality can reveal much about the misuse of the autobiographical impulse in modern fiction."

538. Underwood, V.P. *Verlaine et l'Angleterre.* Paris: Nizet, 1956.

A chronological study of the role of England in PV's life and art. Gives a full account of the 1893-94 lectures in London and Oxford, emphasizing personal rather than literary relations with English writers of the period. [In French]

539. Untermeyer, Louis. *Modern British Poetry*. NY: Harcourt
     Brace, 1921.

     Notes seven characteristic tendencies of post-1885 literature:
(1) the decay of Victorianism and the growth of a purely decorative
art; (2) the rise and decline of the aesthetic philosophy; (3) the
muscular influence of Henley; (4) the Celtic revival; (5) Kipling
and the ascendancy of mechanism in art; (6) Masefield and the return
of the rhymed narrative; (7) the Georgian and war poets.

540. Urban, Wilbur M. "Arthur Symons and Impressionism,"
     Atlantic Monthly, 114 (1914), 384-393.

     Unsympathetic assessment of AS's impressionistic sketches that
notes that for all his variety of scene, "there is a persistent mo-
notony of realization" which can lead to "a vicious abstractionism,
turning realities into appearances, a lust for realization moving
about in worlds unrealized. To this unsophisticated use of the metaphysical instinct the philosophy of impressionism naturally gravi-
tates. And the end thereof is decadence. Frustration of this instinct for the real is of necessity followed by perversion and steri-
lization of the emotions."

541. Van Bever, Pierre. "Signification du 'décadentisme',"
     RLV, 34 (1968), 366-372.

     Discusses the meaning of the term for French symbolists and
their successors in France and Italy. Considers its use as a polemi-
cal nom de guerre before "symbolisme" became the movement's defini-
tive name, its possibilities for irony, its identification with the
avant-garde concern with language as expressive rather than communi-
cative. Notes that the term continues useful in Italy, though im-
precisely defined; suggests that the term may be given a second life
in France thanks to Marxist polemic. [In French]

542. Van Doren, Carl and Mark Van Doren. *American and British
     Literature since 1890*. NY and London: Century, 1925.

     Stresses the intense intellectual ferment of the period and its
reaction against Tennysonian practice in verse. Finds "decadent"
not necessarily a term suggesting diminution of power; rather, the
term "more specifically and perhaps more justly given to a group of
effete and exotic poets who were bent upon destroying as swiftly and
insolently as they could the old proprieties which they considered
hostile to the free spirit of their art."

543. Van Roosbroeck, G.L. *The Legend of the Decadents*.
     NY: Institut des Etudes Françaises, 1927.

     Argues that the French "decadents" of the 1880s were poseurs and self-parodists whose claims were not only taken seriously at the time but continue to confirm bourgeois critics in their opinion of modern poetry as "decadent." Includes chapters on Rimbaud's "Sonnet des Voyelles," which, it is argued, offers itself neither as a poetic program nor as a proof of mental disease, and on *A Rebours*, which is read as "a caricature of the New Esthetes of the Eighties." Insists that artistic decadence "can have but one meaning: It is the stereotyped and weakened repetition of a superior form of art . . . . The notion of decadence includes, esthetically, the notion of imitation."

544. Vessey, David. "Arthur Machen's *The Hill of Dreams:* A Novel of the 'Nineties," *ContempR*, 223 (1973), 124-128.

Analysis of Machen's "masterpiece," a "paradigm of the literary trends which we associate with the 'nineties." Finds AM's portrayal of his hero "an act of self-dramatisation"; "Lucian Taylor is possessed by a demonic urge to self-destruction which may be traced in the lives of such writers as Verlaine, Swinburne, Lionel Johnson and indeed Oscar Wilde himself."

545. Vinciguerra, M. *Romantici e decadenti inglese*. Foligno: F. Campitelli, 1926.

Includes chapters on Poe, Wilde, Hardy, Stevenson, Moore and Synge. [In Italian]

546. Waterhouse, Keith and Guy Deghy. *Café Royal: Ninety Years of Bohemia*. London: Hutchinson, 1956.

See #126.

547. Waugh, Arthur. "Reticence in Fiction," *Yellow Book*, 1 (April 1894), 201-219.

Argues for a literature that adheres to the "moral idea," a poetry that is a criticism of life, a golden mean between "the excess of effeminacy" and the "excess of virile brutality" he perceives in the impressionism and realism of contemporary writers. [See #106]

548. Waugh, Arthur. *Tradition and Change: Studies in Contemporary Literature*. London: Chapman and Hall, 1919.

Mainly concerned with Georgian artists, but does include essays on Johnson and Symons. A contemporary of LJ's at New College, Oxford, Waugh stresses Johnson's isolation from the main tendencies of the period, a time characterized by a "restless stirring of literary and spiritual interest" in "emancipation." Believes the nineties "were actually the seed-time of the most characteristic literary harvest of to-day . . . . There never was more secretly alive with revolution than that apparently weary period."

549. Weeks, Donald. *Corvo: Saint or Madman?* NY: McGraw-Hill, 1972.

A biographical account whose extreme partisanship demands of readers sympathies equally Corvine.

550. Weintraub, Joseph. "Andrew Lang: Critic of Romance," *ELT*, 18 (1975), 5-15.

Studies Lang's critical writings on romance: "Lang, with his background in anthropology and folklore and his consequent perception of the relationship of romance to myth, legend, and epic had the tools, perhaps as well-developed as any critic of his time, to create an aesthetic of romance, one that would be based on the primal dreams, fears, and desires of man, one that would account for the romantic element in contemporary authors, such as Dickens, as well as the source and appeal of traditional romance." Concludes Lang failed because he lacked serious belief in his own abilities, in criticism, and in contemporary fiction.

551. Weintraub, Stanley, ed. *The Savoy: Nineties Experiment.* University Park, Pa. and London: Penn State Univ. Press, 1966. "'The Beardsley': An Introduction," pp. xiii-xliv.

Brief account of the founding, contributors and career of the magazine whose appeal was "not to Decadence, or Naturalism or Aestheticism -- its one appeal was to the cult of personality -- Beardsley."

552. Weintraub, Stanley, ed. *The Yellow Book: Quintessence of the Nineties.* NY: Doubleday-Anchor, 1964. "Introduction -- *The Yellow Book*: A Reappraisal," pp. vii-xxv.

Views the nineties as a transitional period; the *YB* is the nineties, publishing some of the most representative work of the period; includes a brief,anecdotal account of the magazine's publishing history. The *Yellow Book* "responsibly served the transition from Swinburne-Wilde decadence and Victorian reticence to the artistic use of realism."

553. Welby, T. Earle. *Arthur Symons: A Critical Study.* London: Philpot, 1925.

Includes chapters on early poems, later poems, tragedies and critical writings. Stresses the interest of AS's poems, particularly the later poems. Depreciates the importance of "the little decadence of the nineties": "With its curiosity, it concern to capture passing impressions and moods, its desire to be modern, to accept as material the artificiality of modern life, he was in sympathy; of the cruder parts of its moral error he was the severest critic."

554. Wellek, René. *A History of Modern Criticism, 1750-1950.*
      Vol. 4, *The Later Nineteenth Century.* New Haven and London:
      Yale Univ. Press, 1965.

      Illuminating if unsympathetic discussions of the works and
critical assumptions of Swinburne, Wilde, Symonds, Pater, Saintsbury
and Shaw. "Much of what is considered 'aestheticism' in England is
simply the defense of the artist against the arrogant moral preten-
tions of his critics, who forbad the treatment of whole areas of
human experience and feelings."

555. Wellek, René. "Walter Pater's Literary Theory and Criticism,"
      VS, 1 (1957-58), 29-46.

      Despite the fame of the "Mona Lisa" passage and the "Conclu-
sion" to *The Renaissance*, Pater's critical method not primarily impressionistic as has been maintained. Includes cogent discussion of
Pater's major aesthetic ideas. Finds that none of Pater's work es-
caped the limits of aestheticism with "its hectic cult of 'Beauty'
(a very narrow and exclusive type of beauty), its Alexandrian eclecticism, which made it impossible for the age to create a style of its
own and which encouraged an historical masquerade."

556. West, Paul. *"The Dome:* An Aesthetic Periodical of the
      1890's," *Book Collector*, 6 (1957), 160-169.

      Brief account of the magazine devoted to all the arts, pub-
lished March 1897-June 1900, at first in quarterly and later in monthly issues. Contributors included Yeats, Symons, Arnold Dolmetsch,
Roger Fry, Frederick Delius, Sharp, Gleeson White, Thompson, Sturge
Moore. Its editor, Ernest J. Oldmeadow, recruited them or discussed
literary affairs with them at Alice Meynell's at-homes in Palace
Court House.

557. West, Paul. "A Note on the 1890s," *English*, 12 (1958), 54-57.

      Argues that the tone of petulance and weary contempt heard in
the *Yellow Book* and the *Savoy* is "the perturbation of young men who
witnessed the decreasing prestige, and foresaw the eventual calling
into question, of the social class from which they had stemmed and to
which they appealed." The campaign on behalf of taste conducted in
those pages thus was done for its own sake and not for the sake of
those the writers would improve and this is the "real decadence for
which the decade seems original."

558. West, Paul. "Pater and the Tribulations of Taste," *UTQ*,
      27 (1957-58), 424-432.

      Urges that Pater's reputation has been unfairly hampered by a
prejudice that views his works as tending to discredit morality;

rather, Pater's real insistence was always upon the "singular im-
portance of art." Critics have too long settled for a version of
Pater's thought derived entirely from the notorious passages of *The
Renaissance*; insists that Pater must not be studied piecemeal.

559. Weygandt, Cornelius. *The Time of Yeats: English Poetry of
Today Against an American Background.* NY and London: Apple-
ton-Century, 1937.

Chapters on the American influences on modernism, on Henley,
Stevenson, Davidson, on the continuation of traditional Victorian
poetry in Bridges, Watson, Binyon and others, on the Empire poets,
Kipling and Newbolt, on the decadents, Symons and Dowson, and on the
Irish Literary Renaissance of Yeats, Johnson and Irish women poets.
Includes some personal reminiscences.

560. Weygandt, Cornelius. *Tuesdays at Ten: A Garnering From
the Talks of Thirty Years on Poets, Dramatists and Essayists.* Philadelphia: Univ. of Pennsylvania Press, 1928.

Included among these biographical and appreciative lectures --
first given at the University of Pennsylvania and heard by Ezra
Pound -- are essays on Yeats, Johnson, Thompson and Austin Dobson.

561. White, Terence de Vere, ed. *A Leaf from the "Yellow Book":
The Correspondence of George Egerton.* London: Richards,
1958.

Biographical account of the plainspoken author of *Keynotes*,
one of Lane's first best-sellers. Her vogue was short-lived -- she
was a one-book author but, even more than this, her gabble, Shaw
tells us, undid her; no one ever wanted to meet her twice.

562. Whittington-Egan, Richard and Geoffrey Smerdon. *The Quest
of the Golden Boy: The Life and Letters of Richard LeGal-
lienne.* London: Unicorn, 1960.

A prolonged and somewhat poetic account of RLG's life and
literary career, including detailed, though not always factually accurate, descriptions of his relationships with the Rhymers, John
Lane and other literary figures of the period.

563. Wick, Peter A., ed. *The Turn of a Century: 1885-1910: Art
Nouveau and Jugendstil Books.* Cambridge, Mass.: Department
of Printing and Graphic Arts, Houghton Library, Harvard
University, 1970.

"We accept the Nineties as a renascent period, despite its
many extravagances and high jinks, a period of mental activity and

quickening imagination, a period when the quality of living and environment was under scrutiny, a period of not only art-for-art's-sake, a *belle époque*, but nonetheless compounded with a certain malaise, a feverish restlessness and confused heterodoxy. Among that intellectual and cultural elite, the *arbiter elegantiarum* of the age, the dominant concern was mode of life, or 'life style,' as we say today."

564. Wiegner, Kathleen. "French Symbolism in England: 1890-1900," *Wisconsin Studies in Literature*, 9 (1969), 50-57.

Discusses the English view of French symbolism which depended almost exclusively upon the example of Verlaine for its emphasis on "self-consciousness, indirect communication, the analogy with music and the decadent mood." Concludes that French symbolism did not deeply affect English poetic practice during the nineties because the effects it pursued -- simplicity, musicality and magic -- "had remained a part of the history of English poetry."

565. Wilcox, John. "The Beginning of *l'art pour l'art*," *JAAC*, 11 (1952-53), 360-377.

Examines the significance of the concept to French writers from 1804-48.

566. Wiley, Paul L. and Harold Orel, eds. *British Poetry 1880-1920: Edwardian Voices*. NY: Appleton-Century-Crofts, 1969. "Introduction," pp. xxix-xliii.

Would reclaim the last two decades of the nineteenth century as "Edwardian" as well as reject the traditional, conservative stereotype of Georgian poetry. Finds these forty years of poetry characterized by (1) an indifference to the established themes of Victorian poetry; (2) technical variation of accepted forms without bold experimentation; (3) a romantic, lyrical, civilized tone and limited religious seriousness. Believes this "pre-modern" poetry with its "relaxed yet perceptive observation of everyday occurences in all their variety" is a revolt both "against the moralistic rhetoric of the Victorians and against the kind of moralism implicit in the retreat of the Aesthetes to the bar or the divan." Sees its aesthetic as primarily impressionist rather than imagist or intellectual: "it is useful to recall that Impressionist porcedures aimed to stimulate visual or sensory acuity by immediate reaction to verbal patterns rather than to promote the exercise of intellectual association by means of images."

567. Williams, Harold. *Modern English Writers: Being a Study of Imaginative Literature, 1890-1914*. London: Sidgwick and Jackson, 1918.

Believes Victorianism died ca. 1890; the succeeding decade shaped by four new influences: the aestheticism of Wilde, the aims of the *Yellow Book* and the *Savoy*, the Henley circle and the Celtic Renaissance. Chapters on "poets of the transition" (Wilde, Austin, Lang, Bridges, Watts-Dunton, Gosse, Blunt, Meynell), "new forces" (Symons, Davidson, Henley, Kipling, Watson, Dowson, Sharp, Thompson), "the poetesses" (Laurence Hope, Marriot-Watson, "Michael Field"), on Irish poets and playwrights, on intellectual and literary drama in England, and on the novel, including a chapter on "women novelists."

568. Williams, Orlo. *"The Yellow Book,"* *London Mercury*, 2 (1920), 567-577.

A rather coy reminiscence of the periodical and its period ("The yellow principle, the original crude but genuine mustard which had so blistered the critics, had given out, and the innocuous saffron that had taken its place held no vitality").

569. Williams, Raymond. *Culture and Society, 1780-1950.* Garden City, NY: Doubleday, 1960.

Studies the idea of "culture" and its relationship to economic and political change. Views the period 1880-1914 as an "interregnum" between Victorian and modern periods: "It is not the period of the masters, of Coleridge or of George Eliot. Nor yet is it the period of our contemporaries, of writers who address themselves, in our kind of language, to the common problems that we recognize." Includes treatment of Gissing, Shaw, Hulme. Sees the "new aesthetics" of the eighties and nineties as "little more than a restatement of an attitude which properly belongs to the first generation of the Romantics." Discussions of Pater, Whistler ("Pater vulgarized") and Wilde (he, rather than Pater, is "the first of the minor inheritors of Arnold").

570. Williamson, C. "The Decadents," *Search Quarterly*, 3 (1933), 56-69.

A rambling, sententious excursus on various aspects of British decadence and decadents: "most of their work will be forgotten, but there will remain a few lyrics gratefully remembered, not, indeed, as the crystallisation of a philosophy of life, but as the finished expression of a morbid mood which many men have passed through on their way to moral health and spiritual sanity."

571. Wilson, Angus. *The Naughty Nineties.* London: Eyre Methuen, 1976.

A chatty picture-book social history of the decade emphasizing its love of pleasure, luxury and scandal. Concludes that the

"Decadents, of course, were the heirs of the Romantic Movement that, steadily working within the healthy body of Victorianism, finally rotted it to pieces. But, perhaps the whole of the Nineties represents the triumph of one prominent strand of romantic thought -- the cult of childhood. However different their purposes, however serious their aims, there is about Rhodes and Barnato, Wilde and Beardsley, Shaw and Wells, Henley and Kipling, a boyishness at once extreme and at times maddening."

572. Wilson, Edmund. *Axel's Castle: A Study in the Imaginative Literature of 1870-1930.* NY: Scribner's, 1931.

Examines the influence of symbolism upon the work of Yeats, Valéry, Eliot, Proust, Joyce and Stein in the belief that "the literary history of our time is to a great extent that of the development of Symbolism and of its fusion or conflict with Naturalism." Takes Villiers' hero as the type of world-renouncing dreamer of the symbolists; their characteristic tendency "to intimate rather than speak plainly and [their] cult of the unique personal point of view are symptomatic of the extent to which they found themselves out of touch with their fellows and thrown in upon their own private imaginations." Predicts that the writers of Axel's school, "though we shall continue to admire them as masters, will no longer serve us as guides."

573. Wilson, Edmund. "Late Violets from the Nineties," *Dial*, 75 (1923), 387-390.

In a review of novels by Van Vechten and Firbank notes that "the school which began with Baudelaire and is now dissolving with Arthur Symons derived its prime vitality and force from its extreme conviction of sin. The decadents talked much about 'paganism' but their point of view was anything but pagan: it was a reaction against Victorian Christianity by people who were still Victorians and Christians."

574. Wilson, Jean. "The 'Nineties' Movement in Poetry: Myth or Reality?" *YES*, 1 (1971), 160-174.

Myth for the most part. Only Dowson and Symons among the major representative writers (and these are not truly representative of the period that was much more heterogeneous than most critics have been willing to admit) can be considered "ninetyish"; points out that a movement can scarcely consist of two poets. "The only possible sense in which the so-called 'decadents' could be seen as the central 'movement' is in their common rejection of 'Tennysonian ideals'."

575. Wimsatt, William K., Jr. and Cleanth Brooks. *Literary Criticism: A Short History.* NY: Random House, 1957.

Chapter on art for art's sake ("Art for art's sake may be seen
as a kind of aesthetico-scientific detachment, an intellectual reaction against the romantic letting down of the hair and flood of personal emotion") examines sources of the notion of art as a terminal
value in German idealism, in Poe and in Baudelaire: "With Baudelaire,
the main fight for 'art' in 19th-century France was won. After him,
the simply aesthetic assertion fritters away into *Parnassien* formalism, the exoticism, the intricate versification of Leconte de Lisle
or Théodore de Banville. The main line of French poetry and poetics,
with Verlaine and even more with Mallarmé, advances into subtler
themes of musical intimation, ironic finesse, and symbol -- above all
else, symbol. The simpler campaign of art for art's sake during the
second half of the 19th century is carried with most flourish into
the new territory of England." Critical ideas of British aestheticism discussed with special reference to Wilde, whose elevation of
criticism to an art is seen as closing the circle of didactic and
aesthetic theory. Thus Wilde and Arnold may be perceived as "Victorian brothers. Both entertained not only a low opinion of the English mind but a vision of art and art criticism as free activities
which were destined to bring about man's salvation from the bondage
of philosophy and religion."

576. Wingfield-Stratford, Esmé. "Panjandrums and Decadents,"
    Bookman (NY), 75 (1932), 657-663.

    "To contemporaries, it seemed like the beginning of a modern
Renaissance, a time of higher values and more exacting standards."

577. Wingfield-Stratford, Esmé. *The Victorian Sunset*.
    NY: Morrow, 1932.

    A breezily written social history of the years 1870-1901 which
includes chapters on the eighties and nineties. 1880s viewed as a
time of transition in which aestheticism had ceased to be a craze,
a time of cultivated intensity. After Tennyson's death in 1892,
everyone was conscious of living in a new age, a time of boundless
experimentation; concludes "lack of inhibition was the real beset-
ting sin of the Naughty Nineties."

578. Winters, Ivor. *Primitivism and Decadence*. NY: Arrow, 1937.

    Unlike the primitive poet, whose work is characterized by
vigorous form and limited range, the decadent poet displays " a fine
sensitivity to language and . . . may have a very wide scope but
[his] work is incomplete formally . . . or is somewhat but not too
seriously weakened by a vice of feeling." Decadent poetry requires
a mature poetry as a background. Declares the decadent poet "may
embody the most economical method of recovery for an old and rich
tradition in a state of collapse, for he offers all the machinery
of a mature and complicated poetry." Cites Pound, Williams and Hopkins as poets who became decadent through self-limitation.

131

579. Witemeyer, Hugh. *The Poetry of Ezra Pound: Forms and Renewal, 1908-1920.* Berkeley and Los Angeles: Univ. of California Press, 1969.

Includes discussion of late nineteenth-century aesthetic poets and decadence and EP's debt to both; believes Pound abandoned this poetry of essences, ecstasy and dreams because of its insubstantiality.

580. Witt, Robert. "Kipling as Representative of the Counter-Aesthetes," *Kipling Journal,* 371 (June 1970), 6-9.

Finds late nineteenth-century literature divided between the decadent aesthetes whose work was escapist and "permeated by a morbid self-pity" and the counter-aesthetes "who took a 'muscular, hair-on-the-chest' approach to life." Citing various works as proof of RK's anti-aesthete attitude, concludes "there is a muscularity about his work which contrasts with the morbidity of the aesthetes . . . . [Kipling is] in every way the antithesis of the decadent aesthetes."

581. Wolff, Joseph. *George Gissing: An Annotated Bibliography of Writings About Him.* Dekalb, Ill.: Northern Illinois Univ. Press, 1974.

582. Woolf, Cecil and Brocard Sewell, eds. *Corvo, 1860-1960: A Collection of Essays by Various Hands to Commemorate the Centenary of the Birth of Fr. Rolfe, Baron Corvo.* Aylesford, Eng.: St. Albert's Press, 1961.

Includes essays on Rolfe's personality, friends and various works.

583. Woolf, James D. *Edmund Gosse.* NY: Twayne, 1972. [TEAS 117]

Analytical evaluation of EG's writing, concentrating on representative criticism. Includes chapters on the life, emphasizing religious and literary setting, on Gosse's poetry, with a brief look at the novels and dramas, on his theory and method of criticism, on applications of this method in a wide range of critical writings, and on EG's style.

584. Woolf, James D. "Sir Edmund Gosse: An Annotated Bibliography of Writings About Him," *ELT,* 11 (1968), 126-172.

Includes a brief introduction.

585. Woolf, James D. "Vers de Société and Decadent Poetry: Descriptive Comments on Continuity," *ELT,* 7 (1964), 13.

Notes several connecting links: Old French forms, color images,
epicureanism, funambulism and art for art's sake.

586. Worth, George J. "The English 'Maupassant' School of the
    1890's: Some Reservations," *MLN*, 72 (1957), 337-340.

    Questions the usefulness of the notion of a "Maupassant school"
when such a construct obscures differences among Dowson, Crackanthorpe, Egerton, Harland, Street, etc. and neglects these writers'
ambivalent reactions to M. Despite "undeniable resemblances," finds
the English writers "not in harmony with the spirit of Maupassant's
oeuvre."

587. Wright, Cuthbert. "Out of Harm's Way: Some Notes on the
    Esthetic Movement of the 'Nineties," *Bookman (NY)*, 70
    (1929-30). 234-243.

    A hostile view of a literary and artistic movement "at present
more dead than the dodo." Concedes "we who perhaps comprehend better the derivative affectations of the 'nineties can say what we
like, but to the men of the period it seemed like a new world."

588. Wright, Samuel. "Richard Charles Jackson," *AntigR*,
    1 (1971), 81-92.

    Relates the peculiar life and fortunes of a tangential and
eccentric figure of the period whose very dubious claim to have been
the model for Marius the Epicurean convinced Pater's first biographer.
Includes a checklist of works by Jackson.

589. Wyndham, Violet. *The Sphinx and Her Circle: A Biographical
    Sketch of Ada Leverson, 1862-1933.* NY: Vanguard, 1963.

    A short anecdotal account of AL by her daughter, focussing on
her friendship with Wilde during the 1890s and that with the Sitwells
during the 1920s. Includes three previously published Leverson
sketches of Wilde at the time of his trial.

590. Yeats, William Butler. *Autobiography*. NY: Macmillan, 1965.

    Includes richly evocative and immensely influential memoirs of
his life in London during the late 1880s and early 1890s, an account
first published in 1922. Yeats's indelible portraits of members of
the "tragic generation" have troubled their biographers ever after.
Treats the period as a symbolic passage in his own vale of poetic
soul-making: "Why should men, who spoke their opinions in low voices,
as though they feared to disturb the readers in some ancient library,
and timidly as though they knew that all subjects had long since been
explored, all questions long since decided upon in books whereon the

dust settled -- live lives of such disorder and seek to rediscover
in verse the syntax of impulsive common life? Was it that we lived
in what is called 'an age of transition' and so lacked coherence, or
did we but pursue antithesis?"

591. Yeats, William Butler. "The Autumn of the Body," *Essays and
      Introductions*. NY: Macmillan, 1961, pp. 189-194. [First pub.
      1898]

      An almost joyfully apocalyptical essay that predicts a new his-
torical phase and a new mode of writing, a poetry at once spiritual
and unemphatic that would continue the struggle against externality,
"a poetry of essences, separated one from another in little and intense poems": "I see, indeed, in the arts of every country those
faint lights and faint colours and faint energies which many call
'the decadence,' and which I, because I believe that the arts lie
dreaming of things to come, prefer to call the autumn of the body."

592. Yeats, William Butler. "Modern Poetry: A Broadcast,"
      Essays and Introductions. NY: Macmillan, 1961,
      pp. 491-508.

      First given in 1936, this talk suggests WBY's persistent sense
of identity with his companions of the Cheshire Cheese; "even two
years ago . . . I should have named three or four poets and said
there was nobody else who mattered." Reminiscences of the Rhymers
include remarks on their pursuit of intensity, their ambitious unam-
bitiousness, their preference for small forms, for purity, their
hatred of rhetoric.

593. Yeats, William Butler, ed. *The Oxford Book of Modern
      Verse, 1892-1935*. NY: Oxford Univ. Press, 1936. "Intro-
      duction," pp. v-xlii.

      An essential if highly idiosyncratic interpretation of fin de
siècle literary history, stressing Pater's revolutionary importance,
the need for tradition and ritual, the pursuit of purity, the appeal
of Catullus, the Jacobean writers, Verlaine and Baudelaire to the
young poets of the 1890s: "The revolt against Victorianism meant to
the young poet a revolt against irrelevant descriptions of nature, the
scientific and moral discursiveness of *In Memoriam* . . . the political eloquence of Swinburne, the psychological curiosity of Browning,
and the poetical diction of everybody."

594. Yeats, William Butler. "The Rhymers' Club," *Letters to the
      New Island*, ed. Horace Reynolds. Cambridge, Mass.: Harvard
      Univ. Press, 1934, pp. 142-148. [First written April 1892]

      "The writers who belong to it resemble each other in but one
thing: they all believe that the deluge of triolets and rondeaus has

passed away, and that we must look once more upon the world with
serious eyes and set to music -- each according to his lights -- the
deep soul of humanity." Discussions of Symons and Davidson.

595. Yohannan, John D. "The Fin de Siècle Cult of FitzGerald's
      Rubaiyat of Omar Khayyam," *RNL*, 2 (1971), 74-91.

      FitzGerald's work inspired a cult and an anti-cult. Concludes
that "the explanation of the extraordinary appeal of the poem to
readers of all sorts may be found in an area bounded on one side by
high art, on another by pop culture, but on the other two sides trail-
ing off into a no-man's land of unsolved anthropological problems."

596. Zabel, Morton D. "The Thinking of the Body: Yeats in the
      Autobiographies," *SoR*, 7 (1941-42), 562-590.

      Believes the nineties experimental curiosity "renewed the re-
sources of art and thought, enriched the possibilities of the creative life, repudiated the apologetic Victorian conformity of the artist that had stultified emotion and thought alike . . . and its personal tragedies and air of impending disaster, issuing from the surrender of personal identity to sensation, flux, and a progressive demoralization of the spirit made the necessity of a reassertion of
will and choice unmistakable." Finds that the artists of the period
"were exorbitantly and histrionically aware that they were living in
an age of transition, of disrupted tradition and comflicting impulse;
their lives dramatized to the point of moral dereliction and nihilism
the tension of oppositions which they felt to be peculiar to the or-
deal of modern sensibility." Yeats, viewing their example, was "com-
pelled, not to abuse the sense of 'transition' by formulating the
theory of irresponsibility, which is the usual mark of such creative
periods as the Nineties, but to resolve antithesis in decision, in
moral choice, in a conception of man and of history that looks beyond transition to the immutable laws of nature and of man."

597. Zagona, Helen G. *The Legend of Salomé and the Principle
      of Art for Art's Sake*. Geneva: Droz, 1960.

      Chapters on Heine, Flaubert, Laforgue, Wilde and minor treat-
ments -- including painting -- of the legend. Finds the subject
"lent itself most effectively to the expression of artistic revulsion
at the excessively utilitarian preoccupations of an era when the
values of the bourgeoisie were seen to be overrunning the sacred
domain or art."

598. Ziegler, Arthur P., Jr. "*The Dome* and Its Editor-Publisher:
      An Exploration," *ABC*, 15, vii (1965), 19-21.

      A brief account of E.J. Oldmeadow whose periodical was devoted
to the arts of literature, music, architecture and graphics and

published Rothenstein, Laurence Housman, Yeats, Sharp, Symons, Sturge Moore and Roger Fry among others.

599. Ziff, Larzer. *The American 1890s: Life and Times of a Lost Generation*. NY: Viking, 1966.

Includes a chapter on the galvanizing effect of the *Yellow Book* on American little magazines.

INDEX

Numbers refer to bibliographical items.

Activism, 42, 76, 115, 446

Aesthetes, Aestheticism, Aesthetic Movement, Art for Art's Sake, 1, 6, 15, 18, 21, 31, 32, 40, 51, 75, 87, 89, 97, 110, 117, 128, 130, 139, 141, 159, 163, 164, 176, 188, 196, 201, 224, 230, 256, 262, 263, 283, 319, 332, 340, 351, 368, 379, 380, 391, 392, 396, 407, 415, 431, 436, 441, 452, 466, 474, 476, 518, 565, 587, 597

Androgyne, 51, 81, 131

Anthologies, 8, 31, 48, 119, 132, 190, 248, 257, 273, 364, 386, 422, 477, 480, 482, 483, 484, 506, 522, 551, 552, 566

Art and interart analogies, 18, 19, 209, 270, 271, 286, 344, 397, 399, 442, 476, 501, 513

Art for Art's Sake. *See* Aestheticism.

Artist-novel. *See* Künstlerroman.

"Artistic" prose. *See* Prose, "artistic."

Arnold, Matthew, 128, 142, 234

Austin, Alfred, 108

Barlas, John, 322, 324, 451

Beardsley, Aubrey, 26, 51, 57, 138, 233, 292, 303, 340, 397, 413

Beerbohm, Max, 161, 214, 223, 298, 433

Bennett, Arnold, 42

Binyon, Laurence, 475

Bodley Head, The, 69, 242, 267, 335, 372

Book design, 68, 69, 372, 514, 563

Carpenter, Edward, 50

Catholicism and the Catholic literary revival, 9, 137, 157, 387, 457

Celtic Revival, 13, 60, 99, 331, 400, 449

Conrad, Joseph, 193, 287, 440

Corvo, Baron. *See* Rolfe, Frederick.

Crackanthorpe, Hubert, 236, 239, 393

Criticism, literary, 71, 112, 199, 216, 222, 231, 256, 284, 328, 356, 431, 463, 467, 488, 500, 517, 533, 550, 554, 575

Custance, Olive, 251, 459

Dance and the dancer, 4, 169, 198, 207, 229, 290, 291

Dandy, the, and dandyism, 223, 298, 348, 490

Davidson, John, 312, 314, 317, 318, 401, 483, 529, 531

Decadence and decadents, 12, 17, 19, 27, 28, 31, 39, 61, 62, 72, 74, 75, 84, 94, 96, 97, 107, 123, 135, 136, 144, 146, 159, 176, 196, 203, 205, 215, 240, 241, 249, 269, 274, 277, 281, 282, 286, 294, 297, 299, 304, 305, 320, 336, 344, 362, 363, 377, 387, 392, 398, 402, 408, 409, 414, 416, 421, 430, 440, 445, 447, 454, 472, 473, 498, 503, 508, 511, 518, 541, 543, 545, 570, 573, 578, 591

De Tabley, Lord, 405

Dobson, Austin, 147, 435, 560

Douglas, Olive Custance. *See* Custance, Olive.

Dowson, Ernest, 12, 20, 113, 135, 136, 175, 178, 204, 211, 292, 321, 373, 406, 417, 424, 483, 502, 526

Drama, 315, 376, 450, 495

Duclaux, Mary, 258

Du Maurier, George, 493

Egerton, George, 561

Eighties, the Eighteen-, 40, 75, 127, 268

Ellis, Havelock, 79, 199

Femme fatale, 49, 70, 160, 343, 481

Fiction, 49, 89, 90, 111, 182, 190, 237, 238, 240, 242, 247, 320, 323, 462, 493, 496

Field, Michael, 271

Fin de siècle. *See* Nineties, the Eighteen-.

FitzGerald, Edward, 595

French literary influence, 23, 82, 116, 120, 186, 275, 309, 330, 487, 516, 525, 532, 538, 564, 586

Galsworthy, John, 42

Gissing, George, 581

Gosse, Edmund, 525, 583, 584

Grahame, Kenneth, 418

Gray, John, 47, 91, 172, 327, 373, 460

Hardy, Thomas, 121

Headlam, Stewart, 198

Henley, W.E. 76, 225

Homosexuality, 50, 51, 107, 118, 370, 396, 422, 474

Hopkins, G.M. 332

Horne, Herbert, 171

Impressionism, 43, 112, 232, 389, 510, 517, 540

Interart analogies. *See* Art.

Irish literary renaissance. *See* Celtic Revival.

Jackson, Richard Charles, 588

James, Montague Rhodes, 105

Johnson, Lionel, 134, 135, 164, 167, 292, 354, 373, 388, 390, 403, 412, 483, 535, 548, 560

Kipling, Rudyard, 195, 301, 402, 580

Künstlerroman, 37, 202

Lane, John. *See* Bodley Head.

Lang, Andrew, 550

Lee, Vernon, 85, 226

Lee-Hamilton, Eugene, 326

Le Gallienne, Richard, 124, 245, 562

Leverson, Ada, 589

Machen, Arthur, 83, 147, 189, 400, 427, 504, 505, 544

Macleod, Fiona. *See* Sharp, William.

Mathews, Elkin. *See* Bodley Head.

Memoirs, 25, 44, 162, 219, 268, 276, 306, 375, 384, 406, 420, 428, 429, 443, 461, 536, 548, 559, 590

Modernism, 35, 217, 289, 304, 337, 391, 394, 478, 489

Moore, George, 147, 191, 192, 200, 261, 403

Morris, William, 213

Newman, J.H. 128

Nietzsche, Friedrich, 64, 355, 519

Nineties, the Eighteen-, 5, 38 (in U.S.), 48, 75, 77, 78, 95, 99, 101, 102, 109, 115, 150, 168, 170, 194, 261, 272, 273, 280, 285 (in Australia), 295, 306, 307, 335, 353, 357, 358, 365, 372, 384, 389 (in U.S.), 419, 423, 434, 442, 448, 479, 484, 501, 557, 569, 571, 576, 577, 587, 599 (in U.S.)

Nordau, Max, 177

O'Shaughnessy, Arthur, 250

Paget, Violet. *See* Lee, Vernon.

Parnassianism, 435, 436, 524, 525, 585

Pater, Walter, 29, 50, 54, 55, 73, 98, 104, 128, 130, 142, 174, 179, 210, 221, 234, 244, 284, 350, 351, 371, 403, 413, 455, 469, 499, 512, 527, 555, 558

Periodicals, literary, 86, 92, 100, 133, 238, 260, 266, 279, 366, 410, 534, 556, 598. *See also Savoy* and *Yellow Book*.

Plarr, Victor, 166

Poetry, 4, 16, 56, 58, 119, 132, 155, 157, 220, 231, 241, 299, 336, 341, 362, 364, 373, 378, 385, 386, 394, 399, 404, 468, 477, 480, 485, 506, 522, 539, 566, 574, 585, 592, 593

Pound, Ezra, 274, 369, 579

Pre-Raphaelitism, 180, 259, 264, 265, 518

Prose, "artistic," 23, 63, 339

Raffalovich, André, 460

Realism, 28, 106, 125, 182, 190, 239, 383, 547, 586

Rhymers' Club, 10, 11, 33, 34, 36, 185, 253, 444, 521, 594

Ricketts, Charles, 68

Rolfe, Frederick, 395, 537, 549, 582

Romanticism, 65, 80, 156, 160, 181, 225, 252, 259, 262, 291, 325, 342, 347, 352, 414, 456, 489, 545

Rossetti, D.G. 311, 343

Ruskin, John, 17, 311

Saintsbury, George, 431

Satires of aestheticism, decadence, 269, 334, 367, 368

Savoy, The, 57, 186, 187, 241, 497, 551

Sharp, William, 7, 228

Shaw, G.B., 1

Short story, 190, 212, 235, 237, 238, 247, 482, 494, 586

Smithers, Leonard, 465

Stenbock, Count, 5

Sturge Moore, T., 129, 227

Surveys, literary, 88, 93, 101, 109, 122, 151, 155, 255, 288, 293, 302, 313, 336, 349, 385, 394, 404, 438, 468, 528, 539, 541, 559, 560, 567

Swinburne, A.C., 413, 464

Symbolism and the symbolist movement, 22, 59, 103, 153, 183, 259, 282, 291, 310, 319, 356, 378, 430, 491, 511, 516, 564, 572

Symonds, J.A. 50, 333, 396

Symons, Arthur, 30, 35, 52, 135, 149, 169, 199, 203, 207, 208, 214, 218, 257, 316, 354, 359, 360, 361, 397, 403, 413, 478, 491, 492, 540, 548, 553

Thompson, Francis, 411, 426, 520, 560

Watson, William, 374

Wells, H.G. 42, 45

Whiteing, Richard, 243, 246

Wilde, Oscar, 68, 117, 148, 154, 179, 184, 217, 234, 311, 334, 370, 379, 380, 403, 413, 420, 448, 500

"Woman, the New," 110, 111, 453, 490

Wratislaw, Theodore, 147

Yeats, W.B. 5, 36, 52, 53, 56, 100, 114, 120, 137, 140, 152, 158, 169, 173, 179, 183, 331, 341, 347, 354, 360, 371, 382, 415, 437, 439, 452, 560, 596

Yellow Book, The, 66, 248, 345, 497, 530, 552, 568

Zangwill, Israel, 2, 3

Hull /
Z
2013
D68

FLORIDA STATE UNIVERSITY

3 1254 02729 7676

DATE DUE

	MAR 2 1 2000
MAY 0 2 1999	
APR 1 5 2004	